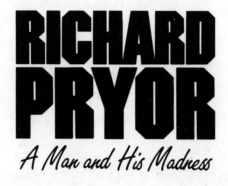

RICHARD PRYOR

A Man and His Madness

SOME RECENT BOOKS
BY JIM HASKINS

Bricktop,
WITH BRICKTOP

The Cotton Club

Lena:
A Personal and Professional Biography
of Lena Horne

Donna Summer

Katherine Dunham

Scott Joplin:
The Man Who Made Ragtime,
WITH KATHLEEN BENSON

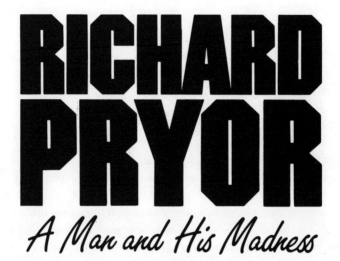

RICHARD PRYOR

A Man and His Madness

A Biography

JIM HASKINS

BEAUFORT BOOKS, INC.
New York / Toronto

The author gratefully acknowledges permission to reprint the following photograph: From the motion picture *Which Way Is Up?* reprinted courtesy of Universal Pictures.

Library of Congress Cataloging in Publication Data

Haskins, Jim, 1941–
    Richard Pryor, a man and his madness.

    Includes index.
    1. Pryor, Richard.   2. Comedians—United States—Biography.
3. Entertainers—United States—Biography.   I. Title.
PN2287.P77H3   1984   792.7′028′0924   [B]   83-21498
ISBN 0-8253-0200-5

Published in the United States by Beaufort Books, Inc., New York.
Published simultaneously in Canada by General Publishing Co. Limited.

Designer: Cindy LaBreacht

Printed in the U.S.A.   First Edition

10   9   8   7   6   5   4   3   2   1

Acknowledgments

I AM DEEPLY GRATEFUL to the people who consented to be interviewed for this book: Kathi Fearn-Banks, Andy Boone, Richie Havens, Jim Hinton, Arnold Johnson, Ray Le Roy, Bob Lucas, D'Urville Martin, LaWanda Page, Michael Schultz, Carol Speed, Melvin Van Peebles, and Juliette Whittaker. I appreciate as well the help of Karolyn Ali, Joan "Halimah" Brooks, Roberta Flack, Lynn Hamilton, Frank Jenkins, Lee Roten, the Peoria Public Library, the *Peoria Journal-Star*, and Laurel Burns. A special thank you to Kathy Benson.

TO KATHY

Contents

Introduction

PICTURE THIS. A POOR black kid from Peoria—high-school dropout, veteran of the Caterpillar tractor assembly line, father at age 16—sets out to seek fame and fortune as a comic, undaunted by the fact that no black comic before him has ever made it out of the "chittlin' circuit." Within seven years he is making ten thousand dollars a week and appearing on *The Ed Sullivan Show* and the *Tonight* show. In another ten years he's a top movie star.

Along the way he acquires—and loses—several wives and quasi-wives, fathers four more children, is the plaintiff or the defendant in a plethora of lawsuits over assault, alimony, child support, broken contracts, misrepresentation, misappropriation of funds, nonpayment of taxes, and possession of controlled substances, and nearly dies in a fire in which he suffers third-degree burns over fifty percent of his body and whose cause has never been definitely established. Yet, he emerges, like a phoenix, from the rubble of his life every time.

Richard Pryor's life is a demonstration of the old adage that truth is stranger than fiction. It is also a manifestation of madness, not only of this man who has been called a genuis, but of the arena in which he plies his talents and of the society that spawned them both. What makes Pryor so engaging is that his own brand of lunacy has proven equal to the insanity that surrounds him. Rather than simply tilting at windmills, he grabs hold of the whirling vanes and hangs on, while the world holds its breath and wonders if he will fall. He is a man who lives on life's edge; a man fascinating to watch, but not to be envied; a man who will never be fully understood, even by himself.

Jim Haskins
New York, November, 1983

CHAPTER I

The Accident of Birth

IN THE NIGHTCLUB ROUTINES he did in the late 1960s, Richard Pryor often talked about his hometown of Peoria, Illinois. He'd say, "Peoria's a model city, you know. That means they've got the Negroes under control." To this observer things haven't changed much since then. In this second largest city in Illinois the sight of a black man in a suit and tie seems to engender puzzlement in whites, as if it is improper attire unless one is a preacher or on his way to a funeral. At one of the city's better hotels the arrival of this observer produced a sudden confusion over the "misplacement" of his reservation, and he was eventually lodged next to the laundry room. There were, however, white folks down there too: progress of sorts since the 1940s and 1950s when, according to Richard Pryor's childhood friend Andy Boone, "racially, Peoria compared to the South."

Peoria's name came from the Peorias, one of the most populous tribes of Illinois Indians. The Indian name is *Pi warea*, "he comes carrying a pack on his back." Appropriately, the first Europeans in the area were French fur traders, eighteenth-century backpackers in the North American wilderness. After the French ceded the Illinois country to Great Britain in 1763, the European settlement grew slowly: by 1833 there were only twenty-five families in the area. But eleven years later, after the first distillery was built there, the town started to grow; it was established as a municipal entity in 1847 and within twenty years after that first distillery was built, eleven more were in operation. According to Ernest E. East, who published a pamphlet on the history of Peoria in 1941, except for the fourteen years of Prohibition whiskey-making was the chief industry in Peoria. After repeal of the Volstead Act, Hiram Walker & Sons, National Distillers Products

1

Corp., and Century Distilling Co. all erected plants in Peoria; and in 1940, the year Richard Pryor was born, IRS collections at Peoria, consisting almost entirely of taxes on spiritous liquors, reached an all-time high of $60,227,146.46.

There were other industries, of course. The automobile industry was not well represented. Back in the early years of the century Charles E. Duryea tried and failed to get financial support for his Motor Wagon Company in Peoria. According to a 1968 *Students' History of Peoria County*, "It is generally agreed that Peoria's denial of aid may have cost the area the automobile industry to Detroit." In the 1980s, this doesn't seem such a tragedy—people may not be buying cars, but they're still buying liquor.

Peoria also manufactured, among other items, washing machines, animal and poultry foods, work gloves, vinegar, fences and wire products, shopping bags, dresses, brick and tile, domestic heating furnaces, and heavy earth-moving equipment. By the time Richard Pryor was doing his Peoria's a Model City routine, the Caterpillar Tractor Company of east Peoria was the area's largest manufacturing concern. Pryor had worked there himself.

Still, it is somehow fitting to emphasize the wetness of Peoria, since its development as a manufacturing hub was accompanied by a similarly virile growth as a center for gambling, prostitution, and political corruption. Its mid position on the important Lakes-to-Gulf waterway, and its access via a dozen leading truck and railroad lines, among them the famous Rock Island Line, made it an ideal stopping place for drifters and show people. And since, according to the 1968 *Students' History*, Peoria considered itself "innocently liberal," the atmosphere was conducive to the development of a large and healthy tenderloin.

"Peoria was a great show town once," says veteran vaudevillian Ray Le Roy. "I even worked all the strip joints here when they were open." There were numerous gambling houses, taverns (the Peoria telephone directory for 1940 lists an inordinate number of taverns for a town with a population of 105,000), and vaudeville houses. The expression "Will it play in Peoria?" dates from the heyday of vaudeville, and the *Students' History* notes rather sourly that "at one time [Peoria] seemed less a city than a vaudeville joke."

In 1940 in the metropolitan area of Peoria, approximately one-and-a-half percent of the people were black, most of them concentrated in the north central section of Peoria proper. No doubt, like Ronald Reagan, the majority of Peoria's white population didn't think there was a race problem, since for most of them it was not necessary even to see blacks very often, much less have problems with them. Still, blacks do have a way of getting into the annals of local history.

There's always at least one memorable crime story. On June 24, 1903, a black named William McCrea allegedly gunned down a city detective named William Murphy. An angry mob threatened to lynch the suspect, but the police managed to save him for a proper hanging. According to the *Students' History*, McCrea asked to see the rope that would be used to hang him, saying, "I'm longin' to go. The rope on which I'm goin' to climb to glory." He was hanged on December 11, 1903, protesting his innocence to the end.

Often, blacks also manage to set records for longevity, if they can manage to avoid lynchings and other existential hazards. When Richard Pryor was growing up, the record for "oldest living Peorian" belonged, posthumously, to Abernathy Paton, who was said to have been 123 when he died in 1933.

On the whole Peoria's blacks lived and worked invisible to the larger white population and were free to form their own social lines. In the black community of Peoria there were two basic classes. There were the bourgeois blacks—the preachers, teachers, doctors, and undertakers—the hard-working, upstanding, educated folks. And there were the others, one of whose primary sociological characteristics was that they were uneducated. These others were further divided into two classes—the takers and those who got taken. The takers were those who decided that, being uneducated and on the bottom, there was no point in expending effort in futile attempts at respectability the. Man wasn't going to let them have anyhow. They chose to use their wits and become ghetto entrepreneurs, providing services to the colored folks, not to mention a substantial number of white folks, who were willing to pay for a little relief from day-to-day life in Peoria, Illinois. Richard Pryor was born into such a family on December 1, 1940.

His father, LeRoy "Buck Carter" Pryor, Jr., born LeRoy Carter at

Decatur, Illinois, in 1915, had come to Peoria with his mother in 1929 at the age of fourteen. He won a Golden Gloves boxing tournament in Chicago in 1933 but did not go on to a boxing career. Instead, he went into vaudeville as a singer, playing the chittlin' circuit and thus returning often to his adopted hometown, since Peoria boasted any number of stops on this particular vaudeville circuit in the 1930s and 1940s. During one such stop he got a girl named Gertrude Thomas pregnant, and not long after the child was born, LeRoy quit vaudeville and settled down in Peoria, apparently at the urging of his mother, Marie Carter Pryor, who was a ghetto entrepreneur par excellence.

In Decatur in 1899 Marie Carter Pryor was born into a family that would eventually include two girls and twenty boys. Her family heritage was New Orleans Creole and she was a proud Catholic. But that didn't keep her from doing what she had to do to be a taker and not one of the taken. Marie Carter Pryor operated whorehouses, or as actress LaWanda Page, who was playing the chittlin' circuit during the 1940s and later, says, "At that time, we called them ho-houses." Marie was a strong woman with a sense of right and wrong that in some instances was beyond the understanding of those who have only a conventional sense of morality; but when she learned that she was to have a grandchild she had conventional opinions about what would be right for the child. Her son should settle down, and her grandchild should be born in a hospital.

LeRoy Pryor left the vaudeville stage and got a job as a construction worker. The child was born not on a kitchen table or in a northside bedroom, but in a hospital. The hospital was St. Francis, and so it might seem that Marie's Catholicism motivated the choice. But Juliette Whittaker, Richard's mentor as an adolescent, explains, "For a long time St. Francis was the only hospital around, so anyone who was born in a hospital was born in St. Francis." Still, the fact that he'd been born in a hospital was impressed upon Richard Pryor by his family. He often speaks about it with pride, as if it made him somehow special, which it did. It was unusual in 1940 for a black child to be born in a hospital.

Richard Pryor was christened Richard Franklin Lennox Thomas Pryor. He says he was given these names by pimps, but at least two are family names—Richard after his uncle and Thomas after his mother's family.

According to Pryor, his parents got married about three years after he was born, but the marriage did not last long. Gertrude Thomas is a shadowy figure. Richard has talked about spying through a keyhole as his mother turned a trick for a white man and his father watched from a more conspicuous vantage point. Perhaps she and her husband did join the family business and she found she didn't like it; perhaps she was simply overwhelmed by her husband's family. Whatever happened, Gertrude Thomas couldn't take care of her child. She left when he was "of an early age" as Richard puts it, but he was supportive of her throughout her life. "My mother went through a lot of hell behind me," he says, "because people would tell her, 'You don't take care of that boy.' She always wanted me to be somebody and she wasn't the strongest person in the world. But I give her a lot of credit. At least she didn't flush me down the toilet like some do."

Gertrude remained in Peoria and later married a man named Emanuel. LeRoy married Viola Anna Hurst, who operated her own "joint" according to Ray Le Roy. Meanwhile, a small child named Richard fell through the gap of broken love into the safety net provided by his grandmother.

Richard has some memories of his father during his childhood. He remembers being a "bird dog" when his father went hunting: "My father was an outdoorsman; he loved to teach young people to hunt . . . squirrels, ducks, geese, and a couple of cows." But his father went off to serve in World War II, and during his childhood and adolescence Richard's grandmother was the most important person to him. Juliette Whittaker, who knew Richard well when he was aged thirteen to about sixteen, says, "I didn't even know Richard had a father and a mother. He always talked about his grandmother and his Aunt Maxine, so if his parents existed, I was not aware of them."

Ray Le Roy, who lived next door to LeRoy and Viola Pryor in the late 1950s, thought LeRoy Pryor was Richard's uncle.

Richard's grandmother married Thomas Bryant on December 22, 1942, when Richard was just two years old. Richard has said that the couple, who were in their forties, had three different whorehouses on North Washington Street—Nos. 313, 317, and 324. The 1944 and 1945 Peoria telephone directories do list a Thomas Bryant at both 313 and 317 North Washington, and until 1953 he is listed at one or the other address but not at both. There is no listing for 324 North Washington in any of these years, but perhaps that particular establishment did not have a phone or had one with an unlisted number. Urban renewal has changed the face of North Washington Street, but back in the 1940s the street was noted for its string of brothels. There were three establishments catering to the white trade, then a cross street, and then a block filled with houses catering to a black clientele. Marie Bryant's houses were on that block.

The Bryants enjoyed a certain prominence in the Peoria sporting community. They were looked down on, according to Pryor, by the more "respectable" blacks, but in some ways they had more influence. Around 1946, after the Sheltons of southern Illinois moved in and took over Peoria's gambling operations, Peoria officials cracked down on vice in the city; but Marie Bryant's businesses survived. Richard remembers that around election time the politicians who were running for office all came around "to tell all the whores that there wouldn't be no busts." These were white politicians, of course —not until 1959 was the first black councilman elected in Peoria.

Juliette Whittaker divides the classes in Peoria's black community in those days into day people and night people. Richard Pryor's family? "They were the night people; the people you didn't see during the day. They only came out in the evening." With United States entry into World War II and the large-scale migration of southern blacks to northern industrial cities, people like the Bryants enjoyed even greater prominence. For one thing there was increased demand for the services they provided. For another more big-name entertainers were attracted to Peoria's increasing black population and, when playing in Peoria, sought the Bryants's hospitality. Miss Whittaker recalls, "When people like Count Basie and Duke Ellington came to town, they would go to the [Bryants's] places afterwards, to refresh themselves." One of the few truthful statements in Richard Pryor's first studio biography, issued by Paramount in 1966, is that at the age of seven he went to the Famous Door nightclub where stars like Ellington and Basie, Louis Armstrong, and Pearl Bailey gave impromptu performances and occasionally he sat in with the house band as drummer.

Marie Bryant enjoyed her prominence in the sporting life of Peoria, and she didn't do any apologizing for the way she made her living.

She was providing necessary services, and if people didn't want them then they wouldn't be willing to pay for them. Perhaps her business was outside the law, but she had her own law. According to it, people helped each other because "you don't get through this life alone." One never resented giving another person food, or a place to stay, and one always accepted graciously the gifts bestowed by other people, even if these gifts were not entirely welcome. Richard Pryor once told David Felton of *Rolling Stone* a wonderful story about his grandmother, a story that epitomizes her outlook. It took place in 1967 when Viola Anna Hurst Pryor died and twenty-six-year-old Richard went back to Peoria for his stepmother's funeral. Among the dishes brought to the wake by friends and neighbors was a bowl of baked dressing prepared by an elderly neighbor. Richard was horrified to see cockroaches in it. Just as he was about to display his distaste, his grandmother held up a cautionary hand, and speaking in a soft voice as if to a child, she said, "Now don' say nuthin' to her. She old an' blind, she can't see no more. She probably lef' the oven door open an' ney crawled in there las' night. But Richard, you have roaches just like ever'body else."

Richard Pryor feels that he learned things like "real morals and honesty and dignity" as a child of people "in the life." He explains, "These people lived the backside of life and they saw things different than if you had money and were careful what you said. My father was devastatingly funny and would tell the truth even if people didn't want to hear it. To a lot of people it might shock. But the words are true. It's a language within a language that's so to the point it makes pictures in your mind." The same can be said of the language in Richard Pryor's routines.

Marie Bryant also had a healthy sense of humor. According to LaWanda Page, who met her in California in the 1970s, Richard's grandmother was a comedian in her own right but was often unaware of how funny she was. To Richard, Marie Bryant was Mama. She raised him and mothered him, and when she died in 1979 she was still worrying about him, wondering if he was equipped to survive in a world she knew could be achingly cruel.

Although she was not ashamed of her life, or her life-style, Marie Bryant wanted something better for her grandson. Richard witnessed plenty of life's raw edges as a child—he says he watched his parents fighting and once on the street found a dead baby in a shoe box—but he also remembers being the neighborhood baby whom someone was always around to look after. His grandfather, his Uncle Dicky, his aunts Jenny and Dee and Maxine, neighbor ladies, visiting entertainers, all seemed to have a tacit agreement among them that young Richard was special and to be protected. As an example, he points out that he was kept away from dope and never even smoked a reefer until he was twenty years old. But as a very young child, surrounded by adults and living in an area where there were few children, Richard was lonely, and he invented an imaginary friend named Charlie Eggy to keep him company.

It is hard not to cite Charlie Eggy as Richard Pryor's first "character," but most lonely children, especially bright ones, invent imaginary friends. They also invest inanimate objects with the thoughts and feelings of human beings, and no doubt Richard Pryor did this too. As a very young child, he didn't understand the differences between people and things, and living surrounded by adults as he did he was especially prone to identifying with inanimate objects that were his size. Richard Pryor probably had chairs and footstools for friends, not to mention mice, roaches, and stray cats and dogs. How else to explain his later ability to invest inanimate objects like sonarscopes and cars, and nonhuman forms of life, like cheetahs, with such human characteristics that his audiences actually suspend reality for a moment and believe that they can talk and feel?

A skinny, wiry little kid with strange, glittering eyes, Richard frazzled his grandmother's nerves but delighted her with his precocity. She hoped he would enjoy the education she'd never had, and when he was six she enrolled him in a Catholic grammar school. School was supposed to put him in contact with children his own age, channel his energy and imagination, and give him some discipline. But the main thing school did for Richard Pryor was to hurl him against the disapproving wall of the conventional, predominantly white society from which he had been sheltered until that time.

It taught him that there was something wrong with his family. When school authorities found out the nature of his grandmother's business, they expelled him. According to Juliette Whittaker, that's when Marie Bryant and her family became Baptists. "The whole family walked away from the Catholic Church." Although this display of family unity must have given young Richard a sense of security in the support of his loved ones, his expulsion from school planted in his mind the idea that his family was somehow different and not acceptable. And when he found out that he himself was different because he was black, he didn't even have the consolation of family support.

Pryor has spoken about two incidents that come to his mind when he thinks back to his first awareness of racism. One occurred when he was six or seven and just finding out that boys are supposed to have girl friends. He decided that he was in love with a little white girl in his class and one day he brought her a gift—one of those erase-a-slate writing boards on which the writing disappears when you lift up the top plastic sheet. The little girl was delighted, but the next day her father stormed into the classroom and told the frightened Richard not to dare give his daughter a present. "When I told my father, he just shook his head," Pryor told Joyce Maynard of *The New York Times*. "You see, nobody had told me about racism, but he knew."

His family's reaction the first time he was called *nigger* was similarly inadequate. Richard remembers it vividly. He didn't know what the word meant, but he knew it must mean something terrible, something that made him want to cover himself up. He still seethes at the outrage, the devastation this epithet wreaks on the psyche of a child. "Black parents should go to school and pitch a bitch, just for their child, just scream and yell, 'There is no nigger in my family!' I mean, they should do that just for that child, so he will know, so he won't accept it." But Richard's family were not the sort to go to school and scream and yell. This was Peoria, Illinois, in the 1940s. Although it pained them to see him hurt, they knew they could not protect him from racism. He would hear the word *nigger* often in his life and might just as well start getting used to it.

But it was hard getting used to the idea of being a nigger when he'd thought he was just a regular kid. He wasn't black, he decided, studying himself in a mirror. He was orange, the color of the sun. He called himself Sun for a while, he says, until a white teacher decided to put a stop to such nonsense. He was a Negro, she told him firmly. "And I didn't want to be this Negro," he recalls. "I said, 'But I'm orange; do I have to be a Negro?' "

Being a Negro seemed a crime of such magnitude that he could not understand it. He must have done something very wrong to be born a Negro. But he couldn't figure out what he might have done, and he was too frightened of finding out to ask anyone who might be able to tell him. He felt completely helpless, and that helpless feeling enraged him. But he couldn't express his rage. He was too small and skinny. It was probably then that he began to develop his keen sense of irony.

He must have been quite young when he first heard the children's ditty "Found a Peanut." It was his favorite song. Even today, when he is concentrating on something else and his unconscious is free, Richard Pryor will hum "Found a Peanut" to himself.

The parody of "Oh My Darling, Clementine" tells the story of a hapless person who finds a peanut, cracks it open, discovers that it is rotten, eats it anyway, gets a stomachache, calls a doctor, and dies anyway. The ditty had a particular meaning to Pryor after he reached school age.

The largely friendly, protective world he had known as a very young child had turned out to be as rotten as that peanut. He couldn't fight it outright, and he couldn't hide from it. He had to come to terms with it, just as the speaker in the ditty eats the rotten peanut anyway. Richard's way of coming to terms with his world was to be funny.

At some point young Richard Pryor found that he could make people laugh. When he contorted his mobile, expressive face, the other kids giggled. When he made odd sounds, they howled. It was very satisfying to get that kind of reaction from his classmates at school, and worth the ire of his teachers. At the public schools he attended after his expulsion from parochial school, he was classified as a problem child and placed in classes for slow learners, which he disrupted as thoroughly as possible, according to his father, often with carefully rehearsed Tarzan yells. "He was always getting into trouble with the teachers at school," LeRoy Pryor told Jean Budd of the *Peoria Journal-Star*. "His mother was always getting notes from school and visiting the teachers. He wasn't mean, but just upset the class with his funny faces and his comedy."

Pryor says his family moved around a lot in Peoria and that he attended three different public elementary schools. Only one teacher at one school cared enough and was sensitive enough to see that what young Richard Pryor needed was attention and that his comic talent was a source of pride for him. She was Miss Marguerite Yingst, and Richard was in her sixth-grade class at the Blaine-Sumner Elementary School.

Miss Yingst, who later became Mrs. Parker, remembers Richard as a perpetually exhausted, perpetually late twelve-year-old, who was very quiet in class and sometimes seemed lonely. He was a poor black kid in a predominantly white school and he did not mingle with his classmates very much. However, she did observe that on the playground he seemed to enjoy entertaining the children who were not playing kickball or climbing the Jungle Jim. He was adept at pantomime; she still remembers him pretending to slurp steaming hot soup—"Oh my, he could roll those eyes back"—and it occurred to Miss Yingst that there might be a way to persuade him to get to school on time. While she suspected that he was up half the night and that this was the main reason for his lateness, she also had an idea that he would get to school for the opening bell if he had an incentive. Thus, in the winter of 1953, she made a deal with him: If he got to school on time each day, he could perform for the class for ten minutes on Friday afternoon. From that time until the end of the school year, the deal was in force and successful. "It was great for Richard," Mrs. Parker recalled in late 1982. "The other pupils loved him. And Richard kept his promise. Got to school on time."

Having a regularly scheduled time to perform helped Richard to feel more accepted and less lonely. It also helped to structure his comic presentations. And, it challenged him to find new material, for he couldn't just pretend to slurp soup every Friday. By now he had access to a television, and he used as his material the routines of the top television comedians of the day. He did Red Skelton's Junior character and a Jerry Lewis imitation. His classmates loved it, and Richard liked being the center of attention. Trouble was, his classmates started getting televisions too. Richard still remembers the time they told him they'd seen Sammy Davis, Jr., on *The Toast of the Town* (the early *Ed Sullivan Show*) and that Davis was pretty good too. "I was jealous," Pryor told Gene Siskel of the *Chicago Tribune*. "It was like I'd been home sick one Friday and some other cat had come in and done my act. Now I knew I was going to have to be even better."

Unfortunately, Richard had Miss Yingst as a teacher for only one year. Other teachers were not as perceptive of his need to express himself, and in schools that were predominantly white there were few teachers who were sensitive to the viewpoints of their black students. Richard remembers being particularly galled by lessons about slavery: he would hear that the slaves *came* from Africa, as if they had a choice. In protest he would act up or boycott school altogether. He became a frequent truant, spending his days at the local movie theaters.

At that time blacks had to sit in "Nigger Heaven" (the balcony) in Peoria theaters. Richard rebelled against this stricture at first—he wanted to be right up front, close to the screen, and, he believed, close to the performers behind it. But after being thrown out several times, he decided to accommodate to racism in order to see the movies he enjoyed.

Once the picture filled the screen, Richard's sensitivity to racism evaporated as did his sense of reality. "One of my first big traumatic experiences was when I went to see a Little Beaver movie," he told Joyce Maynard. "When it was over, I tried to get back behind the screen. I thought Little Beaver would be there, you know. And I wanted to talk to him. I never thought to myself, 'Little Beaver's white.' I didn't think about color—just feelings. My heroes at the movies were the same as everyone else's. I wanted to be John Wayne too. I didn't know John Wayne hated my guts."

Cowboy star Lash La Rue, who dressed in nontraditional all black, was another childhood hero, and so were the Little Rascals, Abbott and Costello, Porky Pig, Bugs Bunny, Baby Huey, the Roadrunner, and Mickey Mouse. On Saturdays the Peoria movie houses offered cartoon marathons when as many as twenty-five cartoons were screened in one afternoon. Richard happily lost himself in this celluloid world where racism, and in most cases blacks, seemed not to exist. Afterward he would act out the cartoons for his friends, delighting them particularly with his voices. He had an almost perfect aural memory.

Among his friends were the Clarks—a big family of big people. "There were twenty of them," says Juliette Whittaker, "and the boys were big, husky guys. Handsome too. Every Clark who ever came into this world seems to have been good looking.

"Their father was a minister, and actually they spent a whole lot of time in church—they had to go to church on Tuesday night, Thursday night, and Saturday night, as well as Sunday. But in between they were out in the community, and when they marched down the street people got out of their way. Because they weren't going to move for you—they were going to just walk through. A Clark's not afraid of anybody."

Small, skinny Richard Pryor seemed out of place among the Clark boys. In fact he was the type of kid they regularly mowed down. But they liked Richard because he made them laugh. "They'd say, 'Richard tell us a joke. Richard, tell us a story,' " according to Miss Whittaker, "and Richard got them off of him by keeping them laughing, so that they became his protectors."

Richard explains his friendship with the community tough guys by saying that he wasn't afraid to be afraid and that he expressed for them the fears they could not admit. But he also had a sense of bravado, and scared or not he usually went along with whatever mischief his friends got into.

They decided one day to make a raft and float down the Illinois River. Richard contributed his family's fence poles to the vessel. Depending on his mood, Richard tells two different versions of the story. In one the boys constructed the raft on the river bank, boarded, pushed off, and discovered that they could not control it. The river current carried it swiftly downstream. Since none of the boys could swim, they clung helplessly to the raft until the Coast Guard rescued them. His grandmother, who was waiting on shore, "whipped him all the way up Washington Street." In the other version the boys never got to build the raft. Richard's grandmother happened to be looking out the big bay window (on which her girls tapped to attract their customers' attention), saw Richard and his friends carrying away portions of his parents' fence, gave chase, and gave him the whipping right then and there.

Whatever the real story, there's no question that Richard was a handful for his grandmother. She may have succeeded in protecting him as a small child, but as he grew older, started school, and widened the boundaries of his world, her control correspondingly diminished. She whipped him, pleaded with him, tried to reason with him. At one point she even tried to get religion into him. Marie Bryant suffered from arthritis and was in the habit of going to revival meetings in hopes of being cured. One time she took her grandson; maybe the preacher could get the "devil out of him." Richard says, "It was kind of embarrassing, in front of all those people, you know. He prayed over me, and says for that devil to come out! And I'm thinking, I didn't feel anything. I couldn't see it. Maybe . . . it's still in there." Although that preacher didn't succeed in getting the devil out of Richard Pryor, he probably contributed to to the store of experiences from which, years later, Pryor would draw to create his own preacher characters.

The difficulty with Richard was that it was hard to put one's finger on what was wrong with him. He was quiet, soft-spoken, well mannered around his family and their friends. But when he got away from home with his own friends, he was always getting into trouble. They took to till-tapping in the stores on Washington Street, he says. Inevitably, they were caught, and inevitably Richard got a whipping. At Trewyn Junior High School he behaved as incorrigibly as ever and was a frequent truant, spending many school-day afternoons at the movies and dreaming of being a movie star. Stars, he was convinced, led special lives. "I always wondered if stars went to the bathroom," he told Henry Allen of *The Washington Post*. "I figured they'd get somebody else to do it for them." Although denied an official forum for his comedy since leaving Miss Yingst's sixth-grade classroom he found other ways of expressing himself in his own special way. When he was thirteen, he was given the opportunity to appear on a real stage for the first time.

CHAPTER II

Playing in Peoria

THE STAGE WAS AT Carver Community Center, 219 North Sheridan, a few blocks from North Washington. Its purpose was to keep kids off the streets or, as Pryor once put it, "to keep gang fights from happening." One of the supervisors at the Center was Juliette Whittaker. Born in Houston, Texas, the daughter of a lawyer, Whittaker had majored in drama at the University of Iowa and come to Peoria in the late 1940s, almost directly after graduation, having met the director of the Carver Center at a conference at Fisk University and been invited to stage children's plays.

"So I came to Peoria," Whittaker recalls, "and Mr. Harper showed me that stage at Carver Center. They had no sets, no scenery, no costumes—just a bare stage with a front curtain and all these little kids. And I said to them, 'You think you'd like to act?' and they all said, 'Yeah, I'd like to act!' And so I said to Mr. Harper, 'Let me try it for two years and see if I can put some sort of program together for you. And if I can't, I'll go on back to college.'

"And that's where my learning really began . . . here," says Whittaker, who except for a brief time in New York has been in Peoria ever since. She wasn't prepared for Peoria or for the children who came to the Center. She'd been raised in an upper-middle-class home, filled with books, with a father who came home from the office every evening in a neighborhood where all the fathers came home from their offices every evening. She'd spent most of her life going to school, had grown up in an intellectual atmosphere. She was not accustomed, she says, to talking to "ordinary people." Peoria taught her "a great deal."

One of the first things she learned was not to worry about too many specifics in registering children for her new Youth Theater Guild. "I'd say, 'What's your mother's name? What's your father's name?' And somebody would say, 'He ain't got no father.'

15

"I'd say, 'Don't be silly. Everybody's got a father.'

" 'But he ain't got no father.'

"And I began to see that there were children who really did not know who their fathers were. They'd never even seen them."

Juliette Whittaker was willing to learn, and by the time Richard Pryor showed up at the Carver Center she was overseeing an active adult theater group as well as the Youth Theater Guild.

Among the most active members of the youth group were the Clarks. "I had seven of them in my theater group, and they could act, yes they could." Among the seven was Matthew Clark, who was closest in age to Richard and his best friend among the Clarks. Matthew, Whittaker recalls, liked to do magic tricks and had considerable talent at it. It was probably because of Matthew that Richard started going to the Center. Whittaker remembers him as "a skinny little kid. He was thirteen, but he looked about nine."

By the time Richard showed up, the Youth Theater Guild members were in the midst of rehearsals for *Rumpelstiltskin*. All the major parts had been cast, primarily with students from local high schools. Matt Clark had a part in the play as well. But young Richard Pryor seemed so eager to be in the play that Whittaker was loathe to disappoint him. "I don't care. I'll do anything," he pleaded. She offered him a minor part, as a servant. Richard took what he could get, but he persuaded Miss Whittaker to let him take home a copy of the entire script, which he memorized completely. When the boy who was playing the king was absent from rehearsal one day Richard piped up, "Miss Whittaker, I know that part." "Well," Juliette Whittaker recalls with a chuckle, "he brought so many new lines and expressions to the part, everybody was amazed. The other kids just broke up; he was so funny. When the original king returned, even he had to admit that Richard was better in the part than he was. So Richard stayed on the throne. And he hasn't come down since."

From then on Richard was a regular at the Carver Community Center, appearing in many of the productions staged by the Youth Theater Guild, which were often not the customary children's plays. Finding herself with more male actors than were called for in conventional plays, Whittaker began writing her own and setting them to classical music in order to introduce the children to yet another art form. One such play was *Ali Baba and the Forty Thieves* set to the music of Bizet (Richard played Ali Baba). Her plays usually had a definite moral. *The Vanishing Pearl*, in which a pearl is stolen from its owner, shows that you have to work for what you get. Richard played the lead, Ku the thief, in that play.

Like the others, Richard also did his share of behind-the-scenes work, helping with scenery and props and costumes and lighting. For a kid who couldn't sit still for more than a minute, his loyalty to the Center was remarkable. Of course, it gave him the opportunity to perform and be on a stage, which he needed and enjoyed; but for Richard part of the attraction of the Carver Center was Miss Whittaker herself. Shapely and attractive now, some thirty years later, the twenty-seven-year-old Miss Whittaker must have been a knockout when Richard Pryor first came into contact with her.

Andy Boone was already in the Youth Theater Guild when Richard joined. He lived right across the street from the Center. He was, Whittaker remembers, "a clean-cut little kid. A devil, but clean-cut." Andy was not in *Rumpelstiltskin*—"No, I worked on the crew for that one," he says—but he had his share of good parts and of Miss Whittaker's attention. "She was real popular with the young kids. She had a lot of patience, and she introduced us to classical music, drama, and different things. . . . I was, I would say, close to her." Soon, Andy says, he found himself in competition with Richard for Miss Whittaker. "I think he kind of wanted to be closer than he was or closer than I was."

Juliette Whittaker had some awareness that the two felt competitive toward one another, but most of the kids were competitive to some extent. "I know that Andy used to come into the office and if he wanted to clear the room he'd put on Rachmaninoff's Prelude in C-Flat Minor because nobody liked that music but him. He'd put that record on, and everyone would say, 'Aw man, puttin' on that old sad music.' He'd say, 'If you don't like it, get out!' and naturally they would drift on out." She didn't know that, out of earshot, Richard would get back at Andy, puttin' them night names on him, ridiculing him.

Not living in the same neighborhood or having gone to the same schools, Andy and Richard were in contact only at the Carver Center. But in ninth grade they attended the same junior high school, Richard having transferred to Roosevelt Junior High because of a family move. They shared a social studies class and, according to Richard, competed in "jack-off" contests. Andy Boone professes not to remember this. He does remember that they got into several fights and that he won. "I was bigger," he explains, "but not a whole lot bigger. Richard was kind of frail. He wasn't a fighter. He had a tendency to hang around with the tough guys, who would protect him a little. I thought he was kinda mouthy. And some people that he ran around with, I didn't particularly like, so there was a lot of conflict." Richard never forgot that conflict or apparently, how Andy—bigger, but not much bigger—had won their fights.

More than twenty years later Juliette Whittaker started the Learning Tree Day School. Andy Boone's daughter was among her first students. Richard Pryor, who had helped fund the school, returned to Peoria for a reception in his honor. When he was meeting the students, Miss Whittaker introduced Boone's daughter to Richard and told him who she was. According to Boone, Richard said to the little girl, "Oh yes, your daddy used to beat me up all the time"; and when she got home from school she told her father. Boone and his wife attended the reception for Pryor later in the day.

"He was standing around and going from group to group. He comes up to me and says, 'Hello, Andy, how you doin'?'

"He says 'Is this your wife?' and I say, 'Yeah,' kinda lost for words. I didn't know what to say to a big celebrity. So I said, 'Boy, we used to clown it up in school, didn't we?'

"He says, 'Yeah, we sure did.' And he gets a real serious look on his face and say, 'You know, I remember when you got caught masturbating.'

"I think it was a little retaliation for years past. But it stunned me that he would say something like this in front of my wife."

Boone says the masturbating story isn't true. Pryor told David Felton of *Rolling Stone* about "jacking off" in class, but in that telling Pryor was the one who got caught, since he was the only one in the contest who didn't have a front to his desk.

Miss Whittaker was blissfully unaware that the two adolescent boys vied with each other for her attention. When told in the summer of 1982, some thirty years later, that they had actually fought over her, she was flabbergasted. "I didn't know they had come to blows. I had no idea. Oh my goodness!"

In Juliette Whittaker's eyes Richard Pryor was just a bright young kid who would benefit from exposure to drama and literature and music. He was a cutup, but he was controllable. "You know that label they use now—hyperactive? Well, they didn't have that label then. He was . . . frisky and quick. He had a quick mind, was very good with puns. He could see the biting satire in things people would say. He could take your words, twist them, and throw them back at you. And this used to make the other kids very angry, because they weren't used to fighting with words. He had a very good vocabulary, and so he must have done a lot of reading. I think he was a lonely child, and lonely children, if they are intellectually inclined at all, do a lot of reading. They live in a world of their own, and so they have imaginary companions."

Juliette Whittaker thought enough of Richard to go out looking for him when he didn't show up for rehearsals, and by about the mid-1950s she knew exactly where he would be. Prior to that time, he could be in any number of places where kids hung out. There was a confectionary store across the street from the Carver Center and a barbecue place nearby. Between 1953 and 1955 Richard's grandfather, Thomas Bryant, operated a confectionary called Pop's Place at 414 McBean Street. But around 1955 Pop Bryant opened a pool hall, Pop's Pool Hall, at 618 West 6th Avenue, corner of Sixth and Sheridan. Both LeRoy and Dicky helped out there, and Richard was given the quasi-job of racking balls. He was the only kid allowed in the place. Women like Juliette Whittaker were even a rarer sight, and if she wasn't aware of the effect she had on the regulars at Pop's Pool Hall when she walked in, she found out later. "Richard told me, 'When you walked in that joint to get me, they'd be cussin' and fussin', and you'd walk in and that place would be just like a church.'

"Nobody would say anything," Whittaker recalls. "They'd just freeze. And his uncle would say, 'Take him, take him, take him.' " And Juliette Whittaker would take Richard in tow and march him over to the Carver Center, scolding him for skipping rehearsal.

It wasn't easy for her to invade Pop's Pool Hall to get Richard. She knew that the silence that fell over the place was more disapproving than respectful toward this uppity young woman with her notions of turning Richard into a sissy. There was no place for sissies in the Bryants' and Pryors' world, except as butts for jokes. One of the joking lines Richard remembers from his childhood was "I'm as happy as a sissy in a CCC [Civilian Conservation Corps] camp." According to Juliette Whittaker, Richard even had to conceal his brightness from his family. "It wasn't quite masculine," she explains. "We lose so much by that. We don't know what losses we have suffered from that approach to human potential. The dramatic arts offer an outlet for precocious children who have no interest in athletics. Drama offers a chance to take a spotlight for what they can do, perhaps better than sports."

The Pryor and Bryant men had no quarrel with other forms of on-stage entertainment. Their world was full of musicians and singers and comics. Why, Buck himself had been in vaudeville. But drama was for sissies. Says Whittaker, "Nobody from the family, as I recall, would ever come to the plays. They didn't take it seriously. This was just something that Richard did."

When Richard was about fifteen, he began to act as MC at the Carver Community Center talent shows. He fell into the role naturally. Andy Boone recalls, "We'd be in the auditorium working on scenery or something and he'd get up on the stage and start telling jokes or play master of ceremonies." Miss Whittaker saw him doing this and asked him to be the official host at the next talent show. "The first time, he was kind of scared," she remembers, "but he warmed up to it. At first he had just a small comic bit that he did in the show, but then he started expanding his material. Across from the Carver Center there was a kind of confectionary shop where the teenagers used to hang out. He would try out his material over there."

Just as he had looked to television for new material when he was performing Friday afternoons in Miss Yingst's sixth-grade classroom, Richard borrowed from television for his routines on the Carver Center stage. At the time Edward R. Murrow had a very popular show called *Person to Person* in which Murrow would interview celebrities in their lavish homes and receive the grand tour. Richard did a takeoff on the show. In his version Murrow visited the home of a poor black sharecropper in the South.

Juliette Whittaker recalls how Richard played the sharecropper to perfection, even though it is highly unlikely that he had ever met one. "He'd say, 'Mr. Murrow, this my table, and that there's my chair. And that's my chair, and this is my table.' And he began to work with those two objects, and it was hilarious.

" 'Now the table lost a leg in forty-four and we put—oh, yassuh, the wall? We papered it with newspaper. Goes all the way back to 1914.'

"I've never forgotten this routine, because just when you'd think he'd exhausted the possibilities of this chair, this table, and this newspaper, he would say something else.

" 'Oh yeah, that reminds me. . . .' And on and on he would go. No props. He was just showing it to us. And we were seeing it, because he could do that.

"He had another bit where a scuba diver meets up with a shark. The diver is just swimming along, looking at everything, and suddenly this shark confronts him. It was so funny, the way he got out of the water, backing up from this shark. It's hard to show someone backing up, swimming, but Richard did."

His family—or at least his Uncle Dicky—did start attending the Carver talent shows after Richard became the MC.

When he was around sixteen, Richard stopped going to the Carver Center. Juliette Whittaker does not remember the circumstances, just that she didn't see him as often anymore. Perhaps the break was related to her own absence from the Center when she left Peoria for a while. She turned thirty in 1956 and had been at the Carver Center for some eight years. Since childhood she had dreamed of being a star on Broadway, and she may have fallen prey to what Gail Sheehy has dubbed the Catch-30 Syndrome. Life was passing by; if she didn't at least go to New York and try to get on Broadway, she might regret it. Although she soon returned to Peoria, deciding that "I wasn't really interested in the high degree of cutthroat competition that goes on there [New York]," she left at a critical time in Richard's life, and he may have felt that she had abandoned him.

Richard may have stopped going to Carver Center after he was expelled from school. He says he was kicked out because he punched a science teacher appropriately named Mr. Think. If he hadn't been expelled, he would probably have quit school anyway. School hadn't gotten any better for him in the higher grades. The classes were still predominantly white, and the teachers were all white. Peoria's first black secondary school teacher wasn't hired until 1962. Back in 1954, when Richard and Andy entered ninth grade at Roosevelt Junior High School, "their lines," as Boone describes white's idea of of the boundaries beyond which blacks are not supposed to go, were still firmly drawn.

"I'll give you an example," says Boone. "In the ninth grade we had a social dance in the gymnasium. Everyone formed a big circle to learn the fox trot. The girls were on the outside ring, and the boys on the inside ring, and the boys and girls were supposed to change partners every time the circles stopped. But when one of us came to a white girl, we had to skip her and go on until we found a black girl."

This was the same year that Look magazine selected Peoria, Illinois, as a model city.

"And I remember," Boone continues, "when I was in fifth grade I was flunking badly, but they passed me on. And there was this white girl who was doing better than I was, but they held her back. I couldn't understand it then. Later I realized that they were just pushing me through the system, to get me out and into the work force."

Both Andy and Richard rebelled by cutting up in class. Their social studies teacher, a Hawaiian named Mr. Yang, once got so furious with Andy that he grabbed him by the shirt and ripped all the buttons off. And Andy wasn't even the reigning class clown. That distinction belonged to Richard.

Richard entered Central High School in the following year. Some of his studio biographies state that he was a high-school athlete who won letters in football and basketball, but that was either wishful thinking or a gleeful put-on. The only sport Richard Pryor ever went in for was shooting, both as a "bird-dog" for his father and as a sidekick for his grandfather during the time Thomas Bryant had a garbage collection service. When they went to the town dump early in the morning, they took along their guns. "Even now," boasts Pryor, "rats see me, they run." Shooting was not one of the sports offered in Peoria's high schools. In Richard's opinion high school had nothing to offer at all. He managed to attend only infrequently, and on one of the days when he did manage to get to school he had the confrontation with Mr. Think that resulted in his expulsion. Andy Boone does not remember the incident, for he attended a different high school, but he feels that Richard was more likely to have had a verbal confrontation than a physical confrontation with a teacher. Pryor himself has said on occasion that he was kicked out because of his "attitude." Whatever happened, Richard Pryor's formal education ended prematurely; studio biographies notwithstanding, he did not graduate from Central High.

Pryor is loath to give advice to kids, explaining that he feels like a hypocrite doing so. But he will tell young people that they should stay in school. In 1972 an interviewer for *Ebony* asked Pryor what he would say if he could speak directly to the brothers on the block. Pryor replied, "Get off the block, and get on the square. *Knowledge.* Get something into your head. . . . Go to school. They are there to teach you and schools can actually teach you something if you try. . . . It's your right to go to school. . . . But standing on the corner, you ain't going to learn nothing . . . because it's the same old corner; it's the same old thing; it's wasting time. . . . You know, like that commercial says, 'A mind is a terrible thing to waste.' "

But back then, when Richard was a teenager, he believed that his mind was just fine, thank you, and that he didn't need school. He could get his education on the corner. After all, his grandmother had told him, "Son, one thing a white man can't take from you is the knowledge." Pryor explained his grandmother's point to Joyce Maynard of *The New York Times*: "You take some sixty-three-year-old cat on the street—ugly, spit coming out of his mouth—he's still got something you can't have. You can't say he didn't see that gutter or he didn't drink that wine. That's the knowledge."

But Richard Pryor, the teenager, had taken his grandmother's advice literally. He didn't understand that her intent was for her grandson to look charitably toward old drunks like the elderly wino who visited the family occasionally. She did not mean that a bright young boy should seek only after the kind of knowledge possessed by a wino. She knew, as he did not, that this kind of knowledge alone was poor preparation for survival in the world. Years later, after he had become successful, Richard Pryor would feel keenly his lack of formal education.

Richard was sixteen years old when he became a father for the first time. Renée was born in April 1957. Renée's mother was a local girl and probably one of the first girls Richard ever dated, since he was very shy around girls. Elaborating on his checkered childhood in an interview with Barbara Walters, Pryor said that he was very upset when he learned his girl friend was pregnant. He thought he was the first she'd ever had. Then his father informed him that he himself had "had" the girl. Richard did not marry her, nor did he publicly acknowledge Renée as his daughter for years.

Within the space of a year in his young life, Richard was expelled from school, had fathered a child, and suffered the loss of his close relationship with Miss Whittaker. It was a lot for a young kid to handle. He found himself with a lot of time on his hands and not much to do to fill it, and for the first time in his life he had nothing to look forward to. School had at least provided some structure to his life, dividing the months by holidays and vacations, and the years by grades. Now he didn't even have that sense of structure, and for the next year or so he moved from one thing to another with little or no direction.

He worked at a variety of jobs. On occasion he's told gullible interviewers that his first job was steering sailors to the family joints. But to others he has admitted that if there's one thing sailors know, it's how to find whorehouses. He may indeed have worked at the houses in some capacity, for by the age of seventeen he was spending a lot of time over on North Aiken Street where, according to Ray Le Roy, his stepmother operated a joint. He worked "shaking hides" in a meatpacking house, did janitorial duty at a North Washington Street tavern, racked balls at Pop's Pool Hall, and shined shoes in a barbershop. In his off-hours he dreamed—of getting out of Peoria, of being famous and showing everyone that he was special. He went to the movies and engaged in a typically adolescent form of identity display by pasting his own name over Marlon Brando's on movie posters. And by the time he was seventeen, he had started to work on his comedy routines in the hope that he might be able to make a living at it.

Ray Le Roy lived next door to Richard's father and stepmother at the time; right on Aiken Alley in the heart of the red light district known as the Merry-Go-Round. A native of Chicago, Le Roy had by this time adopted Peoria as his home. "I was the house comedian at Mike and Mike's Show Lounge. Jimmy Lewis, the owner, had a house next door which he rented out to the performers, and I lived in that house. It was at four-hundred-seven North Aiken, and right next door, at four-hundred-nine was Anna and Bucky's. All the entertainers would come over to my house, sit around and talk, have a few drinks. And Richard started showing up. I don't know how it happened or exactly when it happened, but suddenly he was always there. And we [adults] would say to each other, 'Isn't he the politest little fella?' He was about seventeen, I guess—real thin then."

At first Richard just sat and listened, but eventually he got the courage to ask Ray Le Roy if he could look through his gag books. Le Roy was flattered: "He was just breaking in. I think I was sort of an inspiration to him.

"I had a lot of material for him to look at—wrote most of it myself. It was mostly stand-up material. He used to sit for hours going through my scripts and books and gags. He said he wanted to work down at Bris Collins's place."

Bris Collins was a big man in Peoria's black community, and more than a little influential in the white community as well. Ray Le Roy remembers, "he was a big, fat man. He did a little time once, but he was a real gentle man. And generous. He helped a lot of white people in town to start businesses." Juliette Whittaker refers to him as Uncle Bris. His place at 405 North Washington had been a fixture in the district since at least 1941, although by the mid-1950s it was much tamer than it had been in earlier days.

LaWanda Page remembers how it was then. A native of East St. Louis, Illinois, Page, who played Aunt Esther in the *Sanford and Son* television series, started out as a shake dancer. Her first engagement outside East St. Louis was at Bris Collins's place. "Back then they called 'em taverns," she says. "It was a dump. It was the kind of place where if you ain't home by nine o'clock at night you can be declared *legally dead*. They all walked around with knives in there. *You* better had one, too—knife or gun or something!"

By the mid-1950s Bris Collins's place was "fairly well appointed," according to Ray Le Roy, and offered live entertainment on weekends—a band and once in a while a dancer or a comic. Bris Collins let

Richard do his routines occasionally. So did Harold Parker, who operated Harold's Club at 103 North Washington.

Pryor says he got the job at Harold's by saying that he could play the piano and sing. Juliette Whittaker adds that Richard told Harold he was twenty-one. Since Parker was probably new to Peoria (he is first listed in the 1953 telephone directory), he was taken in. Richard knew perhaps five chords on the piano and as many songs, but he counted on his comedy routines to get him through. Fortunately for him, his routines were received well by Harold's patrons.

Richard got enough work to feel he needed more help from Ray Le Roy. "He asked me for advice about talking over the mike, getting on the floor, taking bows. I think he used to watch my show, watch me work; you know how a kid will follow you around?" But he didn't get enough work, or enough money when he worked, to earn a living at comedy. Juliette Whittaker says, "I don't think he was actually paid a salary. The customers would throw money, and whatever they threw he could keep."

He had to keep working at odd jobs, low-grade jobs, and the few nights he managed to find a forum for his comedy in North Washington Street taverns were not enough to maintain his idea that he was special. Seventeen years old with nowhere to go, Richard started doing a lot of hanging out on the corner with the colorful street characters of Peoria's district—the winos and the dice and domino players, the pimps and the dope dealers, men whose survival mechanisms included big doses of bravado and humor: the old, toothless southern black man playing his harmonica and understating his skills at dice in order to outwit the northern dudes who thought they'd found a sucker; the wino swaying as he stands, preaching that he's got the secret to success. On the corner verbal creativity was highly prized, and Richard's vocabulary and comic talent gave him an undisputed edge in such favorite corner pastimes as the "The Dozens."

"We used to have good sessions sometimes," he told David Felton of *Rolling Stone*. "I remember once I came up with a beaut, man. I killed them one day. We was doin' it all day to each other, you know? Bang, bang—'Your shoes are run over so much, look like your *ankles* is broke,' and shit like that. And I came up with, I called the motherfucker The Rummage Sale Ranger, you know what I mean? 'Cause that's where he got his clothes. The Rummage Sale Ranger—that was a knockout. I saved that one for the last, that ended it."

Looking back on his time on the corner, Pryor believes not only that it put him into contact with many of the ghetto characters that are now his trademark but that it also challenged him to perform at his best; for there is no audience more critical than a bunch of dudes on the corner. "That's where niggers rehearse. If you want to be a speaker, you rehearse your speeches. You tell your stories. . . . Singers start there. Groups do their thing. Players run their game. It's like that. That was my stage."

But he was up against tough competition, and for all their respect of verbal prowess the men on the corner were not above using whatever they had to win a contest. A purely verbal confrontation could degenerate quickly into a physical one, and small, skinny Richard Pryor with his smart mouth was no doubt a frequent target. That may have been one reason why he entered Golden Gloves boxing competition.

His boxing career was short lived. His father may have won a Golden Gloves tournament in Chicago in 1933 and thought that his son would benefit from channeling his aggressive tendencies in a similar forum, but Richard didn't show much pugilistic promise. Up against the ropes he relied on his wit as usual. "He won his first fight in the first round," LeRoy Pryor told a newspaper reporter. "And I think he did it by telling a joke, which made the guy double up. And then he punched him out." Not every opponent had such an accessible funny bone, and Richard was soon knocked out of Golden Gloves competition.

Pryor says he preferred street fighting and tells of a war between two gangs with the improbable names of Love Licks and the Love Veedles. He says the police arrested the whole lot of them and confiscated a varied street arsenal of knives, pipes, and rubber hoses. Andy Boone disputes this story. "Peoria's a little midwestern town. It wasn't Chicago. Nobody was walking around with chains and switchblades. You had a few roughnecks and some people who were a little whacko in the head, but every place has got that."

Still, Richard was getting into enough trouble to alarm his father. LeRoy Pryor told Jean Budd of the Peoria Journal-Star that Richard "was beginning to run around with the wrong group. So I said one day to my wife, okay, that's it—he goes. That's probably the best thing we ever did for him—make him go out on his own." Richard says his father threw him out because he failed at pimping. Whatever the reason, Richard Pryor left Peoria and joined the Army.

CHAPTER III

On the Chittlin' Circuit

AS HE TOLD THE story in later comedy routines, Richard Pryor left
Peoria the first time under duress—the gangs "had to get out of
Peoria, so we all went to the Army together." If his father is to be
believed, he joined the Army because he had no place else to go. The
reasons for Pryor's doing anything are never simple, particularly in
his own recollection.

He tells a funny story about not being accepted into the service the
first time he tried. Having informed everyone that he was going to join
the Army, he went to Chicago and flunked the entrance examination.
He was so embarrassed he stayed in the house for months, and when
he did go out he donned a bogus Army uniform. "I fooled a lot of my
friends," he told Janet Maslin of *The New York Times*. "Didn't fool
any of their parents, though." After the Army did accept him, he was
trained as a plumber, although studio biographies sometimes say he
was a paratrooper. When Richard Pryor was in the Army, it had yet to
be completely desegregated, although President Truman's directive
to that effect had provided for the process to begin in 1950. In the late
1950s blacks were still consigned to jobs as laborers and body ser-
vants more often than to regular soldiering duties, and this situation
would not change appreciably until the United States became ac-
tively involved in the Vietnam conflict.

Richard was a cold-war soldier. Stationed at Kaiserslautern, a town
in southwestern West Germany that had been severely damaged in
World War II, he was at least in the same country where the major
crisis of the cold war took place in 1961: construction of the Berlin
Wall. Richard's eighteen months in Germany were long enough for
him to know that he wanted to leave. He says he had entertained the
notion of an Army career but that it was dashed by the racism of his

29

white superiors and fellow soldiers. United States involvement in Vietnam had not yet begun, and the only action he saw was on base. He once stabbed a man seven times, and on a separate occasion he hit another guy on the head with a pipe. "Really?" asked David Felton when Pryor told him about the latter incident, "An enemy or one of ours?" Pryor answered, "No, a white cat. One of yours."

Pryor pleads self-defense in both cases. The time he hit a guy with a pipe he was being beaten up in a deserted armory by three crackers with tire irons. More positive experiences during this time included his "giving head" for the first time and appearing in several Army amateur variety shows where his comic talents were well received.

On his discharge from the Army Pryor returned to Peoria where his family welcomed him and he tried for a while to settle down. He married a local girl named Patricia, who bore him a son, Richard Jr., in 1961. (Sometimes he is referred to as Richard III, since Uncle Dicky is the first Richard.) Pryor also got a job at the Caterpillar Tractor Company, and for a time he tried to content himself with the idea that he was following the normal course of life. But he soon got the urge to be on stage again. He went to Bris Collins and got a job at Collins's Cafe for seventy-two dollars a week. He performed at other Peoria clubs whenever he got a chance. But he could not devote all his energy to his comedy—he had a wife and child to support. Trying to think responsibly, he decided that he had no right to expect more out of the future than forty years at Caterpillar in his steel-soled shoes.

But he found it increasingly difficult to keep his mind in that narrow channel. He kept thinking about performing, about how good it felt to be on stage, making people laugh. Going home to Patricia and the baby just made him feel trapped. But spending time in the clubs in the district made him feel guilty. Ray Le Roy had fallen heir to Mike and Mike's Show Lounge by this time, and he remembers that weeks would pass when he would not see Richard. "One day I looked up and he was sitting at the end of the bar. He never spoke or anything, just sat there watching the stripper. When I looked up again, he was gone."

He struggled with his conflicting notions of who he wanted to be and who he thought he should be. In the end he chose the stage. Juliette Whittaker recalls that she had lost contact with Richard for a while; he had not joined her adult theater group and she had not tried to influence him. He was no longer an adolescent who needed to be collared for rehearsals. But when he suddenly appeared at the Carver Center to tell her he couldn't take working at the Caterpillar Tractor Company anymore, she understood immediately. "One day he walks into my office and says, 'I cannot put the widget on the digit one more time. I can't do that. I don't care how much money they give me. I'm gonna try show business. I've gotta do something.'"

Whittaker understood that Richard hadn't made his decision easily. It meant abandoning his family and all the familiar things about life in Peoria. "He was leaving all of his roots," she explains. "He had this dream of being on *The Ed Sullivan Show*, and I told him he'd have to go to the East Coast for that. He'd have to play Grossinger's. . . . Eventually he did do that, but in leaving he had to walk away from his marriage. He just walked away from it. I guess he did what Gauguin did."

Of all the people Richard knew, only Juliette Whittaker had the sense of romanticism, the idea of dedication to one's art, to compare him to the nineteenth-century French painter who left his family in Paris and traveled to the South Sea Islands to produce some of the most famous paintings in the history of Western art. Richard would not forget Whittaker's support.

Everyone else thought he was either crazy or a no-account. As Pryor once told an interviewer for *Ebony*, "I remember how I left Peoria and what they said to me when I wanted acceptance from them. What they said was, 'Fuck you; you ain't shit!' " But at this point Richard didn't care what anyone else thought. He told his friend Artie Dillon, "Someday, Artie, I'm gonna make it."

Patricia Pryor eventually got a divorce and married a man named Price, but for a time she had to struggle to take care of herself and Richard Jr. She still lives in Peoria, attended Marie Bryant's funeral, and is very supportive of her former husband. Andy Boone said in July 1982, "I saw her down at the tavern the other day. I didn't know her but I was with a friend who did and he pointed her out. He took me over to her and we were standing around talking and I told her, 'I used to beat Richard Pryor's ass all the time.'

"She got very upset and my friend told me later that I shouldn't

have said that because she worships the ground Richard walks on—
because he takes such good care of her."

Steered by contacts he'd made in Peoria and by free-lance talent
scouts, Richard became part of the Midwest chittlin' circuit, which by
then was more often referred to as the blackbelt-nightclub circuit. One
of his first jobs was at the Faust Club in East St. Louis, Illinois.
LaWanda Page was also appearing there. "That was around sixty-one,
sixty-two," she says. "Me, Richard Pryor, Chuck Berry, and Redd
Foxx all worked there around that time. Richard was doing an act
where he sang along with doing comedy. He was a very quiet, polite
person off stage. On stage he was doing true-to-life stuff even then,
and he was very funny."

He was still doing the takeoff on Edward R. Murrow's *Person to
Person* that he'd started doing back in his days as MC at the Carver
Community Center talent shows. He'd mined his Army experiences
for their humor, finding his Army-sergeant impressions particularly
appreciated. He interspersed these routines with one-liners.

He fell in love with a flame dancer at the Faust Club and learned that
women could be very helpful to him. They gave him a place to stay
and often brought gigs his way. "Like, you'd suck a fire dancer's
pussy in the dressing room, and in her next job she'd try to get you as
the MC," Pryor told David Felton. "Shit, if I hadn't been able to give
head, probably still be in St. Louis at the Faust Club."

Pryor did stints across the Midwest, over the Canadian border, and
as far east as Buffalo and Pittsburgh. As a rule, he could count on a
four-week booking as an MC in the clubs where he appeared, but
sometimes he found himself out of work sooner than he'd expected.

He didn't last that long in Windsor, Ontario, where he worked in a
"hillbilly bar." He told Sandor Vanocur of *The Washington Post*, "I
was singing and doing impressions of people they didn't care about.
Jimmy Cagney. They didn't give a damn. They wanted to see the
big-chested singer. I mean, I would get comments like: 'Get the fuck
off.' Simple, subtle." Nor did he last long in another club whose
owner told him he had guts, but no talent.

Sometimes he played for the full four weeks and then had trouble
collecting his pay. At the Zanzibar in Youngstown, Ohio, he says

he had to pull a blank pistol on the Arab owners to get his money.

Even when he was paid on time, the money often wasn't enough to see him through until his next gig, and he had to swallow his pride and call home to Peoria. "We was so poor even poor folks didn't speak to us," says LaWanda Page about life on the road. "We traveled by bus or train, couldn't afford hotels most of the time. Stayed in boarding houses in the Negro neighborhoods. Every once in a while you'd get lucky and stay in somebody's house. But most folks wouldn't let you, because most of those show people would steal." Quiet, polite, shy Richard Pryor had the advantage of being very attractive to women and more often than not he found a place to stay. But at a salary of $125.00 a week, tops, the hotels he did stay in were hardly the Ritz. Once in Toronto he checked into a hotel that he later learned was favored by gay wrestlers. "I couldn't believe it," he told Sandor Vanocur. "I mean, you'd see them brutally murdering each other in Saturday night wrestling matches. And then you'd see them back at the hotel kissing and holding hands."

As unsettling as it was to stay in that hotel, playing in the club was equally so, since he couldn't seem to get away from wrestlers. He opened the show for the main act, a bear that drank beer and wrestled with his human handler. "One night the bear got drunk and he got a little bit carried away with the wrestling. He went after me. You know—a bear's a bear. You can't out wrestle a bear, especially a bear that's had a few. And then the bear would get gentle, and stroke you and sit on you."

During one stint in East St. Louis, Pryor MC'd a show that featured a group of female impersonators, several of whom were actually females. He was still as far away from *The Ed Sullivan Show* as he would have been if he'd stayed in Peoria.

One of the lowest points of this period in his life occurred in Pittsburgh when he messed up his good record with women on the road by beating up a nightclub singer, the first of many times when the rage that festered just below the surface in him erupted against a woman.

The singer brought assault and battery charges against him. "It was a valid charge," he later admitted. "We had this misunderstanding. I really assaulted her and I really battered her." Found guilty and sentenced to thirty-five days in jail, plus a fine, Pryor was broke and feeling hopeless, but he was too proud to ask for help from his family—or simply aware that they would refuse. Luckily, his cellmate just happened to be a former boyfriend of one of Richard's aunts. The man took it upon himself to get in touch with his old girl friend and tell her about her nephew's predicament. The aunt wired Richard some money, so at least he wasn't broke when he was released from jail. But as he tells it, he was the most reluctant free man those Pittsburgh jailers had ever seen. "I begged them to let me stay. It was fourteen degrees below outside."

In June 1963 *Newsweek* ran an article on an up-and-coming young black comedian named Bill Cosby. Its title, "Riiight," was a reference to the comedy routine that had catapulted him to stardom: his now-famous Noah routine in which a skeptical Noah hears from God that he is supposed to build an ark and load it up with pairs of living creatures. Each time the Lord adds to the list of things he wants Noah to do, Noah answers "riiight." Cosby had appeared on *The Ed Sullivan Show* and was in great demand on other talk and variety shows. His comedy record was selling hundreds of thousands of copies and he was getting bookings in big white clubs. He was even getting written about in *Newsweek*. His was a success never before achieved by a black comedian, and that fact wasn't lost on Richard Pryor.

Pryor had left Peoria promising himself, and Miss Whittaker, that he would make it to *The Ed Sullivan Show*, and that was not an entirely unrealistic dream. From the beginning of his television show Sullivan had defied custom, and sometimes outright industry opposition, not to mention angry sponsors and southern TV-network affiliates, and insisted on presenting black talent as well as white. By 1963 his show had been on the air for some fifteen years, and dozens of black entertainers, including comedians like Slappy White, Nipsey Russell, Pigmeat Markham, George Kirby, Moms Mabley, and Dick Gregory, had received their first national exposure because of Sullivan. But except for the Sullivan show and *The Jack Benny Show*—given the presence of Eddie Anderson's Rochester character—television was a pale wasteland for blacks. In 1964 the New York Ethical Culture Society scored the television industry for both failing to improve the image of blacks on television and for the lack of black presence on the screen. The campaign was soon taken up by other organizations that promoted ethics, equality, and blacks in America.

Richard Pryor had entertained no serious notions of doing television other than *The Ed Sullivan Show*, or of ever seeing the inside of a big white club. All he hoped to do was to get bookings in the better black clubs in major cities and perhaps MC an occasional rock 'n' roll show. But here was Bill Cosby doing the impossible, and Richard Pryor decided that if Cosby could do it, then he could too.

Cosby had started out in Greenwich Village clubs, and not long after Pryor read the *Newsweek* article he, too, headed for New York. He says he arrived in the city with about two dollars in his pocket, and after paying for a shower, having his suit pressed and his shoes shined, and buying a pack of cigarettes, he was left with exactly thirty-three cents. But he survived in the big city, in the way that fresh-faced eager youngsters were able to in the 1960s in New York.

Somehow he managed to get to Harlem, and like Langston Hughes and countless others before him, he would never forget his awe at seeing so many people who looked like him. As he told a correspondent for *People* in 1978, "Jesus, just knowing there were that many of us made me feel better." The 1964–65, 1965–66, and 1966–67 New York City telephone directories list a Richard Pryor at 217 West 110th Street, the "Mason-Dixon Line" in Manhattan; there is no listing for a Richard Pryor in either the 1963–64 or 1967–68 directories, and if Pryor had a telephone while he was in New York from 1963 to sometime in 1966, the listing probably was his. It stands to reason that he would have chosen to live among lots of other black people once he'd found a place where they were. Besides, he soon decided that people in the Village were snobbish toward him, although he didn't know why.

New York City was another world for Richard Pryor. It took him months just to figure out the subway system, and he never did get used to the crowds. The pace of life, even of talk, was faster than he'd ever experienced; but if he felt out of his element in other areas of Manhattan, he suffered downright cuture shock in Greenwich Village.

The Village was a freewheeling intellectual bohemia where folk music, beat poetry, pacifism, and the writings of Herbert Marcuse were the going street talk, not The Dozens. Village denizens affected long hair and beards, Indian shirts, dashikis, and beads. Richard Pryor, with his processed pompadour à la Jackie Wilson (or Bobby Rydell or Fabian Forte), his tight-fitting suit, and his jive walk may as well have worn a sandwich board that read *Bumpkin*.

Moondog, a white street character who dressed in Viking robes and a crown, and Lamp Man, a black street character who favored leopard-skin loincloths, roamed the streets enjoying their considerable celebrity. Beat poets accosted passersby with readings of their work. Street peddlers offered intricately crafted jewelry and leather goods on the sidewalks in front of craft shops that stayed open all night. Intense singing pedestrians somehow avoided collisions with equally intense walking guitarists; and in the hundreds of sidewalk cafes and dimly lit bistros, the talk was of the meaning of life, art, and politics, and the air was spicy with the scent of marijuana.

"It was a time," recalls screenwriter Buck Henry, who was there, "when every doorway late at night had someone standing in it who would later be famous." Richie Havens, who had escaped to the Village from Brooklyn because no one in his old neighborhood understood his love of folk music or his flower-child philosophy, concurs: "Everybody who is out there was down in the Village in those days— Joan Baez, Pete Seeger, Allen Ginsberg, LeRoi Jones, Lou Gossett— beating on the guitar and singing work songs." Barbra Streisand sported vintage clothing and sang at sidewalk cafes. Bob Dylan strummed his guitar and put politics to song. And a host of young humorists plied their comic wares in the hospitable Village clubs where the controversial Lenny Bruce was always welcomed—no matter how much trouble he was in with the law. Richard Pryor never felt comfortable in this atmosphere, never "made the Village scene," as he put it.

At first he hoped he could find work in uptown and midtown clubs and stay out of the Village. D'Urville Martin remembers seeing him at a midtown club on the West Side in the early sixties.

Martin, a native New Yorker who identifies with Pryor because he was raised by prostitutes in his youth, was doing a variety of acting work at the time: *Cabin in the Sky*, off-Broadway; commercials; and roles in TV dramas like *Naked City*. He recalls, "I first met Richard at a place called Steve Hall's The Scene, on Forty-eighth Street between Eighth and Ninth avenues. At that time, I think, he was working for nothing. He played drums, sang, and told jokes. Sammy Davis, Jr., was doing *Golden Boy* on Broadway at the time, and he used to drop in there. People like that used to come in."

But Richard needed to get paid, and most clubs in the theater district, though great places to meet important people, were not as hospitable as Steve Hall's to young, untried comics. Pryor soon recognized that if he was going to make it in comedy, he would have to be in the Village, if not *of* it.

A number of clubs had what were called hootenanny nights, which were amateur nights when young people with aspirations as entertainers could show their stuff on stage. Comedians were welcome, and the list of young humorists who got their start at these hootenanny nights is as impressive as the list of singers and poets and musicians: David Frye, George Carlin, Robert Klein, Stiller and Meara, Bill Cosby. Monday night was hootenanny night at the Cafe Wha?, Tuesday night at the Bitter End, and so on. The young comics made the rounds, honing their material, improving their live-audience presentations, and hoping to attract the attention of a club owner or agent who could get them a steady booking. Within a month Richard was appearing regularly at the Cafe Wha?, earning five dollars a night (ten dollars on Saturdays) as the opening act for Superman Victor Brady and his Trinidadian Steel Band. After that he shared the bill with Richie Havens.

"He was doing straight comedy—no cussing," says Havens. "He was better than Cosby, but Cosby was more middle-America, more attractive to the TV people. Richard was a little too crazy, a little too political—topics like Vietnam were a no-no for the TV people. But he was still fantastic."

By the end of March 1964 Richard was appearing at the Living Room and being reviewed, although hardly with raves, in *Variety*:

> There is much in Richard Pryor's turn to remind of Bill Cosby. However, it seems to be natural rather than a consciously imitated mannerism. Colored comedian has strong

*and definite ideas on humor. Has an avant garde viewpoint, a
healthy instinct for irreverence and a feel for expression.*

*However, there is still much for him to learn before he can
go into commercial rooms. He is still in the coffeehouse stages
as far as this audience was concerned on his opening night.
He has the approach of an intellectual rather than an entertainer and writing seems to be for clever effect rather than
laughs.*

*Pryor needs a reexamination of his material best done with
more forays in the offbeaters before hoving into the uptown
spots.*

Far be it from a nigger to be an intellectual! America didn't want a
black Lenny Bruce. Richard Pryor didn't want to be compared to
Lenny Bruce anyway. Why not Bob Newhart and Shelley Berman, not
to mention Redd Foxx and Dick Gregory? The Cosby comparison was
okay; in fact it must have pleased him, especially the reviewer's
feeling that the imitation looked natural. Reading the television list-
ings in March 1964, Pryor had to feel that the way to success for him
was on Bill Cosby's coattails. Early that month it was announced that
Cosby had been signed to do *That Was the Week That Was* as well as
The Jack Paar Show and *The Ed Sullivan Show.*

Cosby was acceptable. Pryor still had to work on becoming acceptable: He was told outright when he visited the offices of Cosby's
former agent, Roy Silver. The late writer/comedian Murray Roman
was there, and he took pains to explain to Richard the difference
between him and Cosby: Roman would introduce Cosby to his
mother, but Richard Pryor? . . . Richard Pryor made too much of the
fact that he was black, and that was in bad taste.

Richard admits now that he bought that. He wanted to be successful, and if that meant pretending that he was somehow colorless, then
he was prepared to do it. And if Bill Cosby was what white people
wanted, then he would give them Bill Cosby. "I just started doing
him. I just became him," Pryor has said. If Cosby did Noah, then Pryor
did Adam and Eve. If Cosby never mentioned that he was black, then
Pryor would get up on stage and be Invisible Man.

Once he started doing Bill Cosby, Richard Pryor's career moved
quickly. He appeared at all the Village clubs and sometimes at the

Apollo Theatre in Harlem, where he was at the bottom of the bill, but awed at the mere fact that he was there. He was seen and talked about, and in the late spring of 1964 he got a chance to audition for Rudy Vallee's summer replacement show, *On Broadway Tonight*. Pryor says, "Irving Mansfield, the producer of Vallee's show, liked me, but thought I was way out. Rudy got me the chance, and that's how it began." His first appearance on television was scheduled for the first week of September 1964.

Elated by his success, Richard's first thought was to let the folks back home know he'd made good. He called Tom and Marie Bryant. "All I said was 'Grandpa,' and without letting me finish, he said, 'I ain't got a quarter,' then hung up."

The *Peoria Journal-Star* took him more seriously. PEORIAN TO HAVE NATIONAL TV DEBUT read the headline on August 31, 1964. The article described him as a "comic, singer, dancer, impressionist, and pantomimist." The photograph was a typical publicity shot: Richard in a checked suit, hair still in the pompadour style, resting his jaw on his fist. He mentioned Miss Whittaker's influence on his career.

LeRoy Pryor and his wife read the article and intended to watch the show. Richard called them before the show to make sure they would be watching. But somehow they managed to turn to the wrong channel. When he called after the show to ask what they had thought of his performance, they had to admit they hadn't seen it. "But we saw his next show," said LeRoy Pryor later, "and the thrill of our son making it good tugged at our hearts and brought a tear or two."

White America still wasn't crazy about niggers, even colorless ones, and it was several months before Pryor appeared on television again. He continued playing Village coffeehouses, among them the Village Gate. That is where Arnold Johnson first saw him. Johnson, who appeared regularly as Hutch on *Sanford and Son* and who is often seen on series like *Hill Street Blues*, was doing off-Broadway plays at the time. "Richard was doing a solo act," says Johnson, "and I remember I asked him at that time where he'd studied acting. He said no; he'd never studied it. Then I knew he was somebody special. He was doing skits—an Indian learning karate, an old redneck and a grandmother. He could do voices like you couldn't believe—the redneck hillbilly's *and* the woman's."

The other thing Johnson remembers about Pryor in those days was his attractiveness to women. "Girls used to come to the Village Gate just to see him. Always been a lot of women with that guy."

Pryor played Borscht Belt resort spots in the Catskills, the Uptown Theatre in Philadelphia, the Blue Angel in Chicago. His parents went to see him there. "Sure enough high above in big lights was the name Richard Pryor," his father recalled with some awe. "We knew then that he had found what he'd always wanted."

In 1965 he appeared on Merv Griffin's then new syndicated talk show, and in the same year he achieved his dream at last and made it to *The Ed Sullivan Show*. Sullivan spotted Pryor when he was working in the Village. "Sullivan liked me and the next day he sent for me," Pryor told a correspondent for the *Peoria Journal-Star*, trying to be blasé.

He wore a red, double-breasted suit, buttoned high. His skinny body seemed to consist entirely of right angles. He giggled nervously as the applause at his introduction subsided.

> *Thank you very much. I-I-I'm really happy to be here in show business and stuff, 'cause it's exciting, you know, 'cause people ask you questions and stuff—they always want to talk to you, and ev'thing. And the question people ask me most of all . . . people ask me, "Hey, why ain't you in th' Army?"*
> *[Pause. Laughter.]*
> *And I say, "The reason I'm not in the Army now is 'cause I was in th' Army. We had to get out of Peoria—the gangs—so we all went to th' Army together. And it was all very exciting, except we had little hangups. Like we couldn't understand the people in charge of you, 'cause they talk in funny language. You know: "hup, hap, hup . . . hup, hmmmph, hup . . . nuuumph, nnnaa, nup." [Pause. Laughter.]*
> *And I couldn't understand that, and you couldn't talk to 'em unless you knew that secret language: "uhnamur-nahmph." [Pause. Laughter.]*
> *And they had little guys going around: "minimirnimini-min." [Laughter.]*
> *And it really was wild, because the first day I got in th' Army the guy said, "Hey, who, hup, heep, ho, hup-ap-op-hup-hap-hop, hup . . . Is that understood?" [Laughter.]*

And the guys were too scared to say anything. Said, "Yeah, we'll pick up a bush, sure, anything; we'll do that."

[Pause. Laughter.]

To me, all this talk about bein' in the Army . . . I said, "Why don't they have guys in th' Army doin' the war stuff that like to do it? You know, like the Mafia." [Pause. Laughter.]

I figure, like, say, if you hired the Mafia, they take care ol' Ho Chi Minh, right? [Laughter.]

[Pryor in a deep voice.] "Mr. Mafia, we'll give you seventy billion dollars, you take care ol' Ho Chi Minh."

[Pryor in a godfather voice.] It shall be done.

[Rrriiing.] "Hello, Chicago."

"Hello, Louie? I wantcha ta hit Ho Chi Minh."

"Okay, Chief, it shall be done. . . . What's a Ho Chi Minh?"

[Laughter.]

[Pryor in his normal voice.] Can you imagine the guy goin' to make what they call the hit?

[Ding-dong. Polite voice.] Wh-who is it?

[Mafia voice.] Avon callin'.

[Loud laughter and applause.]

Pryor then did a routine on submarines. In one segment a jivin', obviously black sailor tells a newcomer, "Mens, we goin' inta combat, mens, so I wantcha to mop the deck and poop the ship."

In another a medic in charge of the morphine supply is asked how much morphine is left. "Aaah, I don't know, baby. I'm just sailin' along with the breeze."

And in another he plays not only a sonarscope operator, but also the captain, and the sonarscope, plus assorted other crewmen and torpedoes.

His eyes changed with each character, hardening when he played the captain, becoming heavy-lidded as he played the enlisted men, round and wide when he was being the sonarscope. His mouth was fascinating; it seemed to travel across his jaw in the short frame changes of a cartoon.

On television Pryor seemed to be in his element. He reveled in the realization of his dream so much that he wasn't even overwhelmed when he appeared on the *Tonight* show. He was spontaneous and downright crazy when he sat on the famous couch on this show that represented the pinnacle for a stand-up comedian. In fact his host was somewhat nonplussed at Pryor's show-stealing tactics. But the audience loved it.

Pryor, though still intent on being Bill Cosby, was showing his own stuff, almost in spite of himself. To David Felton, who still remembers vividly the first time he saw Pryor on the Carson show, there was little comparison. Pryor, says Felton, "was far better, far blacker, and truer to life than television's official black comic of the time, Bill Cosby. During his stand-up routine Pryor did his Rumpelstiltskin piece, about some frightened school kids performing the classic children's story; Cosby was currently doing a number of bits drawn from childhood nostalgia, and I was struck by the difference between Pryor's and Cosby's. Pryor's kids seemed very naturally and specifically black, whereas Cosby's could have been white. . . . More likely it was just that Pryor's kids were real—they completely took over his brain and body, while Cosby's kids were caricatures, exaggerated, and filtered through the paternalistic eye of a grown-up."

Fortunately for Richard Pryor television was beginning to open up a bit for performers like him. In the wake of Bill Cosby's success—not one television in a white home was reported to have disintegrated when he was on the screen—and in the atmosphere of greater racial consciousness brought on by the civil rights movement in the South and the liberal awakening in the North, the Eastern Establishment that still controlled television in those days was taking a few tentative steps toward presenting blacks as blacks on the screen.

In fact the world was opening up for Richard Pryor, and as he traveled and met new people, he acquired at least a thin veneer of sophistication. He let his hair go natural, had put on some weight, and was dressing more suitably for an up-and-coming young comedian. Still shy and polite with people he did not know, he had learned not to seem completely tongue-tied with strangers. And when he returned to Peoria for visits, he felt that he could hold his head high, because he had proved himself.

His grandmother was especially proud of him. Juliette Whittaker says she kept a bulletin board full of clippings about his shows and appearances. "That's when they were living over on Millman [1319

West Millman]—one of those houses they kept adding onto, grew like Topsie. They added this large paneled den, and as you'd come inside the door, there was this great big bulletin board, and everything was on that bulletin board. I kept up with Richard through his grand-mother."

But then, everyone was proud of him. Says Andy Boone, "You'd be surprised at how many people knew him after he started to get famous." They naturally had the idea that Richard was getting rich from his TV and club appearances, and he began to get requests for money. He helped out as much as he could, especially with people who had helped him.

By Peoria standards, and by a lot of other standards, Richard was indeed rich. Moreover, as they say in the trade, he was hot. D'Urville Martin still has a note of incredulity in his voice when he says, "After seeing him in Steve Hall's working for nothing, he was suddenly averaging ten thousand a week in nightclubs, or something like that. He was on The Ed Sullivan Show, and he was hot then. Not quite as big as he is now, but big for a nigger. Ten thousand a week and The Ed Sullivan Show—that was the ultimate. I came close to being on Sullivan's show—he came to see us in Cabin in the Sky, but we all goofed up."

Any entertainer who was successful in those days, and who wanted more television work, not to mention film work, moved to California. For Richard this was a greater step than it was for most people. His club bookings were still primarily on the East Coast, and he hated to fly. He was deathly afraid of airplanes, petrified of being in the air, and insisted on taking his small alley cat, which he had bought in New York for a quarter, whenever he traveled by plane. But he had some high-powered white managers and press-relations people now, and they said he should move to California, and he did, even though relocating to the West Coast involved more dreaded flying.

D'Urville Martin was already in California when Richard Pryor arrived. "At that time they were looking for New York black actors, as the best actors. They would hire local California actors for the minor roles. I had been doing LeRoi Jones's The Toilet at the St. Mark's Playhouse in New York, and I was the only one who was asked to go out and do it on the West Coast. My part was also upgraded to second lead." After the West Coast run of *The Toilet* was over, Martin stayed in California, deciding to pursue his television career.

"The first show that I guest-starred in, I took from Richard. It was *A Doktori* and when I saw Richard arrive I thought, 'Oh wow, I ain't got this job.' Because he was hot. I remember that Richard came late, and he had an army of guys, his agents and all, with him. And press . . . white guys with suits and ties.

"I went in first, before Richard. I sat down, and the producer said, 'You want this job?' I said, 'Yeah.'

" 'Think you can do it?' I said, 'Yeah.'

"He said, 'Okay, you've got the contract.' I said, 'Yeah? Where's the contract? 'Cause I know Richard's out there and he's hot.'

"And that was the first and last job I ever beat him out of. We talked there outside the producer's office, and we were supposed to meet at a party, and everything. Then when the word came out that I got the job, I couldn't even reach him on the phone. Forget the party."

Richard Pryor's chance was not long in coming. In late September 1966 he was signed to appear in his first film, *The Busy Body* starring Sid Caesar. Produced and directed by William Castle, and released by Paramount, it was a modest, low-budget gangster spoof. Its comedian-studded cast included, besides Caesar and Pryor, Jan Murray, Dom DeLuise, Bill Dana, Godfrey Cambridge, Marty Ingels, and George Jessel. Pryor played a police lieutenant.

Filming lasted about a month, and when it was over, Pryor headed for Peoria to show his family and friends that he was now not just a television star but also a movie star. He got a full-page spread in the *Peoria Journal-Star* of October 29, 1966, wherein it was reported that he was visiting his parents and receiving old friends and well-wishers. Pryor was eager to talk to reporter Jean Budd of his home-town newspaper.

On acting: "It isn't as easy as I thought it would be. But it's a good business because you don't have to be flying around all the time. I love live audiences, too, but you have to travel so much—and I don't dig that flying."

His ambition: "To get married, live in a house, have kids, enjoy life—not have to work ever—anymore—at anything, shape, form or fashion."

In the meantime he was taking all the work he could get. He was booked solidly until February 1967 in clubs from Washington to Florida, with all the dreaded flying that entailed. There was a record contract in the offing, and he had hopes of appearing in a second movie—*Castle Keep* with Burt Lancaster (Columbia). He was also slated for more television work—the *Roger Williams Show* and his second stint on *The Ed Sullivan Show*, both in November.

Jean Budd asked him how he felt about the increased exposure blacks were beginning to get on television, and Pryor dropped his gee-isn't-life-great routine for a moment. His assessment was biting: "It's a sham—a trick that deludes. You see more Negroes on TV because what they are selling, sells to the Negro. Now they are getting worse parts, but more of them."

For all the success he had enjoyed in the past two years, Richard Pryor was a dissatisfied man.

CHAPTER IV

Pryor in the Big Time

WHETHER OR NOT HE knew it when he told Jean Budd that his ambition was to get married and have kids, Richard Pryor was already on his way to his third role as a father. Maxine was a Los Angeles girl, small, with short brown hair and a no-nonsense air. She was not an aspiring actress, and Pryor was attracted to that comparative rarity in southern California. He "did the right thing" and married her before the baby was born. They rented an apartment at 8400 Sunset Boulevard in West Hollywood. Elizabeth Anne was born April 26, 1967, at Cedars of Lebanon Hospital. Richard was on a northern California tour at the time and was not present for the birth of his second daughter.

Richard Pryor was still not ready for a settled life. He was just beginning to enjoy his success. He was getting a chance to do more movies, including a bit part in *The Green Berets*, starring John Wayne, his one-time movie hero. Inexplicably, he wanted to be listed in the credits as Richard "Cactus" Pryor, perhaps because that seemed a fitting moniker for an actor in a Wayne film.

He also played Stanley X, a fifteen-year-old drummer, in the American International picture *Wild in the Streets*. A futuristic drama about a group of kids who take over society, the movie starred Shelley Winters, Christopher Jones, Diane Varsi, Hal Holbrook, Millie Perkins, and Ed Begley, among others. Pryor made a point of hanging around on the set and watching the actual mechanics of filmmaking, and he took advantage of the opportunity to learn as much as he could about the medium that had fascinated him since childhood. "Watching movies being made is equal to watching the finished product on the screen," he pronounced.

Now he was living out his dreams. He was a star, and he was learning to live like one. It was the start of what has been called his

Super Nigger period, although one of his attorneys in later years preferred to call it his syndrome of irresponsibility. Whatever the label, the year 1967 marks the time when Richard Pryor started to become unglued.

The reasons are as complex as Pryor's personality. He was not comfortable with success. The deep-seated guilt that he was somehow responsible for being born black and "in the life" would not allow him to accept stardom as something he had earned and deserved. Deep down, he felt like a fake, as if at any moment the hoax might be discovered. In part he was indeed faking. He was beginning to feel constricted doing the type of comedy material he was forced to do in order to be acceptable on television, or even in the Las Vegas clubs where he was now getting bookings for three thousand dollars a week. Yet he knew he could not change his image or his material without risking the loss of the success and money he had so recently come to possess. In the fall of 1967 a writer for *Cue* described him as being, "Sharp without being angry, rooted in his background but essentially nonracial in character." Richard Pryor had to work hard at preserving that image, and the effort took its toll.

Not only did he have to keep up the image, but he had to keep up with new material that fit that image. Once he started appearing with some regularity on television, he found that his club audiences were already familiar with his routines. "A comedian can't go on the road with the same material that he's done on records or television like singers do," he once told a reporter for *The Detroit News*. "Comedy is a matter of surprise and you can't have the audience mouthing your punch lines. Once in a while an audience likes to hear certain bits. But when they're paying fifteen or twenty dollars a ticket, they want to hear new material. Buddy Hackett taught me an important lesson. You don't do your act on television and then try to take it on the road."

It was hard enough coming up with new material, but he had to edit himself constantly, throwing out routines, expressions, even characters that he knew were not acceptable to his audiences. No matter how much he liked it, he had to put it aside, get his mind back on the right track—the middle-America track. This was especially true for television, where there was constant pressure from sponsors. "They always say 'be clean,'" he lamented to a reporter for *Ebony*. "They want you to be something that doesn't exist at all. . . . I do the shows, but I just get bugged." And he was still bitter about the racism on television. "They would rather use the dirtiest ofay cat in the world, man, than to use a black cat."

But it was hard for a lot of people to feel sympathy for Pryor. After all, he *was* on television; he was making money.

His stepmother died on December 31 of that year and he went back to Peoria for the funeral. He was struck again by his father's absolute honesty and its shock value. It was a cold day, and his father told the minister to hurry up with the graveside eulogy. There wasn't much sobbing over the death of Viola Anna Pryor, but Richard heard plenty of sobbing about his family's money problems. He returned to Los Angeles broke and depressed.

Cocaine seemed to be his only friend. By his own admission, he was a heavy user by this time, having graduated from marijuana, although he still smoked reefers on occasion. In April 1967, the same month Elizabeth Anne was born, Pryor was busted at the San Diego border for possession of less than one ounce of marijuana. He was convicted and placed on probation.

In Hollywood cocaine was, and still is, the fashionable drug. Some people will give up red meat, cigarettes, and all liquor but white wine, but they'll still ask you when they see you, if you've got a snort. Pryor had the money to support his habit, and he indulged freely and openly. Director Michael Schultz, who met him around this time, recalls that there was coke on the table. Pryor says now that cocaine was the cause of a lot of the troubles he got into during that period of his life.

On July 26, 1967, Pryor returned home late at night and asked the desk clerk for the key to his apartment. Apparently, the clerk, forty-three-year-old Fabian Tholkes, didn't respond quickly enough. Pryor punched him in the face and broke his glasses. Wayne Trousper, the building's owner, happened to be there and went to Tholkes's aid. Pryor then attacked Trousper with a knife. That same night Pryor was arrested and charged with assault with a deadly weapon with intent to commit mayhem. Two months later, on September 28, Pryor pleaded innocent to the charges, forcing a jury trial. When he did not appear for his trial in early December, Santa Monica Superior Court

Judge David Williams issued a bench warrant and Pryor was forced to appear on the new trial date. The trial began in early January, with Pryor in attendance; but after two days he interrupted the proceedings to plead no contest. On February 9, 1968, he was fined three hundred dollars and given a suspended sentence. On the basis of the conviction the desk clerk, Fabian Tholkes, who had suffered damage to his right eye from Pryor's punch, later sued and won damages in excess of $75,000. Pryor did not contest the suit.

After the incident at the Sunset Boulevard apartment building, Pryor and family moved to a rented home on Beverly Drive in Beverly Hills, where a reporter and a camera crew from Ebony visited to do the first article on Pryor to appear in that major black magazine. Pryor was not impressed. He was quite willing to clown for the cameras. He showed off his new sixteen millimeter camera and photographed the spot on his lawn where his neighbor's dog had done its business. He displayed his gun collection, demonstrated his quick-draw abilities, and injured his finger. He even took the crew to the intersection of Hollywood and Vine so they could film him directing traffic, for which he got a ticket. But he was hostile to personal questions: "You know, my life ain't really been too interesting," he began in a vain attempt to sidetrack his interviewer. Pressed for answers about his early life, he said he'd grown up in a house of prostitution. The reporter, thinking he was just trying to shock, asked him to be serious. "Your serious and my serious are two different things," he responded. Asked how he felt about making it in show business, he answered, "The it has nothing to do with show business. The it I've been trying to make is me."

Displeased about the paucity of straight answers she had been able to get from Pryor, the reporter got in touch with his press agent, but she was not much help. "He doesn't like to talk about those things, and I don't push him."

The Ebony piece, which appeared in the September 1967 issue, was heavy on pictures and light on text.

Pryor was sick of the responsibilities of being a public figure, of grinning and shuffling and compromising when he wanted to say, "Kiss my ass." The incident with the desk clerk did not relieve the pressure he felt. Perhaps bolstered by cocaine, he continued to strike back in random and destructive ways. In October 1967, in the middle of a seventeen-day engagement at the Aladdin Hotel in Las Vegas, he answered hecklers in the audience with a string of obscenities and was fired. He also chose not to file an income tax return for the year 1967.

On April 4, 1968, the day Martin Luther King, Jr., was assassinated, Pryor was in Chicago, appearing at Mr. Kelly's and earning fifteen to twenty thousand dollars for a week's work. Although Pryor had never taken an active role in civil rights work, he had followed the progress of the struggle for black equality closely, and King was a hero to him. When he heard the news, Pryor wanted to be alone, and he went to a bar. Apparently, many others had gone to the same bar to talk about what had happened. A man tried to talk to Pryor but he moved away. Then, to Pryor's horror, the man angrily reached into his own mouth, twisted one of his teeth out of the gums in his lower jaw, and threw it down on the floor. Pryor got out of that bar, quick.

But the memory of the incident stayed with him. That kind of self-directed violence frightened him so much that even he couldn't put it into words. And yet Richard Pryor was inflicting violence of another kind on himself at that time. Although he managed to show up for his club appearances and function onstage, off stage he was often so coked up that he had little self-control. According to D'Urville Martin, the desk clerk at the apartment building was not the only man Pryor hit during this period: "Richard punched out certain white people." And it was during this period of Pryor's life that he got a reputation for knocking women around his apartment. Whether or not Maxine was among them, their marriage ended, and shortly thereafter Pryor and Shelley Bonus were an item.

"I knew Shelley before Richard did," says D'Urville Martin, who by this time was beginning to concentrate on producing rather than acting in films. "She worked on the production end of my documentary, Mad Game. She is a fantastic comedian; even though she is white, she can write black material. At that time she was passing herself off as a poor, starving white girl, a flower child, and if I hadn't known she came from a very wealthy background, I would have believed it. Her father managed Danny Kaye; once in a while I'd run into her when she had a chinchilla coat on, and I wouldn't recognize her."

Shelley Bonus and Richard Pryor met on the set of one of the movies he was doing, and one thing led to another. Says Martin, "She was a little white girl working on the set . . . and some of the crew had to stay overnight. She was the first one to tell me that they had met. She called me and said, 'Guess who I'm living with? You'll never guess.'

"I said, 'I don't know,' and she said, 'Richard Pryor.'

"At that time there were a lot of bad words being spread about him—punching out white guys, stripping nude on the set of some movie—but she was saying that he was a really beautiful guy."

They moved into a two-story house on Hancock Place in Los Angeles. They tried out their comedy material on each other. Shelley got pregnant, and once again Richard married the mother of his expected child. D'Urville Martin remembers that Shelley's father was very much against the marriage. Rain, Pryor's fourth child and third daughter, was born in June 1969.

By 1968 Pryor had put on weight. His body no longer looked like a mass of right angles. The Afro (sometimes called a freedom cap in those days of raised black consciousness), which he had worn since 1966, was longer and he sported a spotty moustache. He looked very different from the skinny kid who was believable in the role of a fifteen-year-old drummer in Wild in the Streets, which was released that year. The movie was playing in Peoria in late August 1968 when Pryor arrived to play at the brand-new Playboy Club at Lake Geneva, Wisconsin. The ten thousand dollar salary for a week's work was low by Pryor's standards, but it was a prestigious gig that would count in future bookings. Anyway, Pryor liked playing near home, and his hometown newspaper, represented by its associate editor Bill Little, covered his opening night.

By this time Pryor had begun to introduce more off-color humor into his routines. There was a freedom in club work that he could not enjoy on television, and he had decided to exploit it. He was pushing at the limits that had been set for him, and that he had set for himself, in order to feel better about what he was doing. As he had told the hapless Ebony interviewer in a serious moment, he had begun to worry about his manhood. He'd started doing a routine about The

Dozens, for example, and in those days even a line like "Your Mama" could shock. He'd also decided that, bad taste or not, he and his audiences were going to acknowledge the fact that he was black. "My name is Richard and I come from Peoria," he began his routine that night at the Playboy Club. "Peoria's a model city, you know. That means they've got the Negroes under control."

Bill Little duly reported that in the *Peoria Journal-Star* and noted the possible consequences of Pryor's new stage persona: " . . . the dangerous part of Pryor's act is his blue material, of which he uses quite a bit and quite blue. The blue stuff is dangerous, critics think, because it isn't all that funny—although it elicits loud yuks from a handful of people—and it might cost him bookings. And it doesn't take long for a comic to go down hill once his bookings slacken."

There were indeed some rumblings about Pryor's blue material by this time and not just from his hometown newspaper. A Chicago columnist reported that he had used obscenities on the *Joey Bishop Show* and Pryor was henceforth banned from the show. Although Paul Orr, the show's producer, denied that Pryor had been banned, that he had even used profanity, the anti-Pryor campaign had started.

It was fueled by Pryor himself, in public. He talked about the strictures of performing before predominantly white Las Vegas audiences. "Sometimes I get so mad," he said on the *Tonight* show in 1968, "I feel like getting undressed and running across the tables shouting 'Black Jack! Black Jack!' "

As Pryor described it, "the current was happening, and every now and then I'd go for it." It was the current of his independence as a black man and as a black comedian. It was the current of who he really was, running through the schizophrenic role he had to play in order to be successful.

That year, Pryor recorded his first album. Issued by Warner-Reprise in January 1969 and called simply *Richard Pryor*, its cover makes a statement of sorts. The Richard Pryor on the jacket is about as far from the Bill Cosby mold as one can get. Richard squats in the sand practically naked except for a ring in his nose and a necklace of bones around his neck. In his hand he holds a bow and arrows. It is too ridiculous to be a parody of the noble savage. In fact it is telling the white and black audiences that had made him successful to "kiss off."

Judged by the standards of his later humor, the material on the album is comparatively tame. The situations are traditional. One is a panel TV show in which an academic, a cleric, and a black nationalist debate the origin of man. Pryor's realization of three different characters is superb, but the debate itself is contrived. The one piece that foreshadows later Pryor comedy is a parody of Superman called Super Nigger. Like the cover of the album, this piece is a long way from the Cosby pattern. The word *nigger* was not used in polite society and certainly not on television.

Pryor was not doing much television anymore. Occasionally he would appear on one talk show or another, but when he did his material was predictable—the black preacher, the hillbilly preacher, his "cool run" in high school when he was too chicken to fight but still wanted to impress the girls. And he no longer kept up his performance once his standup routine had ended. In fact, sitting with other guests, he had little to say. After he failed to show up for an appearance on *The Ed Sullivan Show*—he explained that he'd got so busy with his movie-camera equipment that he'd just forgotten—he was not invited to be on TV very often.

That was fine with Pryor. He was doing more work in films and thinking that one day he might be able to devote most of his energies to acting and producing. By late 1968 he had been signed for an ABC Movie of the Week called *The Young Lawyers*, which would also feature Dick Bass, halfback with the Los Angeles Rams. He had also formed his own film company, Black Sun Productions, the name no doubt a reference to his childhood, when he decided he was orange in color and called himself Sun. He had made arrangements with the Galey Studios in Westwood to begin the filming in late February of a movie he had written. Called *The Trial*, it was a sort of Uncle Tom's fairy tale in which he and others kidnap a rich white man and put him on trial.

Although *The Trial* was not completed, it was not the only such movie being made at that time. Protest movies, antiestablishment movies, and even anti-white movies were being filmed. Television had already exposed audiences to the anti-war and civil rights movements. Hollywood had been slow to catch up, continuing with its patriotic, brotherly love films far past the time when these had much appeal, particularly to the young people who bought most of the movie tickets. But independent filmmakers were not so slow on the uptake. By the time official Hollywood caught up with the mind of the mass audience, many of these independent filmmakers already had their films in the can.

Pryor's father died in October of that year. If he mourned, he did not do so publicly. He also did not file an income tax return for 1968.

By March 1969 Pryor was happily at work on *The Trial* and simultaneously filming the ABC Movie of the Week *The Young Lawyers*. But he took time out to accept an invitation to perform at a benefit show at the Carver Community Center in Peoria. It was the first time he had actually been asked to perform in his hometown.

The show was sponsored by the newly created and redundantly named Afro-American Black People's Federation of Peoria. Miss Whittaker had been asked to invite Pryor, and he accepted with pleasure. Besides, his mother was ill and in the hospital, and it was a good chance to see her as well.

It was a very satisfying visit for Pryor. Greeted by a crowd at Greater Peoria Airport, where he arrived shortly before noon, and followed every step of the way thereafter by reporters and cameramen from the *Journal-Star*, he went first to Methodist Hospital to visit his mother and present her with a hand mirror. He wanted her to come live with him in California where he could take care of her, he said. His Uncle Dicky was at the hospital and he accompanied Pryor to the next stop, Pop's Pool Hall, where he and Pop and Uncle Dicky staged a pool game for the benefit of photographers and he visited with his grandmother. Next, he went to visit great-uncle Herman Carter and other relatives before heading for the Carver Center and his afternoon performance. Along with the family in the front-row seats sat Juliette Whittaker.

Then Richard did a twenty-minute routine—his standard material about meeting girls, being born, Army life, cops, political jokes, and some down-home Peoria jokes. After a brief interview with a *Journal-Star* reporter, he boarded a plane for Chicago and a concert at the Hilton Hotel that night. The Afro-American Black People's Federation realized several hundred dollars from the benefit, since Pryor had paid all his own expenses. The proceeds were used to support the Federation's programs in the black community.

Later in the year Pryor did a bit in *The Phynx*, a picture chock full of guest stars that was intended to be the ultimate camp spectacle. Produced by Bob Booker and George Foster, and written by Stan Cornyn, the movie was about a rock group called The Phynx that was created for the sole purpose of gaining enough popularity to garner an invitation to Albania, where a host of kidnapped celebrities are being held by Joan Blondell and George Tobias. The ludicrous plot is primarily an armature on which to hang irreverent jokes about everything from the Boy Scouts, to the military, to the clergy, to the KKK. Pryor, as one of the kidnapped celebrities, and billed as a guest star in the credits, was in illustrious company. Among the other guest stars were Busby Berkeley, Dick Clark, Xavier Cugat, Joe Louis, Maureen O'Sullivan, Ed Sullivan, Rona Barrett, James Brown, Butterfly McQueen, Martha Raye, Clint Walker, and Rudy Vallee.

In the fall Pryor played his second ABC Movie of the Week role. In *Carter's Army*, he portrayed a young soldier whose first taste of combat terrifies him. Playing a coward, said Pryor, "was the hardest thing I've ever done. My natural instinct is to be funny and I really had to fight with myself not to make the character a lampoon." Also starring Stephen Boyd, Robert Hooks, Susan Oliver, Roosevelt Grier, Moses Gunn, Glynn Turman, Billy Dee Williams, and Paul Stuart, the movie told the story of an all-black unit during World War II that is sent out to defend a vital dam under the leadership of a tough, prejudiced white officer. Pryor enjoyed the camaraderie among the actors as they worked. "We got to calling ourselves the Soiled Six," he said. "There was a great togetherness that I hope will come through in the film. At one point in the picture one of the men in the unit is killed en route to the dam. When the actor who played him didn't come in to work the day after that scene was filmed, I think we all thought he had really died. It was one of the most unusual experiences I've ever been through."

During the time a movie is being made, particularly if the script calls for filming on location, the actors do begin to feel like a family, and Pryor liked the feeling. It was just one more advantage to working in films that he did not have working in television or on nightclub stages.

By the middle of 1969 Pryor was having trouble finding any advantages to working on television or on stages before white audiences. Even the big money he got for such appearances began to seem dirty to him. He was canceling a lot of nightclub bookings, and he did not care that he was getting a reputation for being irresponsible. He was sick of being responsible, of supporting children he rarely saw and former wives who hadn't understood him. He was tired of the fact that just about every call he got from Peoria was a request for money. His mother died that year, and he hated the guilty feelings he had about not having visited her enough or done enough for her.

But most of all he was sick of not being true to himself in his work. As he described it later, there were characters in his head screaming to get out; but they were black characters, ghetto characters, street characters who used profanity and lived life on the edge, characters that other black people, unless they were uptight, bourgeois types, could understand. By comparison, the material he was supposed to do was so Mickey Mouse that he couldn't stomach it; moreover, it was no longer funny to him. But people around him cautioned him, "telling me to wait until I had really made it and then I could talk to the colored." As he told a reporter for the *Los Angeles Times*, "I knew I had to get away from people who thought like that and the environment that made them think like that.

"I was tired of that whole atmosphere, tired of meeting a parade of people I didn't like. They liked me, I guess, but I hated their guts. I hated shaking hands with most of those people. I would shake hands and look at them and see the devil . . . horns and all.

"In those days I was basically lying to myself about what I was doing. I kept asking myself, 'How can I do this, how can I do this?' I saw how I was going to end up. I was false. I was turning into plastic. It was scary. . . . So I did what I had to do—get out of that situation."

One night, early in 1970 on the stage of the Aladdin Hotel in Las Vegas, in the midst of a seemingly normal presentation, Richard Pryor suddenly stopped, surveyed his audience, and said out loud, "What the fuck am I doing here?" In the silence that followed, he answered his own question. Without a word he turned and walked off the stage—or, more correctly, squeezed off it. He managed to walk toward the wrong end of the stage, the end that was blocked by a technician's panel that left space for only a midget to get through. But Richard Pryor was going to get through. There was no way he was going to go back across that stage. He squeezed through the small opening and never looked back.

"The audience sat there for about five minutes after I was gone, thinking I was joking," he said later. "But I was already in my car driving back to L.A. It just came to me to do that. You know how something like that comes to you? It was like the gods or fate talking to me. I knew right away that it was a moment of judgment for me and I knew I did the right thing."

Thus, in a gesture so symbolic that it might have seemed contrived, if it hadn't been so embarrassing, Richard Pryor freed himself from the constraints of his Mickey Mouse career. From now on, he decided, he was going to do his own material the way he wanted to do it. Unfortunately, most of the big clubs were not willing to pay him to shock their customers. The news that he had walked off the stage of the Aladdin in the middle of a show had reverberated through the club world, and his reputation for irresponsibility had taken a giant leap. But Pryor was popular, and most of the club owners would have forgiven him this transgression if he had tried to show that it had been just a temporary aberration. Everyone knew he was a little bit crazy. Pryor, however, did not intend to apologize, or offer excuses for his behavior at the Aladdin. He was serious about his new direction. Once the club owners realized that, his career went downhill fast.

He canceled a scheduled engagement at Mr. Kelly's in Chicago not because he wanted to but because he'd been forewarned that his new material was not acceptable. Telephoned two weeks before his stint at the club was to begin, he was told by the manager George Merianthal, who has since died, that he would have to clean up his act. Unwilling to do so, and not wishing to cause trouble for a club where he had always been treated well, Pryor canceled the engagement. Only the Cellar Door in Washington, D.C., was willing to pay the fee he had been used to getting. Otherwise, if he wanted to work he would have to take less money at cheaper and smaller establishments, the kinds of places he had played before he had gotten hot.

His income plummeted. His agents and his family were dismayed, and it fitted Pryor's well-developed sense of irony that everyone around him seemed more worried about themselves than about him. He and Shelley split up at this time. D'Urville Martin feels that

Shelley's father was a major cause of the breakup, since he had never approved of the marriage. Apparently, his antagonism was so great that he could not separate his feelings about his daughter's relationship from his feelings about her child with Richard. Says Martin about that period: "He lost the house in Hancock Place and had to go live with his manager. Shelley went back to her parents. But then her father took Rain and threw her up against a wall, trying to kill her. After that, Rain came to stay with me.

"I was sort of caught in the middle between Richard and Shelley. She would call me up and ask to go to the Candy Store, a place where all the stars hung out. Sinatra went there; Richard went there a lot. One time we met Richard, and Shelley started acting all lovey-dovey with me, and I said, 'Now, wait a minute.'

"Not long after that she went to New York and started living with Miles Davis, and Richard ran into the two of them at a disco on Eighth Street in New York—I think it was owned by Trudy Heller. Richard punched her out and broke her nose, because she was with Miles."

Shelley sued Richard and won a thousand dollars a month in alimony and eighteen hundred dollars in medical expenses.

CHAPTER V

Pryor Takes Stock

RICHARD PRYOR SAYS THAT one of the best bits of advice he ever received came from his Uncle Dicky: when you're all confused and don't know which way to turn, turn to yourself. Take some time for yourself and think back on your life. Look at everything you've ever done or thought and don't deny any of it. Own up to it, look it square in the face, see who you are.

Pryor had decided to take his uncle's advice. His life couldn't have been in more of a mess. He'd lost his third wife and fourth child, was saddled with debts he couldn't pay, and could not do the work that he needed to do for his own sanity, not to mention an income. As D'Urville Martin puts it, "He was blacklisted. He couldn't buy a job."

Pryor got out of Hollywood. He moved to a $110-a-month apartment near the freeway in Berkeley. It was all he could afford. When he was making good money, he hadn't bothered to save any of it. What he had went to his coke habit, not to mention assorted dependents. But far from being a comedown, that little apartment was a place where he felt free. It was his, he explained to David Felton, "and every fucking piece of furniture in there was mine; I bought it. I didn't have nobody in that house I didn't like, know what I mean? Didn't no motherfucker come near I didn't want there."

Alone in that apartment, he did exactly what he wanted to do. For a while that meant sleeping—sleeping all day, not even getting up out of bed, except for necessities, from one day to the next. But all the time his mind was working, and he was thinking about all the things he had ever felt or said or done, and after a time he got up and started working on a very personal screenplay, a comedy about a hapless, helpless teenager named Richard who gets shot accidentally by his grandmother in a whorehouse fight and, as he lies dying, sees his life

61

flashing before him. He sees his mother turning a trick with a white man while his father watches; asks a dove-covered priest why he has been expelled from school, and watches as the doves defecate all over the priest's face; tries to free Christ from the crucifix but is foiled by a mob of monks; witnesses his own funeral and watches as his ashes are mixed into a large pot of cocaine and all his pimp and whore friends snort the mixture; is somehow incarnated as Super Nigger; and in the final camera shot is shown walking away wearing a suit whose trousers have no back panel. Highly surreal and full of autobiographical symbolism, the screenplay was a project to which he would return again and again over the next few years.

It was not the first writing he had ever done. He had been dabbling with screenplay writing for several years. Director Michael Schultz remembers that Pryor was writing screenplays when he was a successful comic. "I met Richard when I first came out here to California. I was looking at him to play a part in an ill-fated picture that never got made. It was way ahead of its time—a ghetto musical, a fantasy—and at one point United Artists was interested in it. The producer, Clarence Avon, a record guy, wanted Richard Pryor, and so I met him and interviewed him for it. He gave me a screenplay that he had written— a cowboy movie called *Black Stranger*. I was amazed at what a good writer he was; the writing was exceptional. When the other picture fell through, I spent some time trying to get that cowboy movie made. I had a couple of meetings with Richard about trying to get it off the ground, trying to get it produced. I was living in Godfrey Cambridge's apartment, in town, at the time, and Godfrey came back and needed his apartment and I didn't have a place to stay. Richard offered me his beach house, and I stayed there for a couple of months."

In those days Richard did not have much time for writing because he was too busy with his club work. In his little apartment in Berkeley, during his period of enforced idleness, Pryor did the writing for which he had previously not had the time.

He also did a lot of reading, particularly about the life and philosophy of Malcolm X, the late charismatic black leader who had been assassinated in New York in February 1965 and whose influence may well be greater in death than it was in life. Former street hustler, ex-con, and one-time minister in the Black Muslims (Nation of Islam),

Malcolm's remarkable life, the story of which was published not long after he was shot down, epitomized the black man's journey to self-understanding and self-respect. Street-wise and self-educated, Malcolm had a remarkable political sensitivity and, perhaps more than any other twentieth-century black leader, the willingness to tell the truth as he saw it with a blunt, no-nonsense honesty. Pryor read many of Malcolm's speeches and was struck by statements like, "I've never seen a sincere white man, not when it comes to helping black people. . . . The white man is interested in the black man only to the extent that the black man is of use to him . . . to make money . . . to exploit." Here was a dude who thought like he did.

There was great foment in urban black communities by this time. Since the Watts riots in 1964 and riots in other cities across America, the focus of black energies had shifted from the civil rights movement in the South to the Black Power movement in cities outside the South. Up in Oakland the Black Panther Party had staged a public display of black manhood by converging on the capitol at Sacramento with guns. Ideas of black pride, black nationalism, and black aggressiveness had replaced the philosophies of integration and non-violence that had previously held sway. The new trends mirrored Richard Pryor's new way of thinking, and in the liberal atmosphere of Berkeley he found support for his refusal to do colorless material, material in which the humor was contrived. The new material he began working on was funny because it was real. "He went to the ghetto and started watching people," says Juliette Whittaker, whose news of Richard came from his grandmother. "He began remembering the people he knew here [in Peoria]—the drunks, the braggarts, the bullies—and he started working with that." The characters who had been screaming to get out were now free, and he worked to give them life. Soon he had the opportunity to try out his wino character in front of a camera. He was asked by Peter Locke, a young independent filmmaker, to do a cameo role in the low-budget and ponderously titled film *You've Got to Walk It Like You Talk it Or You Lose That Beat.* Pryor's character was listed in the credits simply as "Wino."

The film is about a luckless, idealistic young man in New York who fails in every attempt to find purpose in his life. He tries to commit suicide and fails, joins the transit authority in an attempt to find a saboteur and fails, is almost raped by a Women's Libber, gets nose-bleeds during intercourse, and gets fired from a job in advertising. The best parts of this socially conscious, slapstick comedy were the cameos by Robert Downey, director of the landmark film *Putney Swope*, as the head of the advertising agency, and by Pryor as the wino.

The film was shot in and around New York, and Pryor welcomed the opportunity to visit some of his old haunts. The Village no longer seemed snobbish to him; in fact it was a refreshing change from the plastic world he had so recently rejected.

In the same year he appeared in another low-budget film called *Dynamite Chicken*, an EYR release, written, produced, and directed by Ernest Pintoff and featuring Paul Krasner. The film was re-released in 1982 in an attempt to capitalize on Pryor's fame.

Pryor did not file an income tax return for 1970 either.

By 1971 Pryor was taking his new material out to clubs in Berkeley and Los Angeles, and in his routines he showed that he was definitely a new Richard Pryor. They were filled with characters—the old wino and the young junkie; Big Bertha, "the three-hundred-pound woman with the two hundred-eighty-pound ass;" Oilwell, "six foot five, two hundred twenty-two pounds of *mannn!*" and who gets beaten up by a policeman anyway. Through Pryor, they became real people, and they interacted in real situations that were often not so much funny as riveting in their truth. A routine like the conversation between the old wino and the young junkie, two losers who have little left but their own bravado, provoked more silence than laughter from audiences, but when it was over the applause was akin to a reaction to an emotional catharsis.

Richard Pryor was not doing traditional comedy anymore. Instead, his act was more like theater, the theater of real life, which he believed was much more entertaining than contrived, unreal gags. Audience reactions seemed to confirm this belief. He shocked and silenced them as well as made them laugh. His act now included liberal use of profanity and many references to racism, and once again people, casting about for a way to label him, began to compare him to the late Lenny Bruce. But there were only a few similarities in their style.

Bruce used profanity for its shock value. Pryor was using it for its reality—it was the way his characters talked, it was the way he talked. It was straight-out ghetto talk, and it belonged in portrayals of straight-out ghetto characters. Bruce's material was strict social commentary. Pryor's just happened to be social commentary, except when he was talking about racism. Although he acknowledged being influenced by Bruce to some extent, Pryor was convinced that his new comic style was uniquely his own, and in small clubs from Detroit to Chicago to Harlem people told him it was.

He recorded his second live album, *Craps After Hours*, that year. Taped live at the Redd Foxx Club in Hollywood, produced by Ala Enterprises, and released on the Laff label, it is poorly recorded, but some people believe it is his funniest. On it the previously "colorless" Richard Pryor positively reveled in talking about niggers—at police lineups, caught with their pants down by irate fathers. He talked about racism: "White folks don't give a nigger a chance. Jackson Five be singing their ass off, they be talking about the Osmond Brothers . . . mothering Osmond Brothers." He did a wino routine and several of his new characters. He ended the record with a "recollection" of something he always wanted to do but never actually did: take off his clothes and run around a Las Vegas casino screaming, "Black, Jack!"

Funny or not, the album's poor quality bothered Pryor, and by the end of the year he had severed his relationship with Ala Enterprises. He asked to be released from the contract he had signed with the company on December 9, 1970; and on November 4, 1971, he paid Ala an unspecified sum of money in exchange for his release from his obligation. It was just about the time he decided to devote himself to writing and acting.

It is difficult to believe that Pryor would give up comedy so soon after he had declared his freedom to do the comedy that he considered his own. But doing his characters on nightclub stages had not given him the satisfaction he'd expected. "The repetition was killing me," he later explained. "I was beginning to feel like a wind-up robot comic, repeating the same lines, getting the same laughs from the same jokes. It was great for a while, but there's more to me than that." Also, of course, he realized that he was not welcome in the big, high-paying clubs with his new material, and that he had very little chance to recapture his earlier success. "I never achieved the success I wanted to as a comic. My success was knowing I was the best stand-up comedian I could be. That satisfied me. But I had to do something else too."

The something else was more acting. Late in 1971 he got his first part in a big movie, Motown's production of Billie Holliday's story, *Lady Sings the Blues.*

Berry Gordy took a risk in asking Pryor to play the part of Piano Man, Holliday's solicitous sidekick who is beaten to death by dope dealers for failing to make payments. Pryor had never before played a straight, non-comic part, except in a couple of made-for-television movies. Also, he had a reputation for irresponsibility. But Gordy was casting Diana Ross as Billie Holliday, and that, too, was a risk, for neither Ross's singing style nor her personal style was at all like Holliday's. Gordy knew Pryor played junkie characters in his routines; and he decided to give him a chance.

Pryor was so grateful to Gordy for giving him that chance that he made a point of being punctual and cooperative. Originally, the scenes involving Piano Man were to have been shot in a week, but as with most others in that film these scenes were shot and reshot so often that Pryor wound up working about eight weeks. Shooting began in the early fall of 1971 and did not end until late February. Everyone did a lot of improvising, and Pryor had the opportunity to see Diana Ross at work. Like just about everyone else, he hadn't been able to picture her in the role. Also like just about everyone else, he was surprised at her acting ability. "I don't think [her role] has much to do with Billie Holliday, but her performance as an actress really tore me up," he told Gregg Kilday of the *Los Angeles Times.*

He was not as pleased with his own performance. "I had a whole acting job planned, but when I got on the set they had something else in mind. It was just as easy as that. I just did what they wanted. I did a lot of terrible work, but thanks to the editing most of it was cut."

He was being modest. His performance was well received by critics. *Variety* said that he registered "strongly," and Howard Kissell of *Women's Wear Daily* wrote, "There is a show-stealing performance by Richard Pryor as Billy Holliday's pianist. . . ." Some die-hard Pryor fans insisted that his was the only real portrayal in the whole fairy-tale film. What he did was to give perhaps the most convincing portrayal ever of a man who is stoned out of his mind. Richard Pryor had been there; he also knew what it felt like to be in terror over how to pay for the stuff.

Although he was on his best behavior during the filming of *Lady Sings the Blues*, Pryor was still using cocaine heavily in 1971. In that year a reporter for *Ebony* tried to interview him, but he was so coked up as to be unintelligible. It is said that he was snorting up between one and two hundred dollars worth of coke a day, and piling up hundreds of thousands of dollars in debts.

Lady Sings the Blues put Pryor, as he once explained it, "into another perspective": "I'd been working in clubs before groups of three hundred people doing my thing and was happy with it until that movie." In films he could be seen by millions of people, and he could enjoy the challenge of getting into characters that were not of his own creation. "Being a character, man, that makes me come alive. You've got to separate who you are and who the character is. There's such excitement in that real moment when you achieve that character—it's like being in your conscious and your subconscious at the same time."

He knew that the rest of the industry still considered him a comedian and not capable of doing serious roles, but he hoped that his performance in *Lady Sings the Blues* would free him of that one-dimensional label. He determined to prove that he could make it as a serious actor. By 1972 he had stopped playing clubs, moved back to Hollywood, and was devoting his time to acting and writing. He also hired a business manager who filed an income tax return for him for 1971.

Pryor got several chances to hone his acting skills in 1972, although not in movies of uniformly good quality. The worst was James Harris's *Some Call It Loving*, which starred Zalman King, the star of *You've Got to Walk It Like You Talk It Or You Lose That Beat*. In this modern-day version of the classic fairy tale, "Sleeping Beauty" (the movie was first titled *Sleeping Beauty*), a leader of a jazz combo visits a carnival and there for twenty thousand dollars buys an act featuring a girl who is said to have been asleep for eight years. He takes the girl, played by Tisa Farrow, to the castle he shares with his bisexual mistress (Carol White) and various hangers-on, including Richard Pryor, who is supposed to be his best friend and who is always high, presumably on drugs. The group indulges in various forms of lesbianism, drug use, fetishism. The Pryor character doesn't get to take part in much of the fun, owing to his sudden death. The sleeping maiden, awakened, takes part in many of these activities and can't seem to decide if she likes King or White, his mistress, better. In the end King puts her back to sleep and he and White take over the Sleeping Beauty act.

Pryor's role puzzled reviewers. A writer for the *Hollywood Reporter* noted that his presence was obscured by jumbled writing. Other reviewers remarked on the suddenness of his death. But though some called his performance "so eccentric it makes no sense" (*Hollywood Reporter*), and characterized his "hey-man, bleary-eyed gibberish" as a demeaning parody of Stepin Fetchit (*Cue*), others praised it. *Playboy:* "There's welcome relief in the performance of Richard Pryor as a dope freak who seems to find mere existence a nightmare, thus perfectly normal." *Boxoffice:* "Only realistic scenes involve Richard Pryor as a character who is continually high."

Pryor also got work that year in two of the current crop of so-called "blaxploitation" films. This phenomenon was another example of Hollywood's jumping belatedly on the bandwagon before it really knew where it was jumping. By the late 1960s white kids were listening to black music and finding it chic to understand black street-talk and street mores. They were also eager to hear antiestablishment dictums from blacks. Black kids, meanwhile, had been identified as significant film consumers. In 1969 Hollywood supplied what it perceived as a new market with five different black movies: *Uptight, Slaves, The Learning Tree, The Last Man,* and *Putney Swope.* Each contained an indictment of the American system, but of them all, *Putney Swope* was the most successful and clever. It didn't just indict the system, it parodied black American middle-class life, and it not only closed out the decade of the 1960s but opened the way for a new era of black films in the 1970s.

Cotton Comes to Harlem, a cops-and-robbers farce, opened that decade. Directed by Ossie Davis and based on a novel by Chester Himes, it relied on black stereotypes. It was Davis's belief that much truth could be told through the presentation of stereotypes, as he had managed to prove on Broadway with *Purlie Victorious*. But somehow the same truths did not come across on the screen. What came across was entertainment and little or no edification, something that black spokesmen had always said they would be able to provide if only given the chance. But audiences didn't especially want edification, as shown by the poorer box-office showings of the critically more well received black films like *The Learning Tree* and *The Last Man*. They wanted see action and glamour, and they got these things in abundance with *Shaft*.

Directed by Gordon Parks, who had also directed *The Learning Tree*, *Shaft* starred an unknown named Richard Roundtree as a cynical, rebellious detective who lives in a booklined Greenwich Village apartment, dresses in expensive, stylish clothes, is seemingly immune to bullets, and ensures that no woman is immune to him. He also does his living and working to the accompaniment of a sensual, moody score by Isaac Hayes that won him an Oscar. Although, except for the score and the image the movie projected, *Shaft* had little to recommend it, it was an immediate hit. When urban graffiti artists adopt the name of a movie hero as their moniker, it has *sold*. Carol Speed, who later appeared with Pryor in another black action film, adds, "*Shaft* put M-G-M out of the red."

By 1972 there was an explosion of black action movies; it was that year when the term "blaxploitation film" was coined. Hollywood is unabashedly imitative: if something works, everybody grabs onto its coattails. *Shaft's Big Score*, a sequel, *Top of the Heap*, *The Legend of Nigger Charley*, *Slaughter*, *Melinda*, *Blacula*, *Blackenstein*, and *Super Fly* were all of the blaxploitation type. Also released that year were Sidney Poitier's *Buck and the Preacher* and *Lady Sings the Blues*, and documentaries on such black political figures as Angela Davis, Fred Hampton, and Malcolm X. But the action films got the publicity and the box-office receipts.

Particularly controversial was *Super Fly*, which was independently produced by Sig Shore and financed by a group of black businessmen. Directed by Gordon Parks, its hero who is played by Ron O'Neal is a romanticized version of a Harlem pimp/drug pusher. Although he defeats the white mob and leaves the cocaine business with a sizeable bankroll, he is not your run-of-the-mill hero, and the film's backers had to take a lot of flack along with their hefty profits.

Critics charged that these films exploited blacks—both audiences and the race in general—by glorifying the least desirable elements in the black community to draw members of that same community in large numbers to the box office. Liberal whites and middle class blacks were among the most vehement critics. Said Stanley Kauffman in *The New Republic*, April 28, 1973, "... black filmmakers and actors, financed and industrially aided by whites, are so willing to exploit their own people... to show young black dope pushers as examples, just because those examples will bring 'em in at the box office. (And the incidental homiletic bows don't cover this up.) All that talk about Black Power and Black is Beautiful, and when they finally get their long-delayed screen time, all they do is show that Black is Ugly—just as ugly as everybody else."

The major black organizations were equally critical. "That term *blaxploitation* came from Roy Wilkins," says Carol Speed. "The NAACP and the Urban League were up in arms about those movies. But all films exploit. There is a producer's manual that comes out once a month and in the back of it there is a section called Exploitips with suggestions on how to exploit each movie.

"Was *Mean Streets* an Italian exploitation movie? What's the difference if kids go and see Clint Eastwood—he fucks broads; he shoots up everybody; he drinks beer; and then he does some more fighting. What's the difference if a black man does it or a white man does it? Black actors and actresses were saying all this at the time. We were saying, 'Hey, at least we're working. There's a thing called eating.' If we didn't have these films, where were we going to work? Do you remember that the guy who starred in *Blacula*, Bill Marshall, was a Shakespearean actor? But nobody wanted to hear what we had to say."

Richard Pryor didn't see what all the fuss was about either. "You know we used to pick cotton," he told an interviewer in early 1973. "Well, now we're making movies. Same thing. I call them pickin'-cotton movies, but they pay the bills. And some people get over them. All that works, man. I mean, when the industry was controlled by white people it took them forty years to discover sound—how dumb can they be? See, it all takes time."

In Pryor's opinion the so-called blaxploitation films were just the latest hustle, the latest game, and he didn't mind playing it. In 1972 he hustled right along in *Hit!* and *The Mack.*

Actually, *Hit!* is not a blaxploitation film, for criminals are not glorified. *Boxoffice* could barely disguise its incredulity when describing it as, "something of an oddity, *Hit!* is a two and a quarter hour action film about a war on a drug ring, starring two black actors, and yet it isn't a black exploitationer." Directed by Sidney J. Furie, who had also directed *Lady Sings the Blues* and who was working again with most of the male leads from the Billie Holliday film biography, it starred Billy Dee Williams as a vengeful father who also happens to be a government agent out to crush the dope syndicate, including the top echelon of the French heroin traffickers, with the help of a gang of eccentrics whom he blackmails into cooperation. Paul Hampton plays a college professor who pushed heroin while serving in Vietnam, and Sid Melton's character has an unexplained criminal record but is willing to help because his son died a junkie. Pryor plays an underwater demolitions expert whose wife was raped and murdered by a junkie.

Among the many locations where the film was shot was Chino Prison. Pryor heard the inmates talk about the bum raps that had put them there, about terms of sentence, about girls outside. He would remember these men, and a couple of years later he would visit the prison to give a free performance.

Hit! was the first film in which the name Richard Pryor was featured in the same size lettering as that of Billy Dee Williams. Although this may not seem very important to the layman, in Hollywood it means a lot. The August 7, 1973, Paramount memo about main title billing for the movie is very specific, as all such memos are.

1. *Paramount Pictures Presents*
2. *Billy Dee Williams*   *100% size of title*
3. *Hit!*   *100%*
   Copyright © 1973 by Paramount Pictures Corporation
   All Rights Reserved

> *Paramount script logo*
> 4. *Also starring*
>   *Richard Pryor*   *(same size as Williams)*

Paul Hampton also got billing of equal size. The size of the names of the rest of the cast was "discretionary."

Hit! was released in October 1973, to mixed reviews. Furie had chosen to improvise the dialogue with the actors, and some critics cited this when complaining that the movie went on and on and on and was self-indulgent. But Pryor got good reviews. "Pryor excels at improvising because he's an outrageous comedian and even makes fun of the plot on camera," wrote a critic for the *Hollywood Reporter.*

Nor was *The Mack* an unabashedly exploitive film, although its look into the world of pimps and their stables of hookers probably could not have been brought to movie audiences at another time. *Mack* was a West Coast word for pimp, derived apparently from the French slang *mec.* Robert Poole, who wrote the script, was himself a pimp for twelve years and plotted the story during a five-year term at San Quentin. When Michael Campus was asked to direct the film, he went to Oakland to consult with real pimps and got promises of full cooperation from the Ward brothers, who claimed to head the pimp community there. Since the filmmakers were mostly white, there was considerable tension between them and the community at first. Then it seemed as if both groups came together in a common effort to produce something that was truthful and real. Unfortunately, a week after the filming was finished, Frank Ward, head of the Ward family, was executed, shot in the back of the head and left in the rear of his car in Berkeley. When it was released, *The Mack* was dedicated to Frank Ward.

The film is about a ghetto kid who has no choice after getting out of prison but to take up pimping. Though he likes the money and prestige, he reproaches a kid who wants to follow in his footsteps. His brother has become a black nationalist, seeking to rid the ghetto of drugs and prostitution, and the two are at odds until their mother is brutally slain by two cops who are harassing the Mack to pay them protection money. After the death of their mother, they unite to clean up the ghetto.

Max Julien played the Mack, and Richard Pryor played the Mack's loyal, hysterical friend. The rest of the cast were relative unknowns. Don Gordon played the black nationalist brother; Carol Speed a prostitute.

Speed had previously made two films in the Philippines for Jean and Roger Corman, including one with Pam Grier called *Big Bird Cage*. She remembers, "On *The Mack* set everybody had a very warm feeling toward one another. You gotta remember, that was our big shot, our chance to get over."

Filming took about five weeks. "It was a very quick film—we didn't have any six-months budget for it," says Speed. Asked if Pryor was in the habit of showing up on time, she said only, "He was on time as much as anyone else was on time. He was quite easy for me to work with. As a matter of fact, I learned a great deal from him. I learned to be more relaxed with acting—instead of letting the scene control you, you control the scene and make it more natural. Richard was far above everybody else, because he knew his character. He knew about pimps—he knew that pimps come in conservative suits and ties and from oil corporations as well as from the streets."

Released in March 1973, the movie was generally panned. Pryor was at least praised with faint damns, an indication of the growing interest in and respect for him as an actor. One critic allowed that he "expends a lot of energy." A critic for *Players* wrote, "Richard Pryor's attempts at humor don't save it."

Pryor himself was pleased enough with his movie career to feel that he had made the right choice in consigning his nightclub stage career to the back burner and concentrating on acting in films. That year he did, however, take time out from straight acting to do some comedy routines for a concert-movie, although he had not actually taken part in the concert.

In 1972 Stax Records staged a benefit performance at the Los Angeles Memorial Coliseum to wrap up the week-long Seventh Annual Watts Summer Festival. For an admission price of a dollar, nearly one hundred thousand people, most of them black, were entertained by such artists as Isaac Hayes, the Staple Singers, Alberta King, Carla Thomas, and Rufus Thomas, all of whom recorded with Stax. Producer Mel Stuart decided to film the concert and produce a documentary called *Wattstax*, intercutting the musical performances with interviews of Watts residents in barber shops, restaurants, and on the corner, interviews that underscored the existence of ghetto pride. But after editing the footage, Stuart realized he didn't have enough recorded music and interviews to sustain a feature film. He could have secured more interviews or added more performance footage, but either way he felt he would throw the whole into imbalance. He needed something different.

Then he had a brainstorm. He called on Richard Pryor to act as a sort of "funky interlocutor" between acts and interviews, to provide bridges between them. The resulting film, *Wattstax*, was one-third Richard Pryor.

The concert was preceded by the playing of the national anthem. A camera pans over the audience, whose members display marked disinterest in the tune. Cut to a group of young black men, one of whom says, "I got no country; I got no flag." Others describe the point at which they discovered that, in America, they were niggers. Cut to Pryor. He talks about how Africans were crazy to have so many different tribal identities and languages. How fortunate, he adds, that the best among them—the princes and princesses—when they were brought to America didn't have to worry about that anymore. In America "they made us one big tribe: niggers."

The Staple Singers sing "Respect Yourself," and the documentary moves on to reflect the forms in which black people have displayed their self-respect—a statue of a black Jesus, a black beauty contest, a black Santa Claus, Malcolm X College, the Black Muslims. Pryor chooses to elaborate on the Black Muslims's proscription of pork. Eating pork is taboo, he explains, because it leads to "porkitis" or "trichinosis of the mind."

It was no small task for Pryor to view the documentary footage, discuss with Stuart where bridges were needed, and then come up with the appropriate comic-serious bit to provide that bridge. But he performed the role admirably. His bridges were the best parts of the film. "Pryor Hit of 'Wattstax' Collage" read the headline of the *Los Angeles Times* review, and a reviewer for *Newsweek* wrote, "it was a superb stroke to use the wickedly funny Richard Pryor as the film's commentator. Perhaps not even Dick Gregory can shape accumulated black experience into such biting bits of humor. Pryor ... is reason enough to see *Wattstax*."

Unfortunately, Pryor did not have time to develop all new material for *Wattstax*, or so Ala Enterprises later charged in a $2,800,000 suit. He had used material from his album *Craps After Hours* in the film, Ala charged, material that it owned. The case went on for several years, its costs adding to Pryor's mounting debts.

CHAPTER VI

Pryor Returns

IN 1973 RICHARD PRYOR began to rise, phoenix-like, from the rubble of his ruined career as a standup comic. His efforts at acting were beginning to bring him attention. In April he learned that three of his films would be showing in Cannes that spring—*Wattstax, Lady Sings the Blues,* and *Some Call It Loving*—and he'd been invited to attend. By April 4 *Variety* listed *The Mack* at number five among the fifteen top-grossing films (three other black films were also in the top fifteen), and by the end of that month, having grossed over two million in its first five weeks of release and broken records in most cities, *The Mack* seemed ripe for further exploitation with a sequel. He had signed to do several other movies, was involved in some first class writing projects, and he was about to return to television.

Pryor had been largely absent from the tube since 1970. During that time the black presence on television had increased markedly. The *Bill Cosby Show* on NBC had not lasted more than a couple of seasons, but it had paved the way for others to follow. The *Flip Wilson Show* premiered on NBC during the 1971–72 season, and Wilson's character Geraldine Jones had been welcomed into American households. Although some critics pointed to the irony of a black man being accepted in the living rooms of middle America only when dressed up as a woman, at least Geraldine was not exploitive. Wilson gave a lot of talented blacks an opportunity to work on his show. Among them was Richard Pryor. Not only did he appear in front of the camera but also he did some writing for the show.

Wilson and Pryor had met several years earlier, and each respected the other's comic talents. Their personal relationship, however, has had its ups and downs. Kathi Fearn-Banks was then, and still is, a publicist with NBC. She met Richard when he worked on the Wilson show. "Flip and Richard have a kind of love-hate relationship," she says. "Richard was always talking about how much he hates white people. And one time Flip said, 'Richard, if you hate white people so much, how come you keep marrying them?'" Wilson was angry, too—no intelligent black man in America isn't—but he was more objective than Pryor, more secure in himself, and not so intent on *showing* everyone by being a star. Wilson's show lasted until 1974, when it was canceled by NBC, and until late 1983 he worked only occasionally and when it suited him. He preferred to spend his time with his family. As he said during a 1982 appearance on the *Tonight* show, he'd made enough money back in the early 1970s to live comfortably for the rest of his life, and once he had done so he was content to stay home and be a father to his children.

Pryor, by contrast, had spent his money, a sizeable portion of it on dope—"Hell, I could have bought Peru!"—and assorted law suits. And he was not much of a father to his children. During an appearance on *The Mike Douglas Show* in 1974, he was asked when he had impressed his kids the most. He answered, "When I admitted I was their father."

Richard did crazy, destructive things. Kathi Fearn-Banks recalls a story Wilson told her: "Richard had a lot of people over to his house for dinner. One of his lady friends was there. He went crazy and started turning tables and chairs over, knocking things down from the walls. All the people left, and then he went to a bedroom and closed himself up in it. When he came out and saw all the mess, he said, 'Who did this?' His lady friend said, 'You did.' He said, 'No, I didn't, you did,' and got angry with her!"

Wilson could not understand such behavior, but he did recognize Pryor's talent and he sympathized with his problems. Knowing he was taking a risk, Wilson invited Pryor to appear on his show and do some writing for it, and the risk paid off. Unfortunately, the show was dropped at the end of that season. The reason cited was low ratings. In February 1974 Roger Rice, vice president of independent TV station KTVU in San Francisco, questioned the validity of ratings by A.C. Nielsen and the American Research Bureau, charging that blacks were under-represented in their samplings. He cited as an example Greenwood, Mississippi, which according to the 1970 census was fifty-eight percent white and forty-two percent black but which was measured for television by an American Research Bureau rating sample that found it eighty-three percent white and seventeen percent black.

A few black shows managed to defy the odds and the skewed TV-rating samples. Perhaps the most successful was *Sanford and Son*, which premiered in 1972. One of the most amusing ironies in the history of television is that Redd Foxx, who over a quarter century had built a solid reputation as a "blue" comic, particularly for his sexually explicit jokes and who because of this reputation had rarely appeared on television, should land a plum like a starring role in a TV series. But he happened to be just the man Bud Yorkin and Norman Lear, coproducers of *All in the Family*, were looking for as the star in their planned American remake of the British TV hit *Steptoe and Son*. Foxx was so perfect in the role of the wily, sarcastic old junkman who takes great pleasure in thwarting the business and social aspirations of his well-meaning son, Lamont (played by Demond Wilson) that the producers even renamed the series in his honor. Foxx's real name is John Elroy Sanford.

The show was an immediate success, and within a month was one of TV's top ten programs in the ratings. And despite conflict between the star and the producers—the problems inherent in a black show scripted by white writers and Foxx's demands for more money and star perquisites like a window in his dressing room—the show remained popular for many years and continues in reruns even today.

The popularity of *Sanford and Son* meant work for many black actresses and actors. Carol Speed appeared in an early show called "Here Comes the Bride, There Goes the Bride," playing Lamont's almost-wife. In fact most of the blacks in Hollywood worked in the series at one time or another. Foxx was responsible for giving a lot of friends and colleagues work on *Sanford and Son*. He suggested that Quincy Jones write the theme, that LaWanda Page play the role of Aunt Esther, that Arnold Johnson play Hutch, and brought in a number of others for one-time appearances. Serving as an unofficial consultant and writer for the show—the white writers would include lines like "Dis hyar," Foxx once explained, "and everybody is always saying ain't. But black people say ain't and isn't in the same paragraph, and sometimes in the same sentence." Foxx also welcomed the few black writers who worked on the show from time to time. Among them was Richard Pryor, who had teamed up with Paul Mooney to do a quartet of *Sanford and Son* episodes.

Mooney, who looks a great deal like the singer Sam Cook and who played Cook in the film *The Buddy Holly Story*, was a frustrated comedian who could write great comedy but who could not seem to deliver it to good effect. Pryor, of course, was superb at delivery. The two made an excellent team, and according to D'Urville Martin, Paul Mooney is perhaps Pryor's closest black friend. "Richard gives him work on everything he does. He is either the casting director, a consultant, a writer for his jokes, etc. On anything Richard does, there's Paul Mooney's name somewhere.

"They have a very strange relationship. Richard puts him down a lot in public. Paul, behind Richard's back, talks about him like a dog. A girl told me that Paul Mooney once took her to Pryor's house. He wanted to impress her, and he was doing his number and acting like a big shot until Richard said, 'You know, I remember when I fucked you right here in this living room, right in the ass.' That just totally blew Mooney away, and he kept quiet the rest of the evening.

"The first time I met Paul Mooney he told me that Richard steals all his material and that he's a better comedian. I'm sure Richard knows Paul Mooney says these things about him, but at least he knows where Mooney's at. They are still together."

The *Sanford and Son* episodes were among Pryor's and Mooney's first important writing assignments. Pryor in particular looked forward to working on the show. Arnold Johnson remembers, "Richard really looked up to Redd when he was writing for *Sanford and Son*, and I think he still does." Redd Foxx had managed to make it on television despite his reputation for blue comedy. Redd Foxx, it appeared, had learned how to compromise with the representatives of middle America, taking the material offered by the primarily white writers and altering it to make it more real. "The cast changed the material," LaWanda Page remembers. But Pryor still found it hard to compromise. His memories of his association with Tandem Productions are tinged with bitterness. He couldn't get along with the series producer, Aaron Reuben. "They say at Sanford they wanted black people writing the scripts," Pryor told Gregg Kilday of the *Los Angeles Times* that year, "but they changed them to the way they thought black people was." Defiantly, Pryor teamed up with Bob Chartoff, a white writer, to develop a new comedy series to be called Love Thy Neighbor about a black militant and his bourgeois sister. But the series never got past the development stage.

Somewhat more satisfying was his work on the two Lily Tomlin specials, for which he was a costar and also was listed in the credits as a cowriter. The first special aired in March 1973, one night after his appearance on a *Flip Wilson Show*, which wasn't bad for someone who had been unofficially black-balled from TV at one time.

Of the two activities in which he engaged for the Tomlin specials, the writing was more rewarding. He and Tomlin were on the same comic wavelength from the moment they had met, and during the writing of the shows they shared that indescribably good feeling of working almost as one. Pryor even brought his former wife Shelley in on the writing, the bitterness between them having been put aside, and Shelly would continue to collaborate with Tomlin on occasion. Pryor could get into Tomlin's characters, and so he could write for them. But he still had trouble with the censors when it came to creating characters of his own in front of the cameras. This was particularly true during the taping of the second special, which aired in November 1973.

On that show Pryor did what he considered to be one of the best comedy bits he'd done so far. In the sketch he played a junkie in a soul food cafe that is invaded by two white social researchers armed with questionnaires. The junkie begins by putting on the two researchers, then subtly reverses the roles so that he becomes the questioner, asking the bewildered couple, "Who's Pigmeat Markham's momma? Wilt Chamberlain the tallest colored chap you ever saw? Have you ever been mugged in the same neighborhood more than once? . . ."

But he also was forced to squelch a scene with Tomlin, a potentially fine sketch between Lily's Edith Ann and his own kid character, Billy.

Asked to play a kid, Pryor became a kid, just as he became Oilwell and Black Bertha and the wino and the junkie when he played them. As the cameras rolled, Pryor's kid, faced with Edith Ann, naturally started talking about anatomy: "I have titties bigger than your

titties. . . . Boys have titties—first, boys have titties . . . then girls. . . ."
The cameras stopped abruptly, and Pryor was told by the censors that
it wouldn't do. His face like a child's who has been told that something he has said in perfect innocence is nasty, he walked off the set.
Tomlin followed him to his dressing room and tried to persuade him
to continue, but Pryor refused. If his kid character couldn't say what
came naturally, then his kid character would be contrived. It was
unfair to the kid character to be manipulated. The piece was scrapped.

Pryor won an Emmy for his writing on the Tomlin specials. It was
gratifying to him to have his talent in that area recognized. He was
devoting as much time as he could to writing. He was still working on
his autobiographical screenplay titled This Can't Be Happening to
Me, and had finally had it copyrighted in January 1973. He was still
peddling his cowboy script, Black Stranger, and was just beginning
work on another cowboy script with Mel Brooks. But writing and
acting in films was not enough. He also wanted to do more television,
albeit on his own terms.

Richard Pryor's relationship with television was characterized by
mutual wariness. To Pryor, television was a nest of vipers, or perhaps
cobras like the ones that come out of baskets and hypnotize their
intended victims with promises of money and exposure, then strike
with their deadly venom. But his agents kept telling him that he
needed television if he ever expected to get his career back up to the
level where it had once been. By this time Pryor had taken on a new
management firm, Wald, DeBlasio, Nanas Associates. The Wald was
Jeff Wald, then Helen Reddy's husband. Ron DeBlasio was Pryor's
personal agent, and he did not understand his client's love-hate
relationship with television. Like most agents, DeBlasio saw things in
terms of money. Pryor was still thinking in terms of his own artistic
integrity. But his ego was also an important factor. He wanted to be
seen by the millions of people who watch television.

Ironically, it was his former idol, Bill Cosby, who gave him a chance
to return to that bastion of middle-American viewing, the Tonight
show, that year. Cosby was guest host on the show and it was his idea
to invite Pryor to appear. It was also Cosby's idea in the course of their
ad-libbing and horsing around for the two of them to mimic weight
lifters. Cosby went first. He went for the slapstick style, clowning

around as he tried to lift an imaginary barbell. Then it was Pryor's turn. For a full ten seconds he concentrated on lifting that barbell, and through the contortions of his face alone he became that weightlifter and the barbell became real. The struggling, as revealed in his face, was so true and funny that the audience broke up, not in polite appreciation, as they had for Cosby, but in outright howls.

In a sense that bit of friendly comic rivalry represented a rite of passage for Richard Pryor. Long a mimic of Bill Cosby, he had struggled to become his own man, and not only had he wrested himself from Cosby's coattails, he had outdone him.

But it was a fleeting triumph. Bill Cosby still had much that Pryor didn't. Cosby had acceptance—no producer thought twice about having him on a talk show. Cosby had a wife, and kids all by the same wife. In partnership with his wife Cosby was investing his money, building up equity. Cosby had a college degree from Temple University and was talking about getting a Masters in Education at the University of Massachusetts. Cosby might not be a comic genius, but he knew how to play the game.

By contrast Richard Pryor could not lay claim to much else but genius, and that didn't keep him warm at night, or give him the financial or personal security to meet on an equal footing others who were more educated or more famous than he.

Nor had he been able to free himself from feeling awe in the presence of stars. Invited to a party at the home of Sammy Davis, Jr., and finding himself in the bathroom with his host, his primary concern, he told David Felton of *Rolling Stone*, was forcing a hard-on so he would appear sufficiently masculine in the eyes of the star. At a prize-fight screening George C. Scott called him by name, and he was so nonplussed at the idea that someone like Scott actually knew who he was that he couldn't find his voice—any of his voices—to answer.

When it came to women, he'd at least had sense enough to stop impregnating them and then feeling obligated to marry them. Law suits for alimony and child support no doubt helped to convince him. Still, he needed women, and he had many brief but intense affairs. Sometimes they were starlets, who appeared in movies with him; but more often they were women who were not in the business, whether because such women gave him more adulation and were more approachable or because they had fewer ego problems is hard to determine. Whoever they were, they didn't last long with Richard Pryor.

Juliette Whittaker feels that Pryor was then, and still is, unrealistic about women. "I guess he saw so much cynicism when he was growing up that he is the undying romantic when it comes to women. He can't deal with the reality in women. He can deal with the romantic part, but not the day-to-day. I think the ideal marriage for Richard would be someone he wouldn't see all the time. In the day-to-day you begin to see the flaws. But if you're only seeing a person, say, when you get off a plane, and you're only going to be there a weekend, it can be very romantic during that period. No problems of any consequence come up—not even a trip to the grocery store."

Pryor's attempts at forming a lasting relationship during this time were futile. The women who stayed in his rented cottage in the Hollywood Hills—a bungalow that had once belonged to the gardener of a famous star—were more likely to be his relatives: his grandmother, his Aunt Dee, or a young niece whose sexual proclivities he didn't approve of.

When he occasionally visited his grandmother back in Peoria, he gained solace from being around her. But his visits also often increased his frustration. Many of the people he had grown up with were dead by now—killed in confrontations with police or by drug overdoses. The ones who were still living seemed to resent his success, to be offended because he had managed to get out of Peoria.

The only friend he seemed able to count on was cocaine. In his filmed concert *Live on Sunset Strip* he does a routine in which he and cocaine talk to one another, and cocaine's argument that he should stick with it seems far more reasonable than his own arguments about getting off the stuff. But cocaine was a false friend, he realized later. Just when he was beginning to be accepted in Hollywood and on TV again, it started to get him into trouble: It took over on movie sets.

In 1973 Pryor started filming *Uptown Saturday Night*, directed by Sidney Poitier and starring Poitier, Bill Cosby, and Harry Belafonte. Billed below these stars, and also below Flip Wilson, who made a cameo appearance, Pryor was listed in the "Also Starring" category along with Rosalind Cash, Roscoe Lee Browne, and Paula Kelly. Pryor played a detective called Sharp Eye Washington whom Poitier and

Cosby try to hire after they lose a wallet containing Poitier's wife's winning lottery ticket during a gambling spree. Penelope Gilliatt, reviewing the film for *The New Yorker*, described his portrayal of the broadly funny and obviously criminal detective this way:

> *Sharp Eye is constantly alert against a leap on him from the law, though the friends take his quick-wittedness to be the mark of a good detective. His face jumps with nerves. He carries on about the strain of his job like a babbling house-wife. . . . He twitches his Venetian blinds, pays no attention to his stammering clients, and talks with concentrated ego-mania about the fatigue for his right eye of keeping such a perpetual lookout for danger, pulling down his left lower lid by mistake to show the optical wear and tear of his career. He takes not the faintest notice of his clients' shy attempt to hire him. His mind is obviously more on making a quick exit, which he does by way of a window and a fire escape—or possibly a water pipe—waving good bye professionally as if he had everything under control. End of any aid from him."*

It was a masterly performance, but behind the scenes on the set, Pryor proved troublesome to work with. Perhaps he wanted to prove something to stars like Poitier, Cosby, and Belafonte. But there are rumors that it was his coke habit that caused the major problems. Poitier will say only that working with Pryor on that movie was difficult.

Pryor's coke habit is also rumored to have cost him the lead role in the Mel Brooks movie that he helped to write, the movie that was originally called Texas, then Black Bart, and finally wound up with the title *Blazing Saddles*. There were five writers on that film—Andrew Bergman, Norman Steinberg, and Alan Unger, in addition to Pryor and Brooks—and they worked for nine months on what they saw as a script that would debunk every myth that had ever existed about the old West. Brooks later said that they had written perhaps ten times more than they were able to use, putting in every cliche: the over-the-hill gunfighter, the timid preacher, the crooked governor, the mean ranch-foreman. "We went all the way," Brooks told the late Kenneth Tynan, who profiled him for *The New Yorker*, " . . . especially Richard Pryor, who was very brave and very far-out and very catalytic." They wrote "berserk, heartfelt stuff about white corruption and racism and Bible-thumping bigotry. We used dirty language on the screen for the first time, and to me the whole thing was like a big psychoanalytic session." To cut the script down to manageable size, the five holed up for a solid month. It was an exciting experience for all of them; the interpersonal chemistry was right; the creative juices flowed. Richard Pryor could feel the character of the slick black sheriff in a town of shabby white bigots, and it was tacitly understood that he would indeed play the part.

When the script was complete, Brooks took it to Warner Brothers, which optioned it immediately and hired Brooks as director. Warner Brothers allowed Brooks considerable freedom, giving in on some of the scenes it feared would be objectionable; but it was adamant about the casting of the black sheriff part, or so Brooks says. Warners did not want Richard Pryor; he was too undisciplined. Rumor had it that the company felt Pryor's reputation as a cocaine user made him too unsavory a character to be a star. Brooks, on occasion, has made subtle references to Pryor's emotional instability. At other times he has insisted that the problem was that Pryor was an unknown. When *Blazing Saddles* was being cast, even *Lady Sings the Blues* was not yet released. Brooks's very equivocation reveals that he is uncomfortable about the entire episode. According to Michael Schultz, who quotes industry gossip, "Richard wrote it, and Mel Brooks chased him out. Mel Brooks was trying to get total credit for the picture. . . . I think Richard had a lot of input into that picture from a writing standpoint, and to be outmaneuvered and ripped off at that early stage in his career is something that's a little hard for him to get over. I'd feel the same way."

Richard Pryor has never forgiven Brooks. As he told a writer for *Gallery Magazine*, "He hurt me. He lied to me. He didn't have the decency to call me up and tell me I wasn't going to star in *Blazing Saddles*. And what hurt me about it was that I was in the car with Cleavon Little and we were going to a nightclub. They asked what I was doing. Naturally I said I was going to do *Blazing Saddles*. And the funny thing is, Cleavon had already been signed for the part. You know what I mean? Shit. Brooks was supposed to call me up and at least tell me that I didn't get the part."

Although Pryor later shared honors for the screenplay from the American Writer's Guild and the American Academy of Humor, these awards were small consolation. Nor was the pronouncement by critics like Pauline Kael that, despite the movie's great success, it would have been even better with Richard Pryor. Kael wrote, "Pryor's demons are what make people laugh. If he had played the sheriff in *Blazing Saddles*, he'd have made him crazy—threatening and funny both." Then, on reflection, she concluded, "Pryor shouldn't be cast at all—he should be realized. He has desperate, mad characters coming out his pores, and we want to see how far he can go with them."

On reading that review Pryor no doubt wondered if the system would ever let him see how far he could go. It seemed that everything about that system was conspiring to keep him down.

Representatives of the larger system called the United States Government came down on Richard Pryor early the next year. There was the small matter of his having failed to file income tax returns for the years 1967 to 1970. The grand jury indictment, which was handed down in mid-March 1974, stated that Pryor had failed to pay taxes on approximately $250,000 in gross income during that four-year period. At first Pryor pleaded innocent to all four counts; but a month later he pleaded guilty to one count. Thanks to behind-the-scenes maneuvering on the part of his attorneys and those for the IRS, he would be held responsible for failure to file a tax return for the year 1967 only, a year in which his income was approximately $68,500. The date for his sentencing was set for mid-May.

Although he faced a possible ten-thousand dollar fine and a year in prison on the one tax charge, Pryor felt he was getting off lightly. The government could have screwed him royally, and it is perhaps no coincidence that he was feeling beneficent at this time. He'd just started making real money again, and the government had chosen not to take it. To Pryor this was a sign that he should start using that money the government was allowing him to keep for something besides cocaine.

He bought his grandparents a new home—a fine house in the southeast section of Peoria called Bartonville. He also started taking more interest in Richard, Jr., sending money to his son's mother, Patricia, and suggesting that Richard, Jr., come to live with him and go to school in Los Angeles. So certain was he that he knew what was best for the boy that he refused to listen to his former wife's objections. He went to Peoria to get Richard, Jr.

By this time Juliette Whittaker had left her job at the Carver Center and started a day-care center. "It was Easter time, and Richard came to visit, came by the day-care center to see me," she recalls. "We were just sitting, watching the kids, and he said, 'I wish we'd had something like this when I was growing up. . . . What would you like for this place?'

"I said, 'I would like a sliding board out in the yard, but it's kind of a special sliding board.'

"He said, 'You got a picture of it?' And I showed him this picture of a frontier-type sliding board with ladders to climb up, a deck, telescopes on each side, and you have the option of coming down a stainless steel slide or a fireman's pole.

"He looked at the picture and said, 'I'll send you a check for it as soon as I get back. I gotta go to Detroit. But when I get back to L.A., I'll send you the money, so you go ahead and order it.' True to his word, the check came from his lawyers about two weeks after he left here, and it was for the entire amount."

In May, Pryor appeared for sentencing on the tax-evasion charge. He was fined $10,000, $7,500 of which was suspended. He was sentenced to a year in prison, all but ten days of which were also suspended. He was placed on three years' probation in addition. The judge ordered that he make his restitution to society by giving ten free performances, and a grateful Richard Pryor promised that he would.

Even ten days in Los Angeles County men's jail were difficult for Pryor. "The hardest part was watching other people being mistreated," he said later. "I was treated with kid gloves in a way. I could tell what would happen if I didn't have some status." The white guards were frightening in the depth of their hatred. Pryor coped with the situation by concentrating on a psychological analysis of what hatred does to a human being. He noted the hate in their eyes and thought about how it must affect their family life, their children. He thought about the destructive progression of hate from prisoner to guard to wife and children to the community. He was glad he didn't have to spend more than ten days in such a psychologically devastating environment.

His first free performances were given for his former fellow inmates who were not so lucky as he. Flip Wilson, in the character of Geraldine Jones, joined him in giving the two forty-five minute shows at the L.A. County men's jail. Soon Pryor would also return to Chino Prison, where portions of *Hit!* had been filmed, to give a free performance there.

It should be pointed out that Pryor had shown some interest in prisoners before he had been one himself. In early May 1974, before he had started serving his own sentence, he had introduced a group of young men who were on leave from a Virginia penal institution to the audience at the Apollo Theatre in Harlem. The reading he had done on the life of Malcolm X had made him sensitive to the plight of the black prisoner, and to the marked imbalance in the proportion of white prisoners to black. In stage routines he did a bit about prisons in which he played on the word *justice* and rendered it as "just us." But his already heightened consciousness was raised a few notches further after his own experience as a prisoner.

In addition to the free performances he was giving under court order, Pryor was beginning to get a lot of paid onstage comedy work. And the stages on which he was appearing were not just any stages. In that year he played to sold-out crowds at the Kennedy Center in Washington, D.C., and at Avery Fisher Hall at Lincoln Center in New York City. Though less lucrative than Las Vegas gigs, these appearances were far more valuable to him psychologically. They represented acceptance with a capital *A*—acceptance by white, middle-class folks who by purchasing every last ticket to one of his performances in these hallowed halls were in effect saying, okay, we're hip, we can understand where you're coming from. As the *Variety* reviewer of Pryor's performance at Avery Fisher Hall put it, "Pryor speaks to blacks in terms blacks understand, but any save a very thin-skinned white can appreciate it."

He ran into trouble only in Richmond, Virginia, where in early August he was arrested on charges of disorderly conduct after allegedly directing obscenities at the city's police bureau.

Television, of course, was not like Avery Fisher Hall. It was more like Richmond, Virginia. Or so went conventional wisdom. Pryor and network television continued their wary love-hate relationship. As host of the *Midnight Special*, broadcast at a time when most children, and certainly most Moral Majoritarians were in bed, Pryor was visibly nervous about his delivery, about saying something censorable. Despite his efforts he was censored anyway. Later, as MC on a tribute to Redd Foxx on ABC, which fortunately was taped, not live, he grew so resentful over censorship of his "natural obscenities" that he forced continued re-taping by saying more loudly and more distinctively with each take words that were TV no-nos.

Still, as the year wore on, Pryor seemed to stop fighting. It may have been because he made a sincere effort to get off drugs, telling himself that cocaine had been no friend and refusing to listen to the arguments of his friend cocaine. No doubt he found support in his struggle from his probation officer, Marcus Woodard, who did not let Pryor renege on the terms of his probation just because he happened to be a star. It may also have been because, for all his rebelliousness, Richard Pryor craved acceptance.

It mattered to him that he had a reputation for irresponsibility. It hurt him that he was criticized by black women for going out with white women. And it mattered to him, suddenly, that the media had painted a picture of him that was, at best, one-dimensional. Richard Pryor, who had previously been about as uncooperative as a mule with the press, was feeling misunderstood.

It seems that writer David Felton approached him at just the right time. Or perhaps Felton was just the right person to approach him. Whatever, the chemistry was there. Felton was intelligent, sympathetic, and persistent. He had followed Pryor's career from the early days and had done his homework. He was a representative of the media, but he was the least obnoxious that Pryor had encountered in a long time. Felton managed to get more out of Richard Pryor than any other interviewer has—before or since. His lengthy biographical piece on Pryor, which appeared in the October 10, 1974, issue of *Rolling Stone* magazine, was the seminal work on Pryor's life; and though the word *seminal* seems rather academic when applied to a piece in a pop-music periodical, it is nevertheless appropriate in this case. David Felton managed to get to the real Richard Pryor in a way that the people who were supposed to be closest to him could only envy.

Pryor allowed Felton to see behind the protective veneer of gleeful put-ons and barely masked hostility. He gave Felton a copy of his autobiographical screenplay and allowed him to quote from it at length. He allowed Felton to see his anger and hurt; he let Felton see him cry. It is possible, of course, that Pryor chose to use Felton for his own purposes, that he'd decided one way to get some of the pressure from the media off him was to choose one sympathetic representative and tell all—or at least what would appear to be all. But the Felton interviews with Pryor seem too real to be contrived. Compared with interviews Pryor gave to others, before and after, the Felton dialogues are tantamount to a series of psychoanalytic sessions. It is more likely that after nearly a decade in the public eye, Richard Pryor gave up trying to guard his privacy so zealously and realized that if he was to be understood and really accepted by his public he would have to start sharing more than his talent with it.

At any rate the fall of 1974 seems to have been this-is-your-life time for Richard Pryor on more than just the magazine front. Back in Peoria the sliding board had arrived at Miss Whittaker's day-care center. "The unit came in; we got it in the ground, and we decided to have a ribbon-cutting ceremony," says Juliette Whittaker. She knew, having kept up with the conflict between Richard and his first wife over where Richard Jr. should go to school, that Richard would be visiting Peoria soon. She scheduled the ceremony for the day he would arrive.

"The mayor proclaimed Richard Pryor Day and that was on the marquee at the Shrine mosque," she recalls. "The YMCA put together a program, and we put on a show that evening at the mosque. That afternoon we held the dedication of the sliding board. We had a band on a flatbed, and after the dedication and the ribbon-cutting, Richard came up to me. He had something wrapped up in a newspaper, and he said, 'Now, I've got a surprise for Miss Whittaker.' And he opened the package and inside it was the Emmy that he had won. He presented it to me, saying 'If it hadn't been for you, I would not have learned anything about the theater. And I certainly wouldn't have learned how to write.' "

Richard's agent accompanied him to Peoria that time. The human-interest angle was not lost on him. He remembered Juliette Whittaker when the producers of *The Mike Douglas Show* decided to have a week devoted to Richard Pryor. Mike Douglas was big on this-is-your-life shows, and on inviting to be his cohosts people who were very much in the news—Richard Pryor and Martha Mitchell appeared on the same show during that year.

In the fall of 1974, Mike Douglas et al decided to have a Richard Pryor Week. Among other people from Peoria who were brought to Philadelphia for the occasion were Richard's grandmother and Juliette Whittaker. Miss Whittaker believes that Ron DeBlasio, Pryor's agent, was the one who suggested she be brought to Philadelphia as a surprise for Richard.

"When Richard came here to dedicate the playground equipment, there was a man with him—his agent, Ron, had a Spanish name.... Later, I got this call, and this girl said, 'Miss Whittaker, can you come to Philadelphia tomorrow?' I said I supposed so, if they could get everything arranged. Well, they did; it was a very quick decision. They kept me hidden in the Green Room, until he got on. In the Green Room were Milton Berle, George C. Scott and his wife, Trish—and they were going on the show, too. I just sat there watching everybody. I didn't get nervous all that time until they sent for me and put me behind this curtain. Suddenly I couldn't see what was on the other side. There was a kind of buzz from the audience, but I couldn't see anything.

"Then the curtain opened, and the lights hit me, and I really couldn't see anything for a time. And then I saw Mike Douglas over on the side and Richard.

"I walked over and shook Mike Douglas's hand, and then I turned to Richard, and he just started to cry. He was so surprised that they had brought me to be on.

"Afterward, we went out to dinner to a beautiful restaurant in the area they were restoring for the upcoming Bicentennial."

The year 1974 saw Richard Pryor back on television, back on selected stages, and even back on records more than in films. This was due more to coincidence than to any conscious career redirection on his part. He was still keenly interested in acting. But there is an ebb and flow to movie projects that has to do primarily with money, and there was a minor recession then. Pryor had yet to receive star billing in a movie, but he had an advantage that other actors did not enjoy. When there was not much movie work around, he had his stand-up comedy to fall back on. His third comedy album was issued that year. *That Nigger's Crazy*, first released by Stax in 1974 and re-released the next year by Warner-Reprise, became the first comedy record in years to break into the top twenty on the charts. It went gold, then platinum.

The gold-record plaque on Richard Pryor's wall has a bullet hole in it, although anyone who knows why is not telling.

CHAPTER VII

The Funniest Man in America

IN EARLY MARCH 1975 Richard Pryor won a Grammy award for Best Comedy Album of the Year. He would also win the Record World award for best comedy album and the NATRA (National Association of Television and Radio Announcers) award as Comedian of the Year. In early April he shared the Writers Guild of America award with Mel Brooks for the screenplay of *Blazing Saddles*. Later in the same month he was the subject of a lengthy profile in the Sunday *New York Times Magazine*, a bastion of arrivaldom if ever there was one. Richard Pryor had indeed arrived or re-emerged. Although he had yet to receive star billing in a film, was still regarded as a risk by the movers and shakers of the television industry, and was still largely unknown to the broader American public, his comedy was not just alive and well but setting new standards for the genre. As James McPherson, writer of the *Times* piece, put it, "Almost single-handedly, he is creating a new style in American comedy, a style that some of his admirers call 'theater' because there is no other category available for what he does."

Before Pryor's very risky leap across the chasm from Cosbyism to Pryorism, there had always been a clear distinction between comedians and actors: a comic projected himself, an actor played a role. But Pryor had somehow managed to blur this traditional distinction—to project himself through playing roles. His was a comic style that clearly struck a chord in the souls of the buyers of comedy records: It was almost unheard of for a comedy album to be in the top twenty. It was also a style that, through his album, echoed and reverberated in ever-widening circles through the broader audience, or at least the portion of that audience that had contact with Richard Pryor or his fans. Pryor himself began to feel these reverberations as he traveled across the country.

He had resumed a heavy club-appearance schedule in the fall of 1974, playing before predominantly black audiences in San Francisco, Detroit, Harlem, and Washington, D.C. In a dressing room in Detroit in early 1975 he was taken aback by a visit from two policemen who wanted to share an experience. They told him they had just arrested a suspect who had used a line from one of Pryor's characterizations: "I-am-reaching-into-my-pocket-for-my-license." Recognizing the line, one of the cops had adopted the Pryor-routine cop-comeback: "Spread your cheeks! Put your face on the ground!" With that, both officers and suspect had stood there laughing together.

Pryor, although not ordinarily a supporter of cops, appreciated the sense of shared humanity that had caused the policemen to visit him and tell their story. He also tried to respond with some warmth to the white hillbilly types who would come up to him and tell him how much they liked his white hillbilly characterizations: "I know a guy just like that!" Such encounters arose from a basic humanity that he generally tried to remind himself existed. For all Pryor's resentment against "the system," and thus against whites as the controllers of the system, James McPherson of *The New York Times* observed, he could see a TV news piece about a paraplegic white girl and remark that he did not wish pain on her just because she was white. But he did have to concentrate on such reminders, for he was still struggling with resentment about the power whites had over him. They seemed to give with one hand and take with the other. They gave him a Grammy but censored him on TV. They welcomed him as a screenwriter but wouldn't give him a starring role in a film. They wanted to be his agents and pretended to be looking out for his best interests, but all they did was use him. (By 1975 Pryor had severed his connections with Wald, DeBlasio, Nanas Associates and taken his business to the William Morris Agency, which was also predominantly white.) And the white women he had known had enticed him with sham understanding and then turned out to be typical women, wanting more than he could give and giving less then he needed.

Richard Pryor was alone in 1975, and perhaps in defense he insisted he wanted it that way. The handwritten sign on the door of his rented Hollywood Hills cottage read: "To avoid ill feeling/or unpleasantness, please be aware of the fact that uninvited guests are not welcome at any time whatsoever. To avoid rejection, please do not take the liberty of 'dropping by.' Sincerely and Respectfully, Occupant.''

There, with his Chicano housekeeper, Mercy, bringing him Courvoisier cognac and otherwise ministering to his needs, he watched cartoons and *Zoom* on television and worked on his screenplay, *This Can't Be Happening To Me*. After the *Blazing Saddles* insult it became very important for him to prove that he could write a screenplay entirely on his own. But he soon put the project aside once again. One reason was that he could not abide isolation very long, despite his determination to play the lonesome traveler. Another was that he was writing material for a new album and trying it out in the clubs.

Is It Something I Said? was recorded live at the Latin Casino in Cherry Hill, New Jersey, and released by Warner/Reprise in August 1975. All the material was Pryor's except for the Just Us routine, which he admitted to having stolen from Paul Mooney. The cover picture shows Pryor bound to a pile of kindling wood and surrounded by torch-carrying, hooded figures.

On this album, Pryor, who still had his drug habit under control, admitted that he had not controlled it very well in the past: "I snorted cocaine for about fifteen years—with my dumb ass.'' He talked about his conviction for income tax evasion and his ten days in jail. This was more serious autobiographical material than he had used in the past, although he managed to render it in hilarious fashion. But it signaled no major change in the Pryor brand of comedy. The album also contained the kinds of characters for which Pryor was becoming uniquely known. Among them was Mudbone, who was based on a man from his childhood days when he hung around Johnnie Mae's Barbecue Pit: "An ol' man who dip snuff an' sit in front the barbecue pit and he spit. . . . That was his job. I'm pretty sure that was his job, 'cause that's all he did.'' The album was a superb blend of comedy and seriousness, autobiography and fantasy. It rose quickly on the charts, placing in the top twenty within a month of its release—and won him his second Grammy in March 1976.

Release of the album and its immediate success brought more club and concert appearances. For several months Pryor subjected himself to the dreaded experience of flying, criss-crossing the country accompanied by his valet, often by his road manager, Bill Cherry, and usually by June Eckstien, daughter of singer Billy Eckstien and a singer in her own right, whom he had begun to date and whom he often introduced as his fiancée. In January he appeared at the Felt Forum at Madison Square Garden in New York City. A writer for *The New Yorker* described his act: "He said things that are usually considered uncomplimentary about blacks, whites, and women, and the audience, which was made up of blacks, whites, and women, laughed and laughed."

Pryor was, according to no less a purveyor of taste than *The New Yorker*, the "funniest man in America," and that kind of praise, coupled with the rest of the publicity and other critical kudos he had been getting lately, naturally brought out the exploiters. He was approached by record entrepreneurs who wanted to release his old material. Although he could have used the money, he turned them down. He didn't want people spending their money expecting material of the caliber of his best-selling albums and being disappointed. As he explained to James McPherson of *The New York Times*, "I'm going to do *mine* right. Whenever they say, 'Richard Pryor,' they can trust me." He probably believed what he was saying—at that moment.

He maintained his integrity when he was guest host on NBC's *Saturday Night* in mid-December of that year and caused the network's censors to put into effect the five-second delay device in order to cut two words from his monologue. The same device had been activated on the first *Saturday Night* show, that time in honor of George Carlin.

Pryor compromised his integrity, or so he believes, by being associated with the film *Adios Amigo* that year. Written, produced, directed, and starred in by Fred Williamson, it was a low-budget comedy-western that seemed deliberately to avoid the violence, sex, and black-versus-white hatred for which the so-called blaxploitation films (in several of which Williamson had starred) were being so roundly criticized. The film was intended to be, and succeeded in being, family entertainment. However, it wasn't very good.

Williamson and Pryor were friends, and off camera they could be a hilarious comedy team. No doubt Williamson hoped they could enjoy the same chemistry in front of a camera. Williamson played Ben, a frontier settler in a racist town who is saved from trouble by a con man named Sam (Pryor). Having saved Ben, Sam proceeds to involve him in a series of schemes that inevitably backfire, leaving Ben holding the bag.

Pryor did the best he could during the nine days in which the film was shot, but he managed to slip in only a few ad libs, and his performance, as described by *Variety,* was characterized by half-hearted fooling around." After the film's release in early 1976, Pryor said, referring to his fans, "Tell them I needed some money. Tell them I promise not to do it again."

Despite generally poor reviews, the movie did well at the box office, but Pryor didn't change his mind about it. *Adios Amigo* was the first movie in which he shared star billing—many reviewers wrote that he was really *the* star, and the release of *Adios Amigo* marks the point at which he became a box-office name of sorts. But he felt that he had sold out himself and his fans by being a part of such a poorly produced film.

Some would charge that both his fans and his name were equally exploited in *Car Wash,* which was also filmed in 1975, and released in April 1976. He played just a cameo role in that film, and yet when it was released it was billed as a "Richard Pryor movie."

Michael Schultz directed the film, and cast Pryor in the role of Reverend Rich. But the Reverend's part had not been written originally with Pryor in mind. According to Schultz, "It was written for Reverend Ike. I was trying to get him in the film, to play himself, because he's got such a great rap. He came and met with us at Universal about it, and at first he was very interested, but then I guess he figured it might not be good for his image. He would have been making fun of himself, in a way. I'd seen Richard do some of his preacher characterizations, and after Reverand Ike turned it down, the part went to Richard."

The film covers a day in the lives of a motley group of characters who work in and around a car wash. Schultz, who'd had considerable experience in the theater, directing several Negro Ensemble Company productions in New York before relocating to Los Angeles and film directing (earlier he had directed *Cooley High*), treated his cast like an ensemble. Before principal photography began on March 1, 1975, he had his actors meet at the sound stage to do preparatory reading, blocking, acting, and interacting. He also staged a run-through at the actual Los Angeles car wash where the film was to be located. By the time principal photography began, the main actors, staff, and crew members were working as a close-knit company.

None of the main actors was a star, although such members of the cast as Ivan Dixon and Clarence Muse were respected veterans of both stage and screen. The big-name comics, George Carlin, Professor Irwin Corey, and Pryor, all had mere cameo roles. The purpose of their cameos was to add interest and box-office appeal, but for Schultz the real point of the film was the everyday lives of ordinary people—a hooker looking for her boyfriend, who had apparently taken a powder, a kid with intimations of Super Flyhood who couldn't even get a date with a diner waitress, a black militant, an aging ex-con who is trying to earn a position of trust. The visit to the car wash by Reverend Rich, in white Cadillac convertible complete with an entourage of Pointer Sisters, was not really germane to the plot.

Still, Schultz enjoyed working with Pryor. "The only direction I gave him was: go here, stand there, do this, do that. Richard's the kind of actor who will give you three or four variations on one theme, and as a director all you have to do is guide him along or pick which one you want. So in that sense he's real good to work with. In his early acting days he played a role the way he acted in his stand-up routines. He'd never do the same thing twice. So, if you captured something and you wanted it again, chances are that you wouldn't get it again— or not the same way."

In Schultz's view although Pryor's—and Carlin's and Corey's— cameo performances added to the film, they were not the main selling point. "The picture worked on its own, but the studio was afraid of the picture. They didn't know who the audience was, so they took what they could sell and sold it. Richard was beginning to get real hot, and the studio, in its infinite marketing wisdom, decided to sell it as a Richard Pryor and George Carlin picture, and it was nothing like that. The strategy may have worked more against the picture than for it, because when people see a picture advertised as a Richard Pryor or Clint Eastwood picture, they want to see those people in more than just a cameo. So I don't think it was smart selling."

The film earned well over ten million dollars. Richard Pryor had nothing to do with how it was marketed, and he could say this to people who complained to him that he was only in *Car Wash* for a few of its ninety-seven minutes. Anyway, by the time *Car Wash* was released, he could tell the complainers that a film would soon be released that was not exploitive of either his audience or his own integrity.

The movie was *The Bingo Long Traveling All-Stars and Motor Kings*, a Motown production in association with Pan Arts. Billy Dee Williams and James Earl Jones were set to star in it, and Pryor, who would be third-billed, was star of a big-budget movie for the first time.

Based on a novel by William Brashler, and set in the late 1930s to early 1940s when black baseball players were denied admittance to the white major leagues, the story is about a barnstorming black baseball team that winds its way through heartland America playing House of David Jewish teams, local black and local white teams, and in the climactic sequence the All-Stars of the Negro National League in a game that will determine whether or not they will be able to enter that league as a self-contained team.

With a $3.8 million budget, the film ranked with Motown's *Lady Sings the Blues* and *Mahogany* as one of the highest-financed black films ever, and its stars were top black actors. Billy Dee Williams would play the title role of pitcher Bingo Long, and James Earl Jones would take the part of the slugger Leon Carter. The third major role, that of third-baseman Charlie Snow who hoped to break into the white leagues by pretending he was Cuban, seemed perfect for Richard Pryor.

When first approached, Pryor had not been eager to sign a contract. Hearing that Williams and Jones had already been signed, he had visions, no doubt, of yet another role as a sidekick, a foil for bigger stars. It took a lot of bargaining and schedule shuffling on the part of the producer, Rob Cohen, to persuade Pryor to sign; but Cohen kept after him, and in mid-June 1975 Cohen finally bagged his prey.

On-location shooting began later in the month in Macon, Georgia, and Pryor deliberately separated himself from the two major stars and the rest of the cast and crew. While everyone else stayed at the Macon Hilton, Pryor rented a house in a white section near Mercer University. Ostensibly, his reason was that he wanted his family with him—he had his grandmother, an aunt, and "a lady friend of Greek extraction," according to one reporter, flown in to stay with him. But though he hosted a party for cast and crew at the house—Marie Bryant cooked up a feast of fried chicken, okra, rice, string beans, white potatoes, oxtail stew, and peach cobbler—this did little to close the gap between him and the others. He played his new album, *Is It Something I Said?*, for his guests, as if to underscore his position as the center of attention. When he was not in such a position of command, he preferred to socialize with non-actors, or lesser actors.

William Brashler, on whose novel the movie was based, was there on location in Macon in July. A few years later, in a 1979 article for *Playboy*, he wrote, "During the long, restless hours of shooting, Pryor was friendly, occasionally withdrawn and private. At times he'd hold court with members of the cast or crew and run into impromptu routines. Or he'd toy with people such as Leon 'Daddy Wags' Wagner or Birmingham Sam Brison, both former pro ballplayers with small roles in the film, and they'd kid him about how awful he was with a bat and ball. It was kidding that Pryor seemed to enjoy."

Pryor did form one close relationship with another actor on the set. Stan Shaw, who would play Alex Haley's father in *Roots II* several years later, had a small part in the film and the two did some hanging out together. Stan Shaw was not a threat to Richard Pryor.

Whether stimulated by a need to prove he was just as talented an actor as Williams or Jones or simply by a desire to make the most of his first important part, or both, Pryor was excellent in the role of Charlie Snow. A reviewer for *Time* magazine called him "an actor-comedian of buckshot brilliance. Pryor calculates every line and gesture for small, explosive effect, and his aim stays true."

"Much of his effort," wrote Martin Weston in *Ebony*, "ended up on the film editor's cutting room floor to allow for more footage of sex symbol Billy Dee Williams."

Still, Richard Pryor was becoming hot in Hollywood. Close on the heels of the filming of *Bingo Long* came the opportunity to co-star with Gene Wilder in *Silver Streak*. It was Pryor's first chance to co-star in a film aimed at the larger (read *white*) audience and thus to reach people who were scarcely aware of his existence—unless they had happened to see him on the *Mike Douglas Show* or the *Tonight* show or *Saturday Night*, or read *Rolling Stone* or *The New York Times Magazine*. With co-stars like Wilder and Jill Clayburgh (most recently seen in *Gable and Lombard*), how could he miss? Although he was not scripted to appear until the movie was half over, he believed that he could make his presence felt.

The setting was a super train that ran between Los Angeles and Chicago. Gene Wilder, a mild-mannered L.A. book publisher, manages to get involved with the sexy secretary of an elderly art historian and then embroiled in a complicated case of art forgery and murder. No one will help him, much less believe him, except Richard Pryor, a thief who turns up in the back seat of a squad car Wilder commandeers, and who repays Wilder for rescuing him by helping to solve the mystery.

Shot in Canada because the producers and director couldn't find an American railroad that offered mountains, desert, prairies, *and* Illinois farmland, the film otherwise paid meticulous attention to the authentic. The final scene, in which the train crashes into what is supposed to be Union Station in Chicago, was not done with miniatures or matte shots but with full-scale mock-ups. And in the scene where Wilder hangs out of a runaway train with Pryor holding onto his belt, no stunt men were used. They rehearsed the scene at ten miles per hour but shot it at fifty miles per hour. Pryor promised Wilder that if he fell off the train and was killed, Pryor would throw himself after him.

They enjoyed working together. Their respective zaniness fit. The Pryor character's active craziness but solid center was an effective counterpoint to the Wilder character's untroubled exterior but manic essence. Director Arthur Hiller allowed them to ad-lib, to rework scenes, and Pryor was responsible for making at least one critical scene work. Police detectives are searching for the Wilder character, and the Pryor character saves him by disguising him as a black, using shoe polish and a hat.

"We were worried about that scene, that it might hurt people's feelings," Wilder told Roger Ebert of the *Chicago Sun-Times* during a promotional interview in which both Wilder and Pryor took part. "The way it was written, after I disguise myself, a white man is fooled by my disguise. That was bad, because then we'd be saying blacks were like that. And so Richie came up with a brilliant structural change, and now the scene gets one of the biggest laughs in the movie."

Pryor took up where Wilder left off. "Instead of a white dude being fooled by the disguise, a black dude comes in and *isn't* fooled. Here's Gene snapping his fingers and holding his portable radio to his ear, and the black dude takes one look and says, 'I don't know what you think you're doing, man, but you got to get the *beat*.' "

Pryor was in a good mood on the day of that dual interview or merely resigned to playing the promotional game. He had resented having to fix up that scene. In fact in the course of filming *Silver Streak*, he had come to resent his very involvement in the film. He'd decided that the *Silver Streak* brass had brought him in primarily to prevent criticism from blacks. At some point something had snapped inside Pryor's supersensitive soul, and he'd stood back and looked at himself having a good time playing second-fiddle to Gene Wilder in a film in which he didn't even make his first appearance until halfway through the story, and he'd suddenly seen a clown instead of Richard Pryor, and he'd hated what he saw. Despite his gee-aren't-we-a-great-team-in-this-great-movie act for the *Chicago Sun Times* interviewer, Pryor rarely had anything good to say about *Silver Streak* once it was released. His remark to Janet Maslin of *The New York Times* in August 1977 was typical: "I put myself in it, but I didn't *do* it, not with my heart. It was a business decision. I was looking to hustle, and I got hustled."

He managed to fool the reviewers, however. Many of them felt that Pryor saved the film, which was released at Christmastime 1976. Wrote Pauline Kael in *The New Yorker*, "For about fifteen minutes, Pryor gives the picture some of his craziness. Not much of it, but some—enough to make you realize how lethargic it was without him." Kael objected, however, to Pryor's being cast as a friend to good-guy whites and suggested that when he was being soft-hearted he was a bad actor. "Interracial brotherly love is probably the one thing that Richard Pryor should never be required to express," she continued. "It violates his demonic, frazzled blackness. The suspense built into watching him is that we don't know what's coming out of him next, or where he's coming from. Those deep-set somewhere-else eyes and that private giggle don't tell us much, but they do tell us this: his comedy doesn't come from love thy white neighbor."

Kael, who had also written that Pryor shouldn't be cast at all, but rather realized, was about one hair breadth away from celebrating him as a 1970s version of the noble savage. Still, she had stumbled onto a truth of sorts.

Pryor and Wilder had meshed professionally in a rare way on that set, and Wilder, perhaps eager to complete his own humanity, had tried to translate that meshing of professional talents into his idea of a personal relationship. But, viewed cynically, Wilder could afford to feel beneficent toward Pryor. Wilder had enjoyed better roles (*The Producers, Young Frankenstein, The Adventures of Sherlock Holmes' Smarter Brother*); and Wilder was top-billed in *Silver Streak*. Wilder, his character in *Silver Streak* notwithstanding, tended to be emotional about his likes and dislikes. D'Urville Martin recalls another dual interview with Wilder and Pryor about *Silver Streak*. "Gene said, "I love this man. I'd do anything for this man.' And Richard said, 'Really? I never realized that. I didn't know that.' "

Pryor did not have the luxury to engage in such effusiveness, especially about a white man. He'd been taught from childhood, learned from some thirty years's experience, that the white man was tricky. He was ever aware of the difference between the meshing of talents and the blurring of racial distinctions. He'd gone along, perhaps with some hopefulness, with the studio hype about how well he and Wilder worked together, and was probably aware, as writer Mark Jacobson reported, that people on the set of *Silver Streak* "seemed to be talking about how Richard hadn't missed a day of shooting, how he's never forgotten a line, how he hasn't been a problem of any kind." But he never let down his guard completely, for all the usual complexity of reasons that governed his life and behavior.

"A great deal of his private moments have been shared with whites," says D'Urville Martin. "But he grew up in an era when the white man was his enemy, and it's a complex situation figuring how to deal with that. The hand that's really feeding you is the white guy's. Richard's relationship with Gene Wilder ... off-screen they do not really associate. When they hear, 'Cut,' they are not as in tune with each other as they are onscreen. They are in competition with each other when they perform together. Richard feels that Gene Wilder is trying to outdo him, and Gene Wilder feels that he is trying to outdo Richard. The chemistry works but not necessarily off camera."

The chemistry between Richard Pryor and film acting worked consistently, on camera and off. By 1976 he had decided definitely to direct his future energies to film. He would continue to write and produce comedy albums and make occasional personal appearances, but he had decided to stop making nationwide tours. His last tour had been so extensive and so grueling that he grew nauseous at the very thought of boarding another plane. He realized he still had to fly, because there was too much additional pressure when he was on a tight touring schedule, trying to get from city to city with little time to spare. By now he was making enough money to hire a private jet, which made flying a little less scary "because I can see the pilot and talk to him and watch what he's doing and keep him as happy and comfortable as I can." But he still preferred occasional flights to flying as a way of life.

Besides, he had such a demanding film schedule coming up that he wouldn't have time for a concert tour. Movies were satisfying work, and movies meant more money. And now that he was making more money, he decided to have it managed properly by hiring a new attorney.

He had met David McCoy Franklin in 1975. The short, rotund, moon-faced attorney was based in Atlanta and was a former law partner of Maynard Jackson, then mayor of Atlanta. He had, in fact, been financial chairman of Jackson's successful mayoral campaign. His roly-poly appearance belied his steely business methods. He was a savvy wheeler-dealer who quickly scouted and understood the labyrinthine intrigues of the business of show business. Besides Atlanta-based friends like Andrew Young and Julian Bond, he represented Roberta Flack and Cicely Tyson. Pryor liked him from the start. "I like David's energy and his creative ability," he told Bob Lucas of *Jet* magazine. "He's not a greedy man. He's much smarter than anyone he's dealing with and he's not afraid of white people."

It took Franklin some time to get Pryor's financial affairs in order, even to find all the loose ends that needed to be tied up. He knew Pryor needed to get some equity, to have some relief from the enormous tax burdens his increasing income engendered. He also knew that far more could be done to exploit Pryor's new position as a hot item in Hollywood, for Pryor still was not getting the money that white stars of similar stature earned.

Meanwhile, Pryor had signed for a role in a comedy version of *Cyrano de Bergerac* for Brut Productions and for what was supposed to be his first starring role in a movie. *Which Way Is Up?*, a comedy take-off on Lina Wertmuller's *The Seduction of Mimi*, was being developed by director Michael Schultz. According to Schultz, "We were developing that for him, to be his first starring vehicle. But while we were developing it, he got tapped by Hannah Weinstein to play Wendell Scott."

Wendell Scott was the first black champion race-car driver, the winner of the 1961 Grand Nationals. *Greased Lightning* was to be the story of his life, and Pryor would play the leading role. Says Schultz, "I think he wanted to be in it because it was a serious role, and he's always seen himself as a serious actor. I think he has a mental resistance to being known as just a comedian. Of course, most dramatic actors would love to be able to play comedy. The grass is always greener on the other side. So anyway, he chose to do that."

Thus, Richard Pryor accepted his first starring role while the movie that was supposed to give him his first top billing was still being developed. He was that hot.

CHAPTER VIII

Greased Lightning

GREASED LIGHTNING WAS PRODUCED by Hannah Weinstein, who had founded Third World Cinema with James Earl Jones, Brock Peters, and the late Diana Sands. Its cast also included Beau Bridges, Pam Grier, Cleavon Little, Vincent Gardenia, Julian Bond, Earl Hindman, Minnie Gentry, and Lucy Saroyan. Although Michael Schultz is listed in the credits as director, Melvin Van Peebles was initially hired for that task. In the credits, Van Peebles is listed only as one of the writers of the screenplay. A lot went on behind the scenes of Greased Lightning; in fact the behind-the-scenes story ought to have been filmed as a documentary of Hollywood film-industry machinations and the problems that blacks in Hollywood experience.

Melvin Van Peebles is accorded by some the dubious distinction of having started the rush of blaxploitation movies in the early 1970s with his independently produced Sweet Sweetback's Baadasssss Song, which he also wrote, directed, and starred in. It is his belief that when Weinstein approached him with the job of directing the Wendell Scott story, she was hoping to acquire in the bargain more than just his directorial talents.

"When I was called in by Hannah Weinstein, the script was little more than a treatment," says Van Peebles. "She asked me if I had any ideas for the script, and it became clear that she wanted me for writing functions also. She wanted two for one—two jobs for one-job pay— which I wouldn't do. After beating her head on the wall and talking about my people, she finally admitted that she wanted me to straighten out the script.

"It had been written by two guys, Kenneth Vose and Lawrence DuKore, and they had a nice concept but they didn't know that much about professional writing. I wasn't about to give them writing class, but I built in a plot.

"One of my requirements before agreeing to work on the script was that I could bring in some other people. At that time Hannah Weinstein was not really a line producer. She'd done *Claudine*, but she was actually an executive producer who'd gotten pushed out of her slot. We needed an associate producer, and that's when Jim Hinton came in."

Van Peebles also took an active part in the casting of the film. "I brought Richard in. He'd never done a feature role. Hannah didn't even know who he was. She had other people in mind. I'd never met him, and I knew he had a very bad press, but I called and went to see him in L.A. We talked and I thought he could do it, and then I talked Hannah Weinstein into using him. I also brought in Richie Havens and Julian Bond."

Later he brought in The Commodores, then an up-and-coming group, to sing a song called "Greased Lightning," which he had copyrighted.

Although Wendell Scott had raced out of Danville, Virginia, on-location shooting for *Greased Lightning* was done in Georgia. Van Peebles had recently shot a movie called *A Sparkle* there, and he had "good vibes" from Georgia. Madison, in the middle of the state, was the main location, but the company also did some shooting in Macon and in the northern part of the state where the dirt racetracks were located. As was his custom, Richard Pryor did not stay in a nearby hotel or motel with the rest of the cast and crew. He rented a place of his own. His girl friend of Greek extraction was not with him this time. She'd been replaced by Deboragh McGuire, a young black aspiring actress whom Pryor was wont to introduce as his fiancée.

Originally the film was to have been done on an extremely low budget. Van Peebles suspected this from the moment he was asked to both direct and write the script. Car crashes are expensive, and with the idea of keeping costs down Van Peebles had not envisioned *Greased Lightning* as being "a film with a lot of car crashes, but a funny, poignant story. And we'd all agreed on that." But even the money for a low-budget film proved difficult to come up with. Says Van Peebles, "Third World did not come up with the money and we were in deep shit. To her credit Hannah went to Warner Brothers— her daughter was a vice-president there—and got Warner Brothers to come up with one and one-third million." Shooting in Madison began on July 4, 1976.

James E. Hinton, film producer and photographic director, met Pryor for the first time while doing that film. "He was introverted," says Hinton, "quiet and removed. He rented a farm for the duration of the production, a place with a little pond on the property. On the set he was very professional—he concentrated on the scene. When he was not doing anything, he would take a chair and sit under a tree. He liked to be around one or two people at a time. If he was in a group, he would just sit quietly."

The one time Hinton remembers Pryor "opening up a little" was when he invited the whole company and their children out to the farm. "Once, Richard gave a party. I think it was to celebrate his fiancée's—Deboragh's—birthday. A lot of people from Atlanta came in, and he invited the whole company, including all the children. It was summertime, and many of the people in the company had their children with them; my sons, Chris and Malaku, were there. There was a barbecue and all kinds of food. He even had the little pond on the property stocked with catfish so the kids could fish. He has a rapport with children. He's got that childlike quality that children are responsive to. In fact I think he probably gets along with children better than with adults. Dizzy Gillespie has that quality too."

But beneath the happy surface of Pryor's party, there were a lot of problems on the film that nearly everyone in the company was aware of. Warner Brothers was not happy with the way the picture was progressing. Jim Hinton feels that Warner Brothers was nervous that Richard Pryor was the star, because of his earlier bad reputation and because, not having starred in a movie before, he might not be a sufficient selling point. Van Peebles feels that the poor box-office showing of his new movie *A Sparkle* worried the studio: "Some of the dealers looked dark, and they thought some of the dealers in this show looked dark."

"We were in the fourth week of shooting," says Van Peebles, "and I was two days ahead of schedule. The director of photography had given us a problem and he'd been changed, but that had been the only major event. Richard had always been on time, courteous, and very helpful. Then, suddenly, I was told I had 'artistic differences' with the producer."

The news, says Van Peebles, did not come as a total surprise: "I had a line to what was happening with Warner Brothers, and I knew what was going to happen." But it did surprise others in the company: "I had brought in many black people—wardrobe people, sound people, producers, actors—and when these people, like Cleavon Little, Pam Grier, Julian Bond, et cetera, heard I was to be let go for artistic differences, they immediately said they were going to walk off."

But in order for such a threat to work, the star of the movie had to go along with it, and Richard Pryor was not prepared to do so. Van Peebles believes Pryor made his decision "on the advice and perhaps prompting of his lawyer."

"He came as a man to the thing," Van Peebles allows. "He came to me and said, 'Hey, man, I hear they're lettin' you go. Cleavon and others going to walk off. . . . I'm not gonna walk. I've been advised not to. Times have been very tough.' Since Richard was the star of the film, I didn't have the ace I needed to put up a fight. That's the last I ever saw of Richard Pryor."

Van Peebles's contract was airtight, and he didn't lose any money. As he puts it, "I was bought out. There was no point in me trying to fight Hannah and Warner Brothers." It rankled with him that certain good things in the film, such as The Commodores sequence and the song, "Greased Lightning," were cut out, "rather than having me be any part of it." He was bothered, too, by the fact that a style he had chosen primarily for budgetary reasons was now deemed insufficient for an increased budget. "I think what I was doing would have been commercial," he said at the time. "My version was more stylized and they wanted it more naturalistic. I can't scream they're destroying my work, it's just a different way of looking at it. I could have gone in their direction, but I wasn't given a chance. I was just summarily dismissed."

Although by the time the picture was released, his formal association with it had been diminished to a credit as one of four writers of the screenplay, Van Peebles knew that a lot of informal credit for the picture was his. According to Jim Hinton, "By the time he left, his stamp was on the film, because he wrote the script, cast it, and designed the look in terms of the cinematography. And it was the first time in the history of the American film industry that there was fifty percent black participation."

Meanwhile, back in Hollywood, Michael Schultz was still at work developing *Which Way Is Up?* for Pryor. It was pure coincidence that he happened to fly to Georgia at that time. "I went down there one week end with Steve Krantz, who had produced *Cooley High*, just to have a story conference with Richard. I got off the plane and heard, 'Boy, you come to save us, huh?' And I said, 'No, no, no, I came to have a story conference. I wouldn't be caught dead down here.' It was *hot*, and I kept saying, 'I'm sure glad I'm not shooting a picture down here.' I knew the picture was in trouble, but I didn't know why. All I knew was that nobody was happy with anybody—Richard was not happy; Hannah was not happy; the studio was not happy."

Schultz got away from that hot, unhappy set as quickly as he could. Another director—"they brought in a white boy," says Van Peebles— was tried, but apparently no one was happy with him either. Back in L.A., Schultz got a call from Hannah Weinstein. "She said they were going to stop production and get a new director, and since Richard and I had a relationship, would I be interested in doing it? I said no. Then Richard called and asked me to do it. His career was at the point where, if he'd been involved in a bad picture, it would have been very shaky. I really wanted to see him succeed, for both personal and professional reasons. I was doing the next picture with him, and I did not want him to come off poorly in a film that would be out before *Which Way Is Up?*. I agreed to do it, much against my better instincts, because I didn't want to inherit anybody else's problems."

By the time Schultz agreed to be the third director of *Greased Lightning*, budgetary matters were less important than saving the picture. The budget, originally $1.3 million, had in the interim been raised to $4 million, and it would go much higher than that. Richard Pryor had something to do with the increased spending; he negotiated more money for Wendell Scott.

Early in his association with the film Melvin Van Peebles had flown to Scott's home to talk with him, but at the time there was no money in the budget to pay him as a consultant. With the production in a mess and Van Peebles gone, Richard Pryor, perhaps aware that he was owed something for not supporting Van Peebles, demanded greater involvement from Scott.

According to Jim Hinton, "In the beginning the picture was divided into two parts—the dramatic, the dialogue, and then the race-car scenes. When the race-car scenes began, Wendell appeared. Richard brought him in as a consultant. Wendell was overwhelmed—he hadn't really thought it was going to happen, that the picture would be done. He had some contractual problems with Warner Brothers, and Richard interceded and got him the money and got the company to use him more than they had originally intended to."

Richard Pryor had a large emotional investment in this film. Trouble-filled though it was, *Greased Lightning* was still to be his first starring vehicle, and his first starring role as a serious character. His own role aside, it was to be Wendell Scott's story. Pryor knew what it had taken for Scott, a black in the South, to become a champion race-car driver. Although he realized this movie represented a pivotal point in his own career, he knew that this was the one chance for Scott, at least in his own lifetime, to see his story put to film. For Scott as well as for himself, Richard Pryor gave *Greased Lightning* everything he had.

"This was my first extended period of working with Richard," says Schultz, "and he was under a lot of stress. The picture was coming apart, but he always had one hundred percent positive energy about working on it because he wanted to do as much as he was capable of at that time. He always felt a little insecure about his ability to deal with dramatic subject matter, so he was looking for a lot of help in that area. He was learning from everybody. Beau Bridges is a very good actor, and a good person too. They had a real tight professional relationship, and it was good for Richard. He watched Beau a lot. He watched everybody a lot. Richie Havens was also not a pro actor, but very real, beautiful—an amazing person. Richard was learning from everything.

"There was only one time that I, in our working relationship, experienced him not being cooperative. At one point he got so furious at something the producer wanted him to do that he refused to show up for a day of shooting. He felt that the producer was being unjust to Wendell Scott. They were trying to run something past Scott—destroy a car of his and not pay for it, or something like that—and

Richard said, 'Well, fuck it. I'll come to work when you treat the man fairly.' What's interesting to me is that the only time I saw him where his anger level took over any other consideration was when he felt that somebody black was getting a raw deal."

With all the problems and changes, Greased Lightning was an extremely long production: filming lasted from July 4 to September 28. It was an expensive production: the budget ran to over seven million dollars. The political maneuvering did not end with the completion of filming. Says Michael Schultz, "I think I had a contract with Warner's that I would spend six weeks after shooting in the editing room. After that, I had to go over to Universal for Which Way Is Up? I think it was about a month and a half between finishing the shooting on one picture and beginning preparation on the other. I was running cross lots trying to get both things in shape, and as soon as I left the editing room Hannah Weinstein fired my editor and recut the picture. That's why it came out the way it did—Goody Two Shoes, it was that bleeding heart, liberal white mentality that did that.

"Once they changed my cut around, I tried to get my name removed from the picture. I didn't want anything to do with it because I saw that they were trying to destroy it. It really disturbed me greatly that we couldn't force the producer to do it our way. I had a whole different way of cutting it so that it was all action—it was hard; it was flashbacks—and she wanted to make a domestic love story out of it."

Aware of all these problems, Pryor was even more nervous than he might have expected to be when he went to a preview of the first movie in which he had a starring role and which, because of its subject matter, he cared about very much. He didn't relax after the preview began. "The audience was laughing in the wrong places," he told Janet Maslin of The New York Times " . . . nervous laughter during the upsetting scenes, maybe laughing so they wouldn't cry. But then there's the scene where Pam Grier comes to visit me in the hospital, when I'm all bandaged up, and she starts saying, 'What've you got left?' One guy in the audience yelled out, 'He got pride,' and right then I knew everything was fine."

Greased Lightning was largely a critical success. Reviewers complained about the uneven screenplay, but they liked the story, the relaxed direction—if they only knew!—and subtle touches like changes in the complexion of members of the grandstand audience over the years as blacks in the South achieved greater social equality. There were universal kudos for Pryor. "Pryor is excellent," wrote Judith Crist. "Pryor is perfectly cast," wrote a reviewer for *The New Yorker*. It was his first starring vehicle: "A project that put him in a position to be superstar," says Jim Hinton; "the turning point for his image as being an incorrigible entity," says Melvin Van Peebles.

Although the film earned over ten million, it was not a box-office hit. On the other hand according to Michael Schultz, "It didn't do anybody's career any harm. Warner's wound up making their investment back, and it saved everybody's ass. It didn't do me any good, though."

Even if *Greased Lightning* had flopped, Pryor had a hefty "insurance policy" to guarantee his continued participation in movies. Back on July 7, 1976, three days after shooting on the film began, the announcement came that he had signed a contract with Universal Pictures that was unprecedented for a black in Hollywood. Under the terms of the three million dollar deal, Pryor would write screenplays for Universal on an exclusive basis. He would have the option to perform in the films or not, but an incentive to star was contained in a contract clause that gave him a share of each movie's profits if he did. Universal would also purchase play rights for him and pay hefty salaries to screen writers to help him finish the movies. He would remain free to act in non-Universal films. He would have offices at Universal, further underscoring his importance on the production end of the movie business. "They told me I can do whatever I want to do," Pryor said, "but I don't think I'll be directing. I can't see spending twelve months in the editing room. I find more enjoyment in front of the camera." It was an unusual contract in the film industry, primarily because of the creative control and freedom Pryor would enjoy. Said Thom Mount of Universal, "We believe it is possible to make money on class A pictures that not only star black people, but are made by black people." Said Pryor, "Well, I guess that means if these movies don't make money, a whole lot of niggers gonna be in trouble."

Blacks in Hollywood were already in trouble, although the change in their film-industry fortunes was just beginning at that time and none but the farsighted could see what lay ahead. Black leaders were

North Aiken Street, Peoria (below). The house at middle left is #409, where Richard's father, Leroy "Buck" Carter Pryor, lived with his wife, Viola Anna Hurst, Richard's stepmother. The white house next door is where Ray Le Roy and other entertainers stayed while working at the neighborhood club. According to Le Roy, it was the only house in the neighborhood that was not a hooker joint. *Credit: Peoria Journal-Star*

Bris Collins (left), owner of Collins Corner in Peoria, let Richard perform at his club but did not pay him. Richard worked for the money customers threw on the floor. *Credit: Ray Le Roy*

Juliette Whittaker and **Ray Le Roy** (below left), two of Pryor's childhood mentors. Whittaker got him interested in drama and gave him the opportunity to do comedy on a stage. Le Roy, a Peoria comedian, let Richard look through his joke books and gave him pointers on performing. *Credit: Ray Le Roy*

Pryor (below) with his **Aunt Maxine** and his **daughters Elizabeth and Rain**. His children visit him often and he is very generous to them, but he has never been able to offer them emotional security. He has not had it to give. *Credit: Frank Edwards © Fotos International*

(Below) **Pryor** "mooning" with his clothes on at a gay rights benefit at the Hollywood Bowl in 1977. His resentment against whites erupted that evening and he shouted, "Kiss my happy, rich black ass!" *Credit: Wide World Photos*

Pryor (right) with **Deboragh McGuire**, his third wife "on paper." The marriage lasted a little over three months, effectively ending in the early hours of New Year's Day, 1978, when Pryor "killed" a car belonging to one of Deboragh's friends. *Credit: United Press International Photo*

Pryor and **Jennifer Lee** (below right), his fourth wife "on paper." Their marriage lasted five months. As of this writing, he has not married again. *Credit: Bob V. Noble © Fotos International*

Pryor (left) with **Pam Grier** in *Greased Lightning* (1977). The movie offered Pryor his first serious dramatic role. He and Grier began to date while working on that trouble-plagued film. *Credit: Wide World Photos*

(Below left) Pryor in **Which Way Is Up?** (1977). He played three different characters in this film directed by Michael Schultz. It was planned as his first starring vehicle and to show his versatility as an actor. *Credit: Universal Studios*

Pryor (below) in **Bustin' Loose.** Begun before the fire and completed nearly two years later, this film was the first over which Pryor was to have complete control. Unfortunately, he lost interest in it before it was released and did little to promote it. *Credit: United Press International Photo*

Pryor (right) walking near **Sherman Oaks Burn Center** after the fire. He believed that God had subjected him to his "trial by fire" in order to make him a new man; but his real friends wondered if he would really be able to change.
Credit: United Press International Photo

still condemning blaxploitation movies, and black actors like Pryor were still countering with, "The black groups that boycott certain films would do better to get the money together to make the films they want to see or stay in church and leave us to our work." But the movies that had caused all the hoopla were on the wane, and since 1975 so was black employment in the industry. By 1979 there wouldn't be any more blaxploitation movies to fight about.

There were a variety of reasons for the mid-1970s decline in black-oriented movies. Rising inflation had increased the cost of making movies, and studios were becoming less willing to make movies for a limited audience. Some say that when *The Wiz*, a thirty-million dollar, all-black movie aimed at the mass audience, flopped in 1978, it was the death knell of the black renaissance in Hollywood. The wisdom of the day was that you could never gross enough money on a black film to justify a big budget.

Other observers suggest that white resentment of blacks in films began to be felt in Hollywood studio offices as the 1970s went on and that it was symptomatic of the larger, more generalized white backlash in the country: blacks had "been given too much."

Sidney Poitier believes that there was also a black backlash against blaxploitation films because these films were too shallow and one-dimensional in their concentration almost exclusively on the "get whitey" formula. He wrote in his autobiography, *This Life*: "The pleasure they [blacks] derived from seeing their actors function on that level was only a momentary satisfaction . . . a nice introduction, a wonderful way for their actors to open up their involvement in film—but not as something to go on repeating forever. Neither the exploitation films nor my films were sufficiently about them, sufficiently representative of what in fact they were. Hollywood was still wide of the mark in relation to their dreams, their aspirations, their frustrations, the things they lived with every day."

What was needed was black films about real black life, in which there was black involvement behind the camera and in front of it. Universal Pictures and Richard Pryor were going to try to fill this need, swimming against an increasingly powerful tide of sentiment and bottom-line realism whose direction was toward a steady decline in black participation in the film industry.

Pryor was feeling good about the opportunity to do something important for black people. He was feeling good about his ability to make movies, both behind and in front of the cameras. He was feeling good about himself in general.

Much of the credit for this era of self-satisfaction was due to David Franklin. Franklin, who had informed Pryor at the start of their relationship that he "didn't represent junkies," was devoting himself to clearing away some of the obstacles that had contributed to Pryor's abuse of drugs and alcohol. "Ninety percent of the black artists are getting ripped off," Franklin once said. "The best service I could give them would be to take a machine gun and wipe out all the people around them and start over." Pursuant to this philosophy, he had set himself up as a buffer between his client and the myriad people who were after him to invest his money in one scheme or another, to make personal appearances, to do movies, to grant interviews. The year 1976 was a particularly ripe time for wild ideas, for it was the nation's bicentennial year and there was a lot of money around for the celebration.

Pryor had agreed to do an album for Warner/Reprise just for the occasion, and the record was called, appropriately, *Bicentennial Nigger*. Recorded live at the Roxy in Hollywood—he'd wanted to do it in San Francisco but that meant flying—the album won a Grammy the following March and was considered by many to be his best work to date. It contained prime examples of his ability to make serious stuff comic without diminishing its seriousness. In one cut his preacher pontificates, "We're celebrating two hundred years of white folks kickin' ass. . . . White folks have had the essence of disunderstanding on their side . . . however, we offer this prayer. . . . How long . . . will the bullshit . . . go on? How long will the bullshit go on? This is the eternal question."

His Bicentennial Nigger character is two hundred years old, in blackface, with stars and stripes painted on his forehead, grinning and snorting, "I'm just thrilled to be here. . . . They brought me over on a boat. There was four hundred of us come over. Three hundred and sixty of us died on the way over. . . . You white folks are just sooo good to us. . . . I don't know what I'm gonna do if I don't get two hundred more years of this. . . ."

Pryor himself did not like the album. In January 1977 he told Gene Siskel of the *Chicago Tribune*, "It's not very good. It's not my best work. I had to rush to get it done. I was under contract to Warner Brothers to produce a record by a certain date. There was no way I could get out of it, so I wrote and produced this thing in less than two weeks."

Scarcely two years earlier, he had been so optimistic about not compromising himself, or his fans, but he was learning that when you are busy and successful, compromises are hard to avoid. As if to distance himself from the money he made in connection with *Bicentennial Nigger*, he donated the eight thousand he received for taping the record at the Roxy in equal shares to the minor children of singer Jackie Wilson, who had suffered a debilitating stroke, and to Dick Gregory, the activist comedian who was currently on a cross-country fund-raising tour.

That year Pryor also bought and donated one thousand tickets for an evening with Alex Haley, author of *Roots*, to the Los Angeles branch of the NAACP. And in December he took out a full-page ad in the small-paged *Jet* magazine celebrating *Kwanza*, the black Christmas ritual, and announcing a five thousand dollar donation to the organization of black actresses of the same name.

He could afford to make such magnanimous gestures. He was making big money now, and David Franklin saw to it that he had something to show for his efforts. All his six hundred thousand dollars in debts had been paid off, and he didn't owe anyone a penny. Thanks to Franklin, his alimony and child-support debts had been settled and the law suits brought against him had been let go by default. Franklin had set up a corporation, Richard Pryor Enterprises, managed by Barbara Wilson, and a production company, Black Rain, named after Rain, Pryor's youngest child.

That year, at Franklin's urging, Pryor bought his first house, a fifty-year-old Spanish villa in the Northridge section of the San Fernando Valley on the other side of the Santa Monica Mountains from Hollywood. The eight-acre estate contained fifty-two fruit trees, two guest houses, a garage, and pool houses. Pryor immediately ordered extensive renovations, including removal of all air conditioners. Although the temperature in the Valley was often ten degrees higher than in the city, Pryor did not like air conditioning.

On the ground floor the house had an indoor garden between the bedroom and a small dining area. Upstairs was a large study and workroom, and there was a screening room in the basement. Outside there were kennels for his pair of Alaskan malamutes, and there would soon be a gym and tennis courts. "I'm gonna take lessons and learn this game," Pryor insisted.

The first month or so after he moved in, he told writer Mark Jacobson, he had dreams of men carrying briefcases coming to his door and saying, "You mean you *own* this house, Mr. Pryor?" Stability was not something he was accustomed to. Owning such a house was something that, deep down, he wasn't sure he deserved. When Martin Weston of *Ebony* visited him at home and Pryor was conducting him and the cameraman on the obligatory tour of the grounds, someone asked Pryor the name of a particular tree. It took him a while to recall the name. After stammering and hemming and hawing, he remembered: "Apricot. Yeah, that's it. Ain't that something, a nigger with an apricot tree."

Pryor would like to have had someone to share it all with, but he was very wary of trusting women, particularly now that he could have just about any woman he wanted. D'Urville Martin says, "After Franklin took over his career, women just threw themselves at him, all the women that he'd wanted but couldn't get, like Enajette Chase, Lynn Moody. . . ." Pryor always had a woman with him, especially when he was filming on location, or on a tour, and if he was in the mood he would introduce her as his fiancée. But he was capable of introducing one woman as his fiancée one week and to accord another woman that distinction the next.

In August and September of 1976 he was still, according to *Ebony*, keeping company with Deboragh McGuire, the actress with whom he'd been linked several times in the past year or so. In November it was reported that he had given a "great big diamond engagement ring" to Lucy Saroyan. The thirty-year-old white aspiring actress, daughter of William Saroyan and step-daughter of Walter Matthau, had played Beau Bridges's wife in *Greased Lightning* and earlier had appeared with Matthau in *The Taking of Pelham One, Two, Three*. If this report was true, the engagement was short-lived. More probably, Pryor, who was in the habit of giving expensive gifts—cars to his driving-age children, jewelry to friends—had simply made one of his customary magnanimous gestures and had not meant the ring to be regarded as an engagement ring. It is also customary for aspiring actresses deliberately to magnify events and gestures in order to get a mention in the press. What made the Pryor and Saroyan relationship especially interesting was that at practically the same time he was also being linked with Pam Grier. When he pledged five thousand dollars to the Kwanza organization that night in December, he also took it upon himself to pledge five thousand dollars of Grier's money, which suggests a more than casual relationship.

Grier, cousin of football star turned actor Roosevelt Grier, had been called by at least one major magazine the "Sex Goddess of the 70s." The designation referred to her having been cast in a series of blax-ploitation films, among them *Foxy Brown; Sheba, Baby; Coffy;* and *Friday Foster*, in each of whch she played a black female crime fighter with a devastating karate chop, a deadly aim with a gun, and a gorgeous face and body. Her role as Wendell Scott's wife in *Greased Lightning* was her first chance to play serious drama in film.

While working on the picture, she and Pryor shared the feeling that this was their big chance to prove themselves, and they wanted to do the best they could. They became very close in Georgia. "It started during the picture," says Michael Schultz, "and I thought it was just a during-movie thing, but it lasted. Pam is a lovely person, very moti-vated and on purpose. California health freak. Just from my own, outside point of view, I thought she was a real good influence on him. She was a very strong woman."

Although Pryor had flirted with vegetarianism before meeting Grier, after he started seeing her he became a true born-again Califor-nian, concerned with his body, what he put into it, and how he used it. The years of drug and alcohol abuse were a closed chapter in his life, he insisted, and his appearance seemed to prove it. His face wasn't puffy play-dough anymore; he'd shaved off his moustache and lost weight. He looked younger than his thirty-five plus years, rather like the Richard Pryor of the mid-sixties, but more solid and less gangling and uncoordinated. But Grier's superb health and athletic ability also seemed to threaten him. According to one often repeated story, he couldn't stand losing to her at tennis and once forced her to play an endless series of matches, saying that he wasn't going to stop until he beat her. Once when she fainted in the middle of a match, he got so mad that he stomped off the court. Still, they managed to stay together for several months, were seen together often, traveled together, and Grier was hostess at parties at Pryor's home.

Bob Lucas, L.A. reporter for *Jet* magazine at the time, remembers, "He had a big party for the crew of *Greased Lightning* after they returned from location. It was at Dillard's, a disco in Westwood; the whole third or fourth floor was turned over to this party. Pam was clinging to his coattails. I'm sure she expected to marry him. I don't know why they didn't. She's a very independent young lady, probably too much so."

As the bicentennial year drew to a close, life was good for Richard Pryor. He had gained control of himself—stopped "on a dime" when he kicked his drug habit, he said—had his finances in order, had put down a couple of roots. He was taking care of his children and their mothers. Rain, seven, and Elizabeth Anne, nine, were in Los Angeles; Richard, Jr., fifteen, was in Peoria; and Renée, nineteen, was at Michigan State College. All four children visited him occasionally, as did his grandmother, his Aunt Dee, and assorted other relatives.

Professionally, he was still best-known for his concerts and comedy albums. It was a satisfying feeling to be considered at the top of his class, and what's more, he'd done it his own way. He'd said no to being the white folks' pet and come back bigger than ever, counting among his fans a sizeable number of whites. He had brought about a marked change in American comedy, and nowhere was the proof of his influence more evident than in the routines of young comics who were just starting out.

Mark Jacobson went to the Comedy Store on Sunset Boulevard one night in the summer of 1976. As he wrote in *New West* magazine, "Not one of the several black comics didn't use the word *nigger*. Every comic, all races, including even American Indian, did Pryor-like characters. But the show really began when Richard himself made an unscheduled appearance ... the word passes fast in the Hollywood Hills, and a half hour before Pryor pulled up, scores of [super] fly-looking people poured in. Big shots too. Redd Foxx peeked through the curtain; Freddie Prinz sat by the bar. Freddie is a special Pryor fan.

Once he said he really felt like he was happening because he was staying in the same room Pryor once had. And as soon as Richard pops on stage wearing a white gangster hat. . . . Freddie starts punching people in the arm, screaming, 'He's the best; he's the goddamn best. . . . Man, Pryor knows what's right; he's paid all the dues.' "

Pryor knew he was the best, and he was not about to display any false modesty about it. He'd helped change comedy as much as Lenny Bruce had. "I'm the Charlie Parker of comedy. I'm doing for black people what Lenny did for white people. . . . I don't mind saying that because I worked hard to get where I am and because it feels good to say it."

But being the best at one thing wasn't enough. He also wanted to be tops at acting. At the end of 1976 most of Pryor's best acting, and his one starring role, were either still in the can or on the script boards. In the major films released that year, he'd had only a cameo in *Car Wash* and hadn't appeared until the middle of *Silver Streak*. Vincent Canby, in a December article in *The New York Times*, included him in a list of "new character faces whose names you should remember." To his credit Canby had the foresight not to pigeonhole Pryor as a character-actor too tightly: "Pryor specializes in comedy performances, but one of these days he may give us an allout dramatic performance. There's also the possibility that he'll suddenly become a star on his own."

That is what Pryor intended.

CHAPTER IX

Movie Star

RICHARD PRYOR BELIEVED HE could achieve major film stardom through *Which Way Is Up?*, his first film under his unique contract with Universal. Rights to Lina Wertmuller's *The Seduction of Mimi* had been secured in June 1976, and director Michael Schultz along with Cecil Brown, author of *The Lives and Loves of a Jiveass Nigger*, and Carl Gottlieb set about shifting the scene of Wertmuller's comedy about sex and politics in Italian wine country to the citrus groves of central California. Preproduction planning had been interrupted by Schultz's stint directing and editing *Greased Lightning*, but by early 1977 the cameras were ready to roll and Richard Pryor was more than ready to attempt a veritable tour de force as an actor, playing three different roles in the film.

He played Leroy Brown, a Fresno orange picker who is working up the ladder in the farmworker's union being advised along the way by his foul-mouthed, dirty-old-man of a father, a role which he also played. Leroy has a mistress, played by Lonette McKee, and a wife, played by Margaret Avery, who herself has an affair with the preacher of the "7-11 Lucky Church of External Salvation." Pryor also played the preacher. Paul Mooney had a small role in the film.

Filming, which was to have begun in October but which was moved forward to early 1977 because of Schultz's commitment to *Greased Lightning*, went smoothly. Schultz had done a great deal of preproduction planning, and he and Pryor agreed on what they wanted the story to convey. Says Schultz, "It was the story of a man who sells out his integrity on every level—business, friendship, love, family—for success. It's an object lesson in what happens to somebody who does that." Pryor could relate to that theme, and by this time he was more secure in his ability to act. The only problem he and Schultz en-

125

countered was resentment from black women over the casting of the movie. The women charged that casting had been done according to racial stereotypes—the very dark farmer's wife, the "high-yaller" mistress.

Schultz believes these critics missed the point. "One of the reasons why I cast it the way I did was . . . he had a beautiful, simple, dark-skinned country wife, and he falls for this light-skinned city girl, somebody else's idea of beauty. I was trying to reflect the faulty reasoning about where love is, where beauty is. Now the preacher's wife, I just cast the best actress for that role. It had nothing to do with skin color.

"People can read into it whatever they want. I don't even try to defend that stuff. You can't win, no matter what you do. I put the whole gamut of colors in, just as I did with Cooley High. If I didn't, the *black* black people would say, 'How come I'm not represented?' Or the *light* black people would ask the same thing. So I thought I'd just put everybody in."

Perhaps if there had been enough acting jobs for blacks to go around, there wouldn't have been so much criticism of the casting in Which Way Is Up?.

Pryor had nothing to do with the casting. He took note of this criticism, however, and decided to learn from it; he would not lay himself open to it in future projects. But he was feeling so good about Which Way Is Up? that he wasn't going to allow anything to mar his euphoria. When filming was completed in April, he celebrated in the way that had become expected of Richard Pryor. He bought two full facing ads in the trade papers to thank the crew. One hundred and seventeen names were listed, everyone from the stand-ins to the painters. And on top of that he paid out twenty thousand dollars to rent a new disco for a wrap party for the entire cast and crew. He also made a special request to Marsha Reed, the project's still photographer. She'd taken some 2,500 pictures during the shooting schedule. Pryor ordered an eight by ten inch copy of every single one of them. "I'm going to save them for the rest of my life," he said. "This film is the most special thing I've ever done."

Released in early November 1977, the film received mixed critical reviews. Many critics, among them Judith Crist, complained of ex-

cess, "Too many stock situations for social satire . . . too much and too heavy-handed sex comedy . . . too much of the good thing Pryor is." Nevertheless, the film was a box-office success, and perhaps it helped to stem, briefly, the tide of anti-black sentiment in Hollywood.

Back in April 1977, when *Which Way Is Up?* was wrapped, there were no critical reviews for Richard Pryor to read. Anyway, he was too busy even to think about the movie, for he was already in the midst of taping his first television special.

Pryor had been conspicuously absent from TV talk shows lately, and it was a voluntary absence on his part. As he told Joyce Maynard of *The New York Times* in January 1977, "There comes a time in your life when the host on the talk show turns to you and says, 'Isn't America great, Richard?' and you're supposed to say 'It sure is,' and then he says, 'See guys, he did it—what's the matter with the rest of you?' I've gone along with that in the past but no more." Pryor didn't like being used, and he especially didn't like being held up as an example, a racial paragon. He'd done a *Saturday Night* guest-host bit and hosted a *Midnight Special,* but he was allowed a modicum of freedom on those programs and in those time slots. And when he was the first black MC on the Oscar telecast in the last winter of 1977, he showed he was neither awed nor grateful for his TV exposure by making the point, which some considered tasteless, that Sidney "Porteer" and Harry Belafonte were the only black members of the Academy. (Bill Cosby has consistently refused to be an Oscar presenter for that very reason.)

Thus it was an historic moment in the life of Richard Pryor when, on May 5, 1977, he appeared in prime time for an entire hour. *The Richard Pryor Special?* was produced by Burt Sugarman, who had produced the *Midnight Special* on which Pryor had been guest host, in association with Richard Pryor Enterprises. Paul Mooney was one of the writers and so were Rocco Urbisci and Alan Thicke. Also on the payroll for the special, according to Arnold Johnson, was a man who was known only as The Prophet. The Prophet, says Johnson, is "a spiritual leader who's around Richard. Just like Muhammad Ali keeps that guy Brown around, Richard keeps The Prophet around. He's black, a very spiritual man." No one seems to know exactly who The Prophet is or where he came from, or what he did to earn his salary, but Richard Pryor was definitely feeling more religious at that time. On May 7, 1977, two days after his special aired on NBC, he returned to Peoria to be inducted into the Masons, specifically the Henry Brown Lodge 22, F&AM Prince Hall Affiliation, and was made a master mason.

God kept popping up in his interviews, too, and when Guy Flatley of the Chicago Tribune mentioned this, Pryor responded, "Yes, I'm religious. God has shown me things, made certain ways clear to me. I believe in divine forces and energies. I believe the ability to think is blessed. If you can think about a situation, you can deal with it. The big struggle is to keep your head clear enough to think."

And to Janet Maslin of The New York Times, he explained, "I'm proof that there's a God, because I'm supposed to be dead by now; the suicide traps of life were set up for me." Implicit in such statements were references to drug abuse, and the numerous violent episodes in his past. But all that was behind him, he believed.

One wonders if his own inability to accept his success also played a part in his increased spirituality. How else to explain his stardom on the comedy stage, in movies, and now a special on television?

Paul Mooney was in charge of casting for The Richard Pryor Special? and he took the opportunity to give work to fellow black entertainers. Arnold Johnson recalls, "Paul Mooney brought me into the NBC things. Richard didn't have anything to do with the casting. Paul did it. I didn't even audition for that." Besides Johnson, there was LaWanda Page from the Sanford and Son days, Shirley Hemphill, who was then in What's Happening?, Maya Angelou, whose autobiographical work, I Know Why the Caged Bird Sings, would soon be made into a television movie, and Glynn Turman, a fine actor who wasn't getting much work except in little theater.

LaWanda Page had seen Richard only rarely since his writing stint on Sanford and Son, and she was pleased to see that "he was the same person, the money and power hadn't changed him. He invited me out to his house one night and I met his grandmother and his Aunt Dee. His grandmother was a beautiful lady—funny as Richard. That woman did comedy and didn't even know she was doing it."

The format of the special aimed at underscoring Richard Pryor as a quiet, polite, nice guy. He is shown walking backstage, on his way to plan the special, in a tuxedo with a yellow rosebud boutonnier. Along the way, he meets people who offer suggestions about who he should have on his show.

He does a hilarious routine around the character, Reverend James L. White, dressed in a white jump suit and high-heeled patent leather shoes and making his unabashed pitch for money: "We're after the Billy Graham dollar." He mugs with John Belushi of *Saturday Night*. In one of the cleverest segments, and the only real guest spot, the Pips, Gladys Knight's backup singing group, are introduced as "——and the Pips," whereupon the group does its usual backup routine while the camera focuses periodically on a lone, spotlighted microphone.

An authentic and poignant dramatic pitch is achieved in a scene in which Pryor, playing a drunk, comes home to Maya Angelou, his long-suffering wife, and she delivers an eloquent essay on love over his passed-out body.

In a clear attempt to mollify those critics who didn't believe Richard Pryor belonged on prime time, a group of children sang and performed to Stevie Wonder's history-lesson-in-song, "Black Man." And a beautiful interpretation of Langston Hughes's poem "Harlem Beauties," which celebrates the range of skin colors of black women, was no doubt Pryor's answer to critics of the casting in *Which Way Is Up?*

The special was a well-balanced presentation of the range of Pryor's talents and concerns. It was critically well received and got good ratings. According to Arnold Johnson, there was a behind-the-scenes feeling of rightness and closeness that contributed to the final product. "Richard was warm to everybody. He always had a smile. One night, I said, 'I want some chicken,' and he sent out for about twelve dozen pieces. He was good to people."

In Johnson's opinion even if Pryor was tethered by the constraints of television while taping that special, he still managed to create characters in an almost magical way. "Where I would start out piece by piece and then put the character all together, he had the whole character right away. With all the training and experience I'd had, I was still learning from him. It was exciting for me to watch him work. Richard was in his own time zone in his own place. The rest of us had to catch up with him, because he was already there."

Even before the special was aired, there was enough excitement about it around NBC for there to be talk about a more permanent arrangement. NBC-TV West Coast vice-president John J. McMahon told the press that the network wanted Pryor for a series of sixty or ninety-minute shows, saying, "We believe he could be the hottest thing to hit TV in many a year."

Pryor wasn't keen on committing himself to a TV series. He thought he could manage a special now and then, but he didn't like having to hold himself in check as much as TV required. All he could get away with on TV was a little naughtiness. But he left the negotiations up to his attorneys. He had to go to Peoria to give his grandmother the keys to the new house he had bought for her and Thomas Bryant, and to introduce Deboragh to his family.

His relationship with Pam Grier had ended, and according to D'Urville Martin it had ended abruptly. "Pam wanted to marry him, and he let her down so cold. I knew her pretty well—we'd done Sheba, Baby together—but I didn't see much of her after she started going with Richard. I ran into her when he was taping his television show. She was on her way to his dressing room. But she was not allowed in. He gave her no warning, just cut her loose. She thought he was going to produce a film starring her about a real-life character named Stagecoach Annie, and he just dumped her cold. That day she didn't even recognize me."

While he was still seeing Pam Grier, Pryor had grown close to Jennifer Lee, who he had hired to decorate his new house. A native of upstate New York, Jennifer had arrived in California with hopes of becoming an actress and had achieved some success earlier in the 1970s, playing a leading role in Act of Vengeance and Walter Matthau's daughter-in-law in The Sunshine Boys. She had also composed songs for films. She had gone into interior decorating to pay the rent, and she proved talented in this area as well. Pryor liked her work, and her, but she was no match for Deboragh McGuire, who came back into his life once Pam Grier was out.

This time Deboragh McGuire was determined to stay. The twenty-three-year-old starlet was not, in D'Urville Martin's opinion, very good for Richard. "There is a certain type of woman who migrates toward stars. Almost every agent or casting director will have a nude photograph of her in his drawer. Some of them are bisexual, or even prefer women, but in order to get ahead in show business they'll hustle guys.

"It amazed me that Richard could be so naive. He is incredibly naive for someone who was raised among prostitutes and a sucker for people who, it's clear to me even from a distance, are out to take him. At the same time he is suspicious of some people who mean well."

Juliette Whittaker also had reservations about Deboragh, whom she had met during the key-presentation visit. When Pryor bought the modest but lovely home for his grandparents in the southwest section of the city, it pleased him to be able to present it to them in person and all the family and friends, including Juliette Whittaker, were invited.

"I remember meeting her," says Whittaker of Deboragh. "It was very strange. He introduced me to her over at the house on Millman Street, and I wanted to talk to her, but she would not talk to me by herself. I couldn't get her into a conversation, and now I realize why. She was afraid of me; she was afraid that if I didn't like her, I would influence him. Why she thought I wouldn't like her is something only she could answer, because I approached her with the greatest neutrality.

"I remember I asked Richard, 'Why her?' He said, 'She's young. She loves me and she's young.' I said, 'All right, if that's your criteria.'

"Deboragh persuaded him to take his Emmy back. The way he did it was kind of cute. He said, 'Miss Whittaker, you know when I talk about how I won an Emmy nobody believes me.' I said, 'Richard, I tell you what. You take it back and put it on your mantel so they can see what you won. I've had it for three years now, and that's plenty. I appreciate having it. It's been inspirational to a lot of people. But you take it back. You earned it.' "

Back in L.A. the spring and summer of 1977 were contract signing time for Pryor. On May 10, five days after his special aired, he signed an "exclusive, five-year personal services contract" with NBC-TV that called for him to do a weekly series of at least ten shows, star in two specials, plus serve in a "creative capacity" on a third special designed to showcase new talent. The contract called for Pryor to receive $750,000 for his work, and after the first year allowed him either to cancel or to renegotiate more money for the next four years.

The terms of the contract were almost unprecedented in television, and NBC was taking a real chance. Says Kathi Fearn-Banks (a network publicist), "I'm sure it was a case of 'Richard's talented. Let's get him before somebody else does.' There's a lot of that going on." Pryor was going against his better instincts in committing that much of himself to television, but apparently the network had made an offer he couldn't refuse. According to Fearn-Banks, "Richard said that NBC flew a plane over his house with skywriting that said, 'Give up, Richard,' plus they offered so much money he couldn't say no."

Meanwhile, Pryor's multi-picture contract with Universal had been renegotiated for five more movies and more money, and he was set to do The Wiz in the fall and tentatively scheduled to film Sting II with Jackie Gleason and without the collaboration of either Paul Newman or Robert Redford. Filming was about to begin on Pryor's second picture under the first Universal contract: Blue Collar in which he would star with Harvey Keitel and Yaphet Kotto.

In late July he signed his second multi-picture pact, this time with Warner Brothers, which called for him to do a minimum of four pictures in four years to be made in association between Warner Brothers and Richard Pryor Enterprises, and with Pryor's attorney, David Franklin, as executive producer. The contract guaranteed him one million dollars per film, plus fifty percent of the profits. Warner Brothers and Universal would alternate in using Pryor's services, with both studios exercising some flexibility as to who got him when. He had his name on so many dotted lines that he couldn't keep track of all his commitments.

With some justification people were calling 1977 Richard Pryor's year. Just seven years earlier he'd been among the persona non grata in the business, reduced to working in small, black clubs for chump change. It had been barely eight months since Vincent Canby had included Pryor in a list of up-and-coming character actors and since other writers had stated, correctly, that he was best known for his concert appearances and comedy albums. When the Richard Pryor Special? was taped, the only film credits he cared to mention on it were The Mack and Adios Amigo (he could have included Silver Streak but chose not to). But now, suddenly, Richard Pryor was the hottest name in Hollywood. One million a picture?! That put him in the big leagues. No other black star had ever come close to demanding that much money, much less getting it.

Unfortunately, Pryor's uniqueness was a problem. He was on a very lonely pinnacle. Happy as he was, convinced as he tried to be that he had earned it all, he had a hard time stanching the guilt feelings that welled up inside him. If he thought it strange to have an apricot tree, how was he going to handle a million a picture? David Franklin once explained to David Felton of *Rolling Stone*, "He does not believe that he should have so much, and so he will try to give it away, to reject it. He will constantly try to prove to people who he should cut loose from—the vultures, the hangers-on—that he's one of them. And he's not. And the only thing they can do is bring him down."

Actress Carol Speed allows that guilt may play a role in the psychic terrain of a black actor who suddenly finds himself on top but suggests, too, that part of the problem is not understanding the business. "Careers are like rollercoasters," she says. "We don't understand the business—how it really works—and we're more or less thrown into it, not in control. Success is very heady, very hard to handle. People treat you differently. When you're up there, you get all kinds of people feeding off of you. Then there are other people who are afraid to approach you. They think you're something special. Meanwhile you're the same person—still have to go to the bathroom, brush your teeth, deal with your family. Then you get a lot of jealous, envious people who want to be around you just so they have a better chance at cutting your jugular vein. I guess it's enough to make anybody hostile. And so what happens is sometimes you take a dive. You don't understand that it's just a business, and you start doing things that aren't in your best interests."

In the months ahead Richard Pryor was going to have a hard time keeping a perspective on his career, not to mention on his life, and where one left off and the other began. He was committed to do and to be so many things for so many people that he would wonder if he, Richard Pryor, had any interests at all. He would be under incredible pressure, and it began in the late spring with the filming of *Blue Collar*.

Pryor had wanted to do more serious dramatic roles, and *Blue Collar* gave him the chance with a vengeance. It was the story of three Detroit auto workers amid the violence and corruption of big business and big unionism. Paul Schrader, thirty-one years old, had written the screenplay with his brother, Leonard, and it was intended to be an exposé, a debunking of the *On the Waterfront* myth that there is any nobility at all in the morass of large organizations. As Schrader once explained, "Large organizations such as businesses, governments, unions, try to keep men fighting horizontally so they can't unite to fight vertically, which is the Marxist truism but one that bears repeating."

The major roles in the screenplay were a white worker and two black workers who decide on an impulse to rob their union. Schrader got both Pryor and white actor Harvey Keitel interested and under contract, and with that ammunition interested Robin French of Norman Lear's T.A.T. Communications to back the film's development. Universal agreed to distribute. Then Yaphet Kotto was signed to play the other black worker. Two black stars and one white star, even if one of the black stars was Richard Pryor, did not seem, somehow, sufficiently commercial, but Schrader was adamant about the casting. "If I have two whites and a black," he explained, "then the black guy has to be a good guy, and good guys are boring." But Schrader also realized he would have a constant struggle to keep the movie from being perceived as a black film.

Pryor hardly knew Schrader. He'd signed to do the picture because he was attracted to the idea of doing a serious dramatic role. Although he was to play a beaten-down man who eventually blows the whistle on his friends, he believed he could bring enough humanity to the role to make it palatable to him and to the audiences. Schrader was young and seemingly politically aware. He had a keen sense of the nature of violence, having written the screenplay for *Taxi Driver*, directed by Martin Scorcese, and of *Obsession*, a takeoff on Alfred Hitchcock's *Vertigo*, directed by Brian DePalma. Both films had consuming, nightmarish qualities, and Pryor did not doubt that Schrader, who would be directing for the first time with *Blue Collar*, would be emphasizing those same qualities this time. That was okay with Pryor. He remembered his time at the Caterpillar Tractor Company in Peoria as nightmarish. But he planned that his character would somehow transcend that quality.

Harvey Keitel and Yaphet Kotto also had plans for their characters, however, and from the moment shooting began on location in Detroit in the third week of May, the tensions off camera were as real, if not more serious, than those that were portrayed in front of the camera.

Schrader had cast three strong men for his three strong characters. Each one had fought his way to his current position and intended to use *Blue Collar* as a vehicle to further his career even more. Each one wanted to be the undisputed star. According to Schrader, the three were like young bulls who locked horns every day. He told reporter Charles Higham, "Each one was determined that every line of dialogue in every scene would belong to him and him only. The ego competition was constant. There were racial arguments that were really transferred ego arguments. Richard would say, 'You're making an anti-black movie.' What he meant was that in the scene we were doing I was giving Harvey more attention. When Harvey would say, 'You're making an anti-white movie,' he meant that I was throwing the scene to Richard."

And then there was Yaphet Kotto, who "had waited fourteen years for a role like Smokey James to come my way. It's going to change my life, at least professionally." Kotto was less worried about whether the movie was anti-black or anti-white as he was that the other two actors would steal his thunder.

"Yaphet has a very powerful ego," says D'Urville Martin. "He is not a very good person to get along with in a film. As far as Yaphet is concerned, when you're in a film it's war. He's always trying to scheme how he's gonna steal a scene from you. He goes back and dreams up all kinds of shit. He's that kind of guy."

Schrader insists that he did not try to create or encourage the tension that existed among the three actors. He says that he knew he had chosen three strong personalities in packaging the movie but that once the packaging was finished he did his best to keep things running smoothly. He admits that he wanted to keep the three under pressure, so that the tension in front of the cameras would be sustained, but he denies exploiting the racial tensions.

Michael Schultz disagrees. "What was happening in that picture was that the director, Paul Schrader, was agitating racism within the guise of a directing approach. He was using it as a technique to create the tension he felt was needed." But when Schultz suggested this possibility to Pryor, Pryor did not agree that Schrader's racial agitation was technique. "That shit was for real," he told Schultz. At the first meeting they had, he said that he was on one side of the table and Harvey Keitel and Yaphet were sitting on the opposite side, and Paul

Schrader said, "Now I'm not real comfortable working with black people." According to Schultz, "Richard said at that point he knew that he was gonna have a hard time. And things just went from bad to worse."

A movie set, especially one where there are a lot of problems, is often a closed set. The *Blue Collar* set was like that. One gets an image of one of those boxes in cartoons; characters disappear inside it and all you see is the box jerking around and biff-boom-pow sounds coming from it. There were fights—verbal and physical. Schrader later said that almost every day shooting had to be closed down for an hour or two while the three main actors battled it out. Who fought who, when, how, and over what, no one is saying. D'Urville Martin doesn't think Pryor would have been foolish enough to get into a physical match with Yaphet Kotto. "I doubt that he would go to blows with Yaphet. Yaphet has very big hands; plus he thinks he's a professional boxer. He used to tell me nothing beats a right cross. He used to work out a lot in the gym. Of course Richard works out a lot in the gym too. In his house he's got a ring, and a punching bag, and all that."

Pryor did make a physical assault on an actor with a minor part. George Memmoli made a reportedly vulgar suggestion to him, and Pryor smashed a chair over his head. Memmoli sued.

Lucy Saroyan was also among the actors with minor parts in the movie; she apparently emerged from the filming unscathed.

As shooting, which lasted five weeks, continued Pryor became more and more concerned that the character he played was a worm, a turncoat. He constantly rewrote lines, as did Keitel and Kotto. His character was required to sell out to the union bosses, and Schrader says he had originally thought about including a scene showing the character ratting on his friends but had decided it was too hard for anyone to play. Pryor insisted that the scene be included. He wanted the audience to see how his character at least tried to put up a fight before he finally capitulated to the union boss's intimidation. He was worried. "People are going to come in expecting laughs and they'll see this different side of me," he explained just before the picture was released. "I don't want to be used to bring in the black audience and then to have them devastated. They have to be prepared. I don't think I could stand the rejection."

Schrader, who after this experience wasn't sure he would ever want to direct another film, listened to Richard's views about not wanting to sell out his public but was not sympathetic. He felt that Pryor was thinking of himself as a personality rather than as an actor, and he felt that such sentiments had no place on a movie set. In Schrader's opinion Pryor was a bundle of contradictions; he felt Pryor's mind was swept constantly by swinging pendula, one swinging back and forth between Richard Pryor, actor, and Richard Pryor, star; and another swinging back and forth between Richard Pryor, black man, and Richard Pryor, success story. What made him so difficult to work with was that one never knew the arc of either pendulum, or what he would do at any given time.

Although *Blue Collar* received excellent critical reviews when it was released in 1978 and was a success at the box office (Pryor's fans, having been forewarned, were not disappointed in his character or in him), few people who were involved in the project looked back on it with fondness. It had been an exhaustive experience for everyone.

Of the actors Pryor was the least able to rest up from it. The schedule ahead of him that summer was worthy of superman. His itinerary included a trip to Europe with all four of his children, who he realized he had neglected. Once he'd started making money, he'd been almost too generous with gifts and was aware that he ought to give of his time as well. On occasion, one or another of his children stayed with him; twenty-year-old Renée was now living with him. But he thought he should do something with all of them together. The trip was as exhausting in its own way as the filming of *Blue Collar* had been, only this time Pryor was the director trying to deal with a lot of young people's ego problems. "I'm not going to make that mistake again," he said afterward. "There was just not enough Daddy to go around."

On his return he had to go to work on the NBC shows.

CHAPTER X

The Year of Richard Pryor

IF EVER THERE WAS a mistake—on the part of everyone concerned—it was NBC's signing of Richard Pryor to do a *series* for the network. From the beginning the two sides were not in agreement over exactly what the agreement was. NBC thought they had committed him to a series, but Richard Pryor thought he had agreed to do a number of specials. Kathi Fearn-Banks had first met Pryor when he worked on the *Flip Wilson Show*, to which she had been specifically assigned. She was not actually assigned to publicize the Richard Pryor shows, but she says, "I somehow get affected by every person who comes to NBC, and that's how it was with Richard."

Although they had met back in the early 1970s, Pryor and Fearn-Banks were not friends. She says the distance between them was his doing. "The first time I saw him with the *Flip Wilson Show*, I asked him about taking pictures or something, and he said, 'Yes, Ma'am, yes, Ma'am, anything you want.' He was just afraid to talk to me. A lot of people find it hard to believe that he would show that kind of respect. I know it was hard to have a casual conversation with him because he put so much distance there. I think that because I was a professional person, I was somehow not a real person. Sometimes he'd talk to Flip and forget that I was there, might use profanity—and then he'd turn to me and say, 'I'm sorry. I didn't mean to do that.' "

NBC held a big press conference at The Improv in Hollywood to publicize its new fall shows. Kathi Fearn-Banks was there, and so were some seventy-five out-of-town television critics all set up to meet Richard Pryor, star of the new *Richard Pryor Show*. She remembers, "Richard came in looking kind of bewildered, and he said to me, 'What am I supposed to do?' I said, 'Just get up there and talk to them, let them ask you questions about the series.' He said, 'I'm not doing a series, I'm doing some specials.' I said, 'Well, no, Richard, you're doing a series.'

"Apparently, he had been signed to do this series without understanding what he was supposed to do. He didn't ever want to do it that way. He was determined he was doing specials."

Pryor was too much of a veteran to show his confusion once he got on the stage of the two-year-old West Coast version of The Improv in New York City. But since he hadn't come prepared to talk about a series, he decided to confine his remarks to what would *not* be in it.

There would not be any sexual activity, he told the assembled critics. "We did audition some people, though."

There would not be any violence, although, "We did kill one 'people' on the first show."

Asked how NBC got him to clean up his act for TV, he replied, "They keep a big stack of money in front of the camera. When I don't curse, it gets bigger. And each time I do curse, it dwindles."

An NBC page turned a long hand-held mike toward him, and he ducked, "Wha's that? A shotgun?"

As soon as he could he walked off the stage and out of the spotlight, leaving it to the six other new stars the network wanted to parade in front of the press—new people on Laugh-In and CPO Sharkey. Pryor got to a phone and called his attorney. He wanted to straighten out this series or specials business—quick.

The difference between a series and a series of specials is this: with a series you are committed to writing enough material to produce a show every week, week after week; with a series of specials you have some breathing room. How the communications broke down is anybody's guess, but where they broke down had to be somewhere between Richard Pryor and his representatives. Perhaps they hadn't fully explained the agreement to him; perhaps Pryor was too occupied with other concerns to hear what was said to him. Whatever happened, Richard Pryor found himself committed not only to produce comedy material on a weekly basis but to produce material on a weekly basis that was acceptable for television. Meanwhile, he already had a busy film schedule and a number of recording commitments. One wonders if the halo above David Franklin's head didn't tarnish just a bit in Pryor's eyes at that time.

No fewer than four Richard Pryor comedy albums were released in 1977, and only one was composed of material from past albums— *Richard Pryor's Greatest Hits*, released by Warner/Reprise. Laff Records released *Are You Serious???* in June and *Who Me? I'm Not Him* in November, and World Sound released *Richard Pryor Live*. He was scheduled to start shooting *The Wiz* in the fall. Meanwhile, he was supposed to find time to put together material for a damn TV series? This was not the way he was accustomed to working. He liked to lay out for a couple of months, work on his stuff, try it out during impromptu visits to the Comedy Store. The whole idea of a series was against his way of doing things: too mechanical, too businesslike. Besides, he'd boasted so often that he wrote all his own material.

To get the requisite amount of material together by the fall, the crew that had worked on *The Richard Pryor Special?* had to take on more writers. Fran Ross, a free-lance writer in New York City, hoped to be one of them. Having read in *TV Guide* at the end of May that NBC's fall lineup would include *The Richard Pryor Show* on Thursdays from nine to ten P.M., she sent samples of her comedy writing to Rocco Urbisci, producer of the first show in the fall. Urbisci expressed interest but said Pryor had final say on his writers. Scheduling an appointment for her to meet Pryor in L.A. was complicated by the fact that Pryor was presently shooting *Blue Collar*, but at last a definite appointment was made for June 30 at the offices of Richard Pryor Enterprises. There at the appointed hour, she met Rocco Urbisci, "a nice, curly-haired California version of Ilie Nastase," Paul Mooney, and David Banks. ("If Paul were a dancer, then David would be an ex-con.")

At that meeting she was told that although Mooney was supposed to be in charge of casting and Banks in charge of the music, both were also doubling as writers. They'd already hired four other writers, then stopped, feeling it wouldn't look good to have too many writers. Ross hoped she could be taken on anyway. The others said it was up to Richard.

Seven days of impatience and innumerable telephone calls later, Ross was informed that a meeting was set for that night at Pryor's house. When she arrived, Mooney, Banks, and Urbisci were there in the second-floor study. Pryor, held up on the Universal set of *Blue*

Collar, didn't arrive until two hours later. After he sat down, he, Banks, Mooney, and Urbisci rehashed ideas they had already come up with for the shows. None of the four people who had been hired specifically as writers—as compared to Mooney and the others, who had other duties and were doubling as writers—were at the meeting. Ross listened and took notes, trying to catch up.

She noticed that although Rocco Urbisci seemed to be part of Pryor's "inner circle," there was an invisible line that he was not supposed to cross because he was white. Ross wrote of the experience in *Essence:* "Richard or Paul could always say something that implied, 'Yeah, man, cool, but you ain't Black and don't you ever forget it.' " She also learned that a stranger, even a black one, did not use the word *nigger* around Richard Pryor.

At a point when none of the ideas for sketches seemed to please Pryor and the conversation lagged, Ross decided to ask him if he'd had any trouble with the cops when jogging through the streets of Detroit for a scene in *Blue Collar.* She reminded him that during an appearance on the *Tonight* show he'd said, "If you see two niggers running in the neighborhood, we're just making a movie."

Ross recalled, "I was definitely quoting, because, unlike many black people who use the term among intimates with affection, *nigger* is not a word that I use. Richard said, a touch coldly, 'I said, "two Black men." ' "

Even at that time Pryor was convinced he could not do a series. "I can't go to Burbank, to NBC, every day. Just like I can't do an album every nine months. . . . There's no art on TV." Ross suggested that he was just tired from making the movie, but Pryor would not be talked out of his funk. "I need a straight, square person like Bob Ellison," he said, referring to the man who had produced his special. "I hated Bob Ellison's motherfucking guts, but he made me work. Y'all love me, sit around nodding and smiling." Pryor was beginning to feel used.

He didn't like being surrounded by yes-men. On the other hand he didn't want to work with anyone he didn't know well. (Fran Ross did not get a job as a writer on the show.) He knew he couldn't come up with enough material for a weekly show on TV, and though he had the money, he didn't want to hire writers to come up with the material he needed. Nor did he want to share his show with big-name guests who, if nothing else, would fill up some minutes in all those empty hours. For the special, he had been involved every step of the way, and if he could not be involved every step of the way in each of the ten weekly shows he was under contract to do, he didn't want to do them.

Taping of the specials was due to begin in August, but in the first week of that month Pryor was off to New York on a publicity tour for *Greased Lightning*. There, Sylviane Gold, a correspondent for *The New York Post*, was treated to a rare hearing of Pryor's political opinions. Speaking of Wendell Scott and of Scott's refusal to play by the rules that said blacks couldn't be race-car drivers, he paraphrased Miss Whittaker's favorite writer, Ayn Rand: "Undoubtedly, the man who discovered fire was burned at the stake."

The main function of most governments, like America's, he said was to "keep us apart so they can work their shit. . . . Nobody bucks nothin'. . . . Most people just go to the slop trough and eat the slop. And if one person says, 'I ain't eatin' that shit no more,' everybody else says, 'Hey, don't cause trouble.' "

He was feeling particularly anticapitalist, perhaps because he was engaging in a capitalist ploy—the publicity tour intended to sell theater tickets. "And the poor people buy. The poor people support us all."

"How can we have equality if we have capitalism?" he wanted to know. Capitalists were worse than looters, he said, and was reminded somehow of the big auto companies. "They can't meet the pollution standards, so they threaten to close down the plants and make millions of people unemployed. . . . Who's the baddest? Nobody calls *their* bluff. . . . "

Of course Pryor was also down on capitalism at the time because a bastion of capitalism called NBC-TV had used the promise of a lot of capital to sucker him into something he was loath to do, and then, through their censorship practices, made a task that was difficult to begin with even harder. He didn't just rant and rave to interviewers, but to anyone who would listen.

One sympathetic listener was Rob Cohen, who had produced *The Bingo Long Traveling All-Stars and Motor Kings* and who was currently with Motown Productions as producer of *The Wiz*. While Pryor was in New York, Cohen wanted him in on some preproduction meetings, so one day he picked Pryor up at his hotel with the intention of taking him to meet the executives behind the movie. But Pryor started talking about being betrayed by the NBC brass, and Cohen realized it was no time to take him to see another bunch of bigwigs. Instead Cohen drove Pryor to the ballroom of the St. George Hotel where some five hundred black dancers were rehearsing for The Wiz. As soon as Pryor and Cohen walked in, a few of the dancers saw them and stopped their leaping and pirouetting. Then they began to clap. Others turned to see what was going on, saw Pryor, and started to clap, too, until the whole huge ballroom thundered with applause. Cohen says it was one of the most moving, spontaneous gestures he's ever witnessed.

Eventually, Pryor had to go back to the West Coast and make good on his part of the bargain with NBC, but he was hardly in shape, physically or mentally, to do so. On August 11 he collapsed and had to be worked on by paramedics. The diagnosis was overwork. Meanwhile, he was still talking about dissolving the contract, and talking publicly. Rona Barrett reported his misgivings on Good Morning America August 3. The people at NBC, worried previously about potential censorship problems, now started worrying about whether or not there would be a Richard Pryor Show at all. Pryor asked for and received a change in the original contract, cutting from ten to four the number of series segments he agreed to do, with the option to do more if he wished, plus two or three specials a year.

Taping of the first show, which was to have begun in August, was delayed until the first week of September, and when the cameras finally rolled there were immediate problems. Some of them were due to Pryor's continued reluctance to do any kind of series. "He didn't want to do it. He didn't want the pace of a regular show, coming every day. In fact, he had trouble coming every day. He fought it the whole time," says Kathi Fearn-Banks. "There was always something to fight about. He fought about the fact that there were not enough black pages on the page staff—pages let in the audience—and he wanted black people to be on the crew. I think that was commendable, but he was insistent.

"He wanted black people in the audience for the taping because he felt that they would be more responsive to his humor than the people

NBC brought in. It *was* almost a lily-white audience, but his show was not aimed at black people particularly, so it made some sense to have white people there at the taping. But NBC realized it would make him feel better if there were black people there, and I think they made some effort to do that."

Still, NBC contributed its share of new troubles to the already problem-ridden show. Somebody in charge of scheduling decided to imprison Pryor in the eight-to-nine P.M. time slot, the traditional family hour. No doubt, the change was made in an effort to challenge ABC's hold on the family hour with its popular shows *Happy Days* and *Laverne and Shirley;* but given Pryor's reputation as a distinctly nonfamily type entertainer, it was a serious tactical error. Pryor immediately renewed his threat to cancel his contract altogether but backed off after Robert Mulholland, NBC's new president, met with him personally and persuaded him to stay. Still, even a network president can exercise little control over his censors, who have nothing to do with time slotting and who must abide by FCC (Federal Communications Commission) rules. The censors, formally known as the Broadcast Standards division, refused to allow the opening spot on the very first *Richard Pryor Show.*

The spot, which lasted about a minute, was supposed to be a Pryor spoof on himself. There was to have been a shot of Pryor, nude from the waist up, saying, "I have given up nothing in order to do a television program." The camera would then have panned a long shot of a supposedly naked host whose flesh-colored tights might have given the impression that he had in fact given up an important part of his anatomy. The censors had approved the segment in script form, but the script had not specified Pryor's physical appearance. The spot had been taped, and Pryor had thought it would thus be allowed. But the way the NBC censoring system worked, a segment could be taped and, to a nonveteran of television like Pryor, seem to have passed muster, when in reality it hadn't even gone through the proper channels yet. While the show was taped in Burbank, the network's Broadcast Standards division was in New York. Thus, a show could be rehearsed, blocked, and taped on the West Coast, but then the tape had to be sent to the East Coast for review. The decision from Broadcast Standards might not come for two days.

Pryor was furious when he heard that the spot had been turned down. He called a press conference and charged that the action was "a violation of an artist's right" and "an offense to our mentality." He said he would tape one more show before deciding whether or not to go on with the programs as planned.

Robert Mulholland allowed that the network's censorship system was imperfect and promised to assign a network representative to the show in Burbank who would have final authority if further questions of censorship should arise. He also agreed to Pryor's demand that the first *Richard Pryor Show* be preceded by a line delivered by a live announcer: a voice over a dark screen saying, "The opening minute of the *Richard Pryor Show* will not be seen—ever."

The first show aired on Tuesday, September 13. Uneven in quality like *The Richard Pryor Special?*, it nevertheless included a couple of clever sketches that showed Pryor at his best. They were the opening and closing sketches of the show. In the first sequence Pryor is a bartender in a *Star Wars*–type bar populated by creatures as strange as in the blockbuster movie. Refusing to notice that there is anything unusual about his customers, Pryor talks about baseball, reminds them that no dancing is allowed, and discovers that one of the crowd looks like a neighbor from Detroit. He also gets a line past the censors that was outrageous by TV standards. Seriously put upon by an octopuslike creature, he summons the bouncer to take it to "de back room." Pryor smiles into the camera and says, " . . . and while you're back there, why don't you get yourself some octopussy?"

In the final sequence, a lengthy one, Pryor develops a character: a soldier returning from World War II to see his old girl friend, who has become a sultry singer in a Harlem nightclub. It was a 1940s period piece, and it showed why Pryor was so far above the ordinary, stand-up comedian. Given the space to develop a character, he put the audience through an emotional wringer and came out with the truth. Reviewers on both coasts cited it as imaginative, bittersweet drama, and Pryor's originality as something network television needed more of. But viewers were yet to be convinced. The first *Richard Pryor Show* was forty-first in the ratings for that week, and in the network ranking third behind *Happy Days/LaVerne and Shirley* and a baseball game for the Tuesday eight P.M. slot.

Meanwhile, the second show had already been taped, which was something else Pryor didn't like about doing a television series: he would have preferred to know the reaction to the first show before taping the second, especially since he was relying on writers other than himself for much of his material.

Arnold Johnson appeared on two of the *Richard Pryor Shows*. He recalls, "His writers [who included Booker Bradshaw, who currently works on *Gimme a Break*] would have the show written, and they would set up at the rehearsal table and he would sit down with them and go over it and make changes. So the final input was his. But sometimes he wouldn't want to go through with the sketches. I remember one time he stayed in his dressing room because he didn't like the material. Burt Sugarman had to go in there and talk with him, and it must have been an hour before he would come out. Meanwhile, Paul Mooney had to come out and improvise jokes for the audience.

"There were problems with what was acceptable on TV, and sometimes he would walk away saying, 'I can't let them do that to me.' It was just one thing right after another."

Johnson remembers that The Prophet was with Pryor during these rehearsals and tapings, but Pryor needed more than spiritual help to cope with the hassles of a weekly television program. The mounting tension exploded on Sunday night, September 18, at of all places the Hollywood Bowl.

The occasion was a benefit for Save Our Human Rights (SOHR), a San Francisco–based homosexual organization founded to combat the recent anti-gay campaigns being waged by former Miss America and then Tropicana Orange Juice spokeswoman Anita Bryant and California Senator John Briggs, among others. The near-capacity audience in the seventeen-thousand-seat amphitheater had paid anywhere from five to fifty dollars to get in and included such stars as Herb Alpert, Cher, Chevy Chase, Truman Capote, Valerie Harper, Alice Cooper, Norman Lear, John Travolta, Jeff Wald, Sue Mengers, Rona Barrett, and Paul Newman.

The show itself starred Lily Tomlin, Bette Midler, and Richard Pryor, as well as the band War, with brief appearances by comedian David Steinberg, singer Tom Waits, disco dancers the Lockers, ballet dancers from the Los Angeles Ballet Company, and others. The whole spectacle was supposed to show Hollywood displaying its liberality and, more specifically, its nonsupport of the current anti-gay campaigns.

Pryor had agreed to do the benefit because Lily Tomlin and Bette Midler were going to be there. He was not getting paid, nor were the others, and this was often not the case with benefits in Hollywood. As it was presented to him, the show was supposed to celebrate human rights, and indeed A Star-Spangled Night for Rights was subtitled A Celebration for Human Rights. But he couldn't miss the fact that the humans whose rights would be emphasized were homosexuals. He was also aware that, for all the entertainment to be presented, the evening was aimed at making a political statement, and he considered himself a nonpolitical entertainer.

Pryor arrived backstage at the Hollywood Bowl with no material prepared, expecting to get a sense of the evening and to ad-lib from there. He was high from the buzz and murmur of the thousands of people out in front and enjoyed watching the opening performances. He was scheduled to appear in the middle of the program.

The show began with actor Christopher Lee reciting "The Ascent of Man," symphonically scored and read to the music of the Hollywood Festival Orchestra. Then Lily Tomlin appeared, to a standing ovation. She did portions of her regular concert show, her 1950s material about good women and bad women: "And of course, no one was gay then—only shy." As she acknowleged the response to some of her more topical material, she surveyed the audience and remarked, "This is the first time my act has sounded like a political tract."

David Steinberg also appeared during the first half of the program, as did War, performing with the group Aalon, and as did the black dance team, the Lockers. John Clifford and Johanna Kirkland of the Los Angeles Ballet Company preceded Pryor on the second half of the program with a pas de deux from "Le Corsaire." Backstage, Pryor noted with some bitterness that the two dance acts were treated differently. As he later told Jim Cleaver of the Los Angeles Sentinel, "When a white dance act went on stage, every damn body and his brother went to fix the lights. They didn't do shit for the Lockers.

"Then a fire marshall started to reprimand a black youngster, and all the white folks simply turned their backs and ignored what was going on and I got mad as hell."

At that point Richard Pryor went out onto the stage, unprepared with any routines but under pressure to say something meaningful, angry at what he had witnessed backstage, and ambivalent from the start about what the show was all about and what he was doing in it.

"I came out here ... for human rights," he began, "and I found out ... that what it really is about ... is about not getting caught with a dick in your mouth." That brought the house down. It was quite extraordinary for a major star to make the statement then and later to repeat it: "Back in 1952 I sucked dick. It was beautiful ... but I couldn't deal with it. I went home and didn't tell nobody."

For a while, Pryor continued in that vein, getting appreciative laughs and even roars of delight as he used the word *faggot* as liberally as he usually used *nigger*. But after five or six minutes something changed. It was clear that he did not feel comfortable doing material about gays. It wasn't his style, and gays were not his customary audience. He began to fumble around for something to say. "Shit," he said at one point, almost to himself, "What the fuck?" At another point he said, "This is really *weird*. ..." He went blindly on. "I never seen this much traffic in my life. ... I seen cars all the way from where to what ... comin' to this motherfucker this evening ... to give us some money ... to suck a dick."

The audience was getting restless. Not everyone appreciated his constant use of the word *faggot*, and there had been some catcalls earlier. But now the audience was murmuring with real hostility. Pryor felt it and returned it.

"I came here for human rights," he said, "but I'm *seeing* what it's really about. Fags are prejudiced. I see the four niggers you have dispersed. White folks are having good fun here tonight. The Locker dancers came backstage dripping with sweat but all you could say is, 'Oh, that was nice.' But when the ballet dancers came out dancing to that funny music, you said, 'Wow, those are some bad mothers.'

"This is an evening about human rights, and I'm a human being. I just wanted to see where you was *really* at, and I wanted to test you to your motherfucking *soul*. I'm doing this shit for *nuthin'*. But I wanted to come here and tell you to kiss my ass ... with your bullshit. You understand? When the niggers was burnin' down Watts, you motherfuckers was doin' what you wanted to do on Hollywood Boulevard ... didn't give a shit about it.

"Kiss my happy, rich black ass!" he yelled, turning his back on the audience and "mooning" with his pants on. Amid jeers and boos he stormed off the stage less than fifteen minutes after he'd come on.

Singer Tom Waits, who quickly appeared in the space vacated by Pryor, hardly had the audience's attention. Bette Midler, who followed Waits, tried to introduce a note of levity with her opening remark, "Who wants to kiss this rich, *white*, ass?" and managed to turn the evening back into a celebration. Pryor didn't stay around to watch. He was on his way back to Northridge. The fireworks display that closed the show was spectacular, but Richard Pryor had already displayed his own brand of fireworks.

For a few days afterward there was a lot of talk about the incident. There were reports that Lily Tomlin was furious with him and would not appear in Universal's *Sting II* with Pryor and Jackie Gleason, that NBC was going to cancel his show, that every gay in the land would boycott his records and movies. But the furor died down quickly. Tomlin insisted that they were still friends. "When you hire Richard Pryor, you get Richard Pryor," she said simply. Still, when Larry Kart of the *Chicago Tribune* asked Pryor a year later about his subsequent relationship with Tomlin, Pryor answered that since the Hollywood Bowl benefit, "I have not spoken with her. But I look at life this way. Friends are always friends if they ever were. They don't turn away from you no matter what. I know I don't. So maybe the relationship wasn't that close in the first place."

Universal went on with plans for *Sting II*, NBC did not cancel Pryor's TV show, and no organized boycott of Pryor by homosexuals ensued. The only public censuring of Pryor by a gay group was of the tongue-in-cheek variety. In the first week of October YOU, Unlimited, a West Hollywood-based organization "dedicated to the principles of self-improvement," granted $120 scholarships to Anita Bryant, Senator John Briggs, and Richard Pryor, with their spouses, in a ceremony at the Universal Sheraton Hotel. Needless to say, none of the winners showed up to accept the awards. As a matter of fact, some people in the Hollywood Bowl audience had felt that it was Pryor's right to speak his mind and that to suggest otherwise was exactly what he had been talking about. Others agreed with John L. Wasserman, a correspondent for the *San Francisco Chronicle*, who wrote, "Richard

Pryor is a genius, but in show-biz genius there is often great pain. Some hide it well, Pryor does not."

Pryor didn't have time to ruminate about his shocking display or about his pain. He was trying to finish up his last NBC shows. Once taping of the fourth and last show was completed, he felt utter relief. So, no doubt, did NBC. The shows, which altogether ran from September 13 to October 18, contained some outrageous moments, some clever sketches, and some hilarious ones, but Pryor aficionados complained that the real Richard Pryor was kept so firmly under the heel of the NBC censors that he was hardly recognizable. Some local network affiliates, on the other hand, found some of the material too objectionable to be aired. In Detroit, located in middle America but hardly considered symbolic of the area, TV station WWJ refused to air the second Pryor show because of the song "Work On Me," performed by the O'Jays. Meanwhile, the song was played on many Detroit-area radio stations and was Number thirteen on the *Billboard* soul list. The station moved the third show from the eight P.M. Tuesday slot to eleven-thirty the following Sunday night because of a sketch about lesbians that was deemed offensive. According to Kathi Fearn-Banks, quite a few affiliates didn't carry the show at all. "Things that were considered very risqué then are not found objectionable now.... I think that in recent years white people have come around to laugh at Richard the way we do, but back then he was a little difficult to take. The ratings were bad, the show didn't stay on long enough to have a lot of publicity."

The whole episode was a fiasco. NBC announced it was canceling the show because of poor ratings. Pryor announced that he was canceling the contract because he wasn't given enough freedom. On Tuesday, October 25, the slot vacated by the ill-fated *Richard Pryor Show* was filled by a one-hour special presentation of *The Gong Show*.

Press releases from NBC mentioned the possibility of Pryor's doing a couple of specials a year for the network, but these never materialized. In the late summer of 1982 a rerun of the first *Richard Pryor Special?* garnered respectable ratings, and says Kathi Fearn-Banks, "If he did, say, two specials a year now, he could be sure of ratings." But Pryor's experience in 1977 confirmed his opinion that he and television just could not get along, and he has had no reason to change his mind since.

Television, in his opinion, was a good thing gone bad. "They've misused it a long time," he told Louie Robinson of *Ebony* toward the end of 1977. "It's just a place where you sell products and they sell information the way they want to sell it to perpetuate their businesses. They're not going to write shows about how to revolutionize America. The top-rated shows are for retarded people."

In the midst of the storm over his NBC shows, Richard Pryor married Deboragh McGuire. The ceremony was a small, quiet one at Pryor's home on the morning of September 22, after which, still in his white tuxedo, he left for Burbank and more taping on one of the shows. On September 23 the newlyweds left for New York where Pryor was to start work on *The Wiz*. It was hardly an auspicious time to get married. Pryor was overworked and hassled and feeling more alienated than usual from the world of white television executives and complaining gays. He had probably started drinking and using drugs again. As in 1974 he was on the edge.

Perhaps he recognized the feeling and married Deboragh in the hope of regaining some stability. When he spoke about her, he often used the word *real*. He told Maureen Orth of *Newsweek*, "Having Deboragh in my life is real . . . and being in my home is real. That's all I've got in life that's real. I find myself talking to people I don't know, shaking hands with them. A lot of people seem to be closing in on me. . . . I want to change my name. Richard Pryor is this actor person, and I need time to just go blank. I'm thinking of moving to a farm in Oregon."

But he had commitments, and he was at the pinnacle of his career. With the release of *Greased Lightning*, *Car Wash*, and *Silver Streak*, with the announcement of his unique film contracts with Universal and Warners, with a second Grammy—for *Bicentennial Nigger*— Pryor was the biggest new name in entertainment. In August *Time* had done a feature story on him called "A New Black Superstar," and in early October, some fourteen-and-a-half years after he had picked up an issue of *Newsweek* and read about Bill Cosby, he was the subject of a feature article in that same magazine. The siren song of fame is a powerful force, and Richard Pryor could not ignore it.

On November 10, 1977, a local L.A. radio station reported the news of Richard Pryor's death. The day before, while on a visit to Peoria to celebrate his grandmother's birthday, Pryor had been rushed to Methodist Medical Center and placed in the coronary unit. Naturally, the speculation was that he had suffered a heart attack, and it stood to reason that for a man with Pryor's history of violence and self-abuse, it was curtains. In fact press coverage of the event seemed to carry the implication that somehow Pryor's health problems were his own fault.

Meanwhile, unaware of the premature reports of his demise, Pryor was resting comfortably. He had asked the hospital not to release any reports on his condition, and the hospital had complied. But Marie Bryant was under no restriction. "He's doing as well as can be expected, considering that he's had a heart attack," she told reporters matter-of-factly.

Pryor and Deboragh had arrived in Peoria the day before for a belated celebration of Marie Bryant's birthday. Her actual birthday had been a few days earlier, but Pryor had had an engagement in New York the previous weekend. He'd spent a quiet day at the new house in Bartonville and had gone fishing in the afternoon with Richard Jr. That evening he had complained of chest pains and been taken to Methodist Medical Center in a private car.

The minimum stay in the coronary unit at the hospital was three days, and Pryor insisted on complete privacy. While he rested, more than five hundred telephone calls and fifty telegrams arrived in the first two days. Among the callers were Sammy Davis, Jr., Aretha Franklin, Diana Ross, Olivia Newton-John, Natalie Cole, and a host of people claiming to be his relatives. According to the hospital's community relations director, all the callers said they knew Pryor would return their calls if only the hospital would relay their messages and numbers to him. But Pryor, who had not suffered a heart attack, had decided to take a brief opportunity to "just go blank." Released from the hospital four days later, Pryor and Deboragh returned to California and went fishing at Big Bear mountain resort. There were no telephones in their rooms, but Pryor couldn't resist finding a pay phone and calling an AP reporter to tell him, "I was on a treadmill, and you often just get on it and don't look back for a while." He'd been close to a nervous breakdown by the time he'd finished *Blue Collar*, he explained, but he hadn't had time to have it. From then on he was going to take things slower and not commit himself to so many projects at once. "Success is no good if you don't have your health."

Although he was traveling frequently to New York to film *The Wiz* and was working on another record album, he did try to slow down in the last months of 1977. It was the waning of the year of Richard Pryor, and he wanted time to enjoy it. He had a mountain of laurels to rest on and a new wife he wanted to get to know better. He was determined that this marriage was going to last. In the fall of 1977 Louie Robinson and a photographer from *Ebony* visited the Pryors at home to do a feature story for the January issue of the magazine. Pryor told Robinson that his marriage to Deboragh was his third on paper and his last. "We're going to be happy together for a long time, because it's the first time that I've admitted that I don't know anything, and we're starting out new together."

He thought he had found love at last. He also had money and stardom. And of course he'd always had talent. He celebrated his good fortune at Christmastime by playing Santa Claus to the hilt—giving individual gifts to all twenty messengers at Universal, not to mention a diamond-studded pinkie ring to his record producer, a Rolls-Royce to his attorney, and big-ticket gifts to other assorted friends and family members. David Franklin, recipient of the Rolls-Royce, played the role of Santa Claus's godfather, telling a correspondent for *Jet*, "Pryor was ready to be fully exposed this year, and quite frankly I was ready too. He is the biggest black star in Hollywood today and by all means this is his richest Christmas."

Pryor, ever wary, tempered his own sense of euphoria when it was taken up by the press. "I'm a little embarrassed about it all," he said. "I guess it has been one of my richest Christmases. But I call this my harvest year. I planted the crop for what happened this year seventeen years ago. I'm just beginning to reap the harvest."

CHAPTER XI

Comeback on the Concert Stage

ON THE FIRST DAY of the new year 1978, Richard Pryor reaped a harvest of another sort. He ended his three-and-a-half month "final" marriage and murdered a car.

In the early hours of the morning of January 1, Pryor and Deboragh were at home with two of Deboragh's friends, Beverly Clayborn, twenty-five, a singer-dancer from Los Angeles, and Edna Solomon, thirty-one, of Washington State. Everyone had been drinking. As reported in the press, the trouble apparently began when Pryor and his wife got into an argument and the two women sided with Deboragh. According to D'Urville Martin, Pryor had just found out that Deboragh was more than friends with at least one of the the two women. Enraged, Pryor gave the women five seconds to get out of his house.

As he started counting, the women ran outside and took refuge in Beverly Clayborn's Buick. But before they could get away, Pryor rammed the car seven times with his Mercedes. The frightened women escaped on foot. Pryor, his fury unabated, ran back into the house, grabbed a .357 magnum pistol, and shot the Buick ten times, causing some five-thousand dollars in damage. *People* magazine quoted a friend of Pryor's as saying, "He shot out the tires, windshield and basically killed the car."

The next day, Monday, January 2, police arrived at the Pryor home with a warrant for his arrest, issued as a result of a complaint filed by Beverly Clayborn and Edna Solomon. The officers were met by friends and employees of Pryor's. Somebody said he was sleeping; somebody else said he wasn't home. The officers agreed not to search the house as long as he surrendered by Tuesday. Accompanied by attorney Leo Branton, Pryor surrendered that evening, was charged

155

with assault with a deadly weapon, and was freed on five thousand dollars bail. At the arraignment in Van Nuys Municipal Court on January 16, he was charged with felonious assault and malicious mischief. A preliminary hearing was set for February 16.

On January 19, Beverly Clayborn filed a personal suit against Pryor in Los Angeles Superior Court. Wearing a neck brace to court, she charged that Pryor had made an unprovoked attack on her person and had caused injury to her "physical and mental well being." She asked for seventeen million dollars. Quipped Pryor, "If she gets it, I'll marry her."

He would soon be free to marry again. On February 3, Deboragh filed for divorce and asked the court to restrain her estranged husband from "annoying, threatening, or harassing" her. Claiming that Pryor earned about fifty-thousand dollars a month and was worth more than a million dollars, she asked for $2,480 a month in alimony. The January issue of Ebony, in which the piece on the happy newlyweds had appeared, was still in the magazine racks or in the yet-to-be-read piles of many American homes and offices, and it was both sad and ironic that the New Year's Day incident notwithstanding, both Richard and Deboragh still felt much as they had when Louie Robinson and the Ebony photographer had visited them a couple of months earlier. Both wondered how things could have gotten so out of hand. But Deboragh felt there was no going back. "A lot of things were said in anger that will be hard to smooth over," she said, "Richard just can't argue. He waits until something gets under his skin so bad he blows up." For his part Pryor admitted to being relieved when Deboragh filed for divorce. He just didn't seem to have any luck with women. He'd found it difficult to balance marriage with his work. He liked the idea that he would be free again to concentrate on working. As he has said many times, "Work is the only thing in my life that's never hurt me, that's given me my fulfillment and let me have my dignity. Never belittled me."

Although he tried to appear casual about it all, it took Pryor several months to come to grips with what he had done. Without specifically naming Beverly Clayborn, he made uncomplimentary references, clearly aimed at her, to a magazine reporter. She sued him for $9,500,000 slander damages and Soul Publications for $18,500,000 libel damages. At a Tribute to the Black Family held at the Shrine Auditorium in Los Angeles in early February, he not altogether jokingly pictured himself as the victim of a larger conspiracy: "Eight hundred police showed up in my yard. . . . I know this is about the family unit. And what's happened to me is part of the family, too. Just use your brain. Maybe I'm talking to myself."

But somehow, blaming other people just didn't seem to work. Eventually, he had to admit that he was still capable of uncontrolled violence, and that he was even capable of it with black people.

Pryor has always professed love for his people and has long been aware of just how much of his success, indeed how much of his comic material, is due to them. He told Louie Robinson of *Ebony*, "You look at them—some Brothers and Sisters who can't read; some who may have their combs sticking in their heads, or a big fat black woman with her hair going every which-way—but when you live with them and hear them talk, you know that they are some of the smartest people on the planet because they know stuff that people out at those institutes at Yale and Harvard are trying to get. If you're born black, you come from Jump Street. . . . You live around rats and roaches and you survive those bites and don't get rabies when everybody in the world gets rabies, and you don't get brain damage from eating the lead paint. You come up and go to school and in spite of them trying not to teach you anything and destroy your character, you hold onto it and try to have your principles about you, and you learn all their stuff and hold yours and you're a proud black person walking the street. It's amazing! It knocks me out! It makes me cry."

And here he'd gone and done violence to black people.

It was to a black reporter for a black magazine that Pryor finally talked about how much he regretted the whole New Year's Day fiasco. Bob Lucas, then a correspondent for *Jet*, was rather surprised to be the chosen one.

Lucas didn't know Pryor well, although he'd been filing reports about him for several years. "*Jet* is like a fan magazine," he explains. "They didn't want much more than the hype stuff. I'd been in his company, but not interviewing him all the time. I remember him at a tennis tournament in San Diego around 1974–75. I remember that his routines back then turned me off, because everything was *nigger*. I'd been to a party at his house in Northridge; he'd been there at the beginning and at the end. Somebody else was giving it. He is very open-hearted and would let other people use his place for parties. One time there was a skating party on his tennis court.

"I was at the court house when he showed up for his hearing about shooting up the car. I was with a photographer from Chicago—Candi Ward—and she took some pictures. He had Rain with him, and Candi took a picture of them there by the court house. It was a Friday, and the hearing was recessed until the following Monday, and when we went back on Monday, Candi gave him an eleven by fourteen of the picture of him and Rain. It was after the court session. He pleaded not guilty and a date for the trial was set. We were in the lobby of the court house, and when Richard saw the picture he just broke down and cried.

"He said, 'Come on and have breakfast,' and he got into his red Mercedes convertible and we followed him out to his house and had breakfast with him. His grandmother was visiting, and she kept scolding him in a good-natured way and he kept making jokes about her pancakes."

After breakfast Pryor talked to Lucas, not about the case but about how he had felt in the court room. "I hate the fact that this black woman pointed at me in court. That hurt me more than anything. The white man asked, 'Who is it?'—ain't nobody else but me in there. I'd rather stood up myself and said, 'I did it. Y'all don't have to point at me.' When I do something that is especially involved with black people, regardless of the circumstances—which I don't want to discuss—it hurts me to my heart because black people have made me rich and famous."

The case, which dragged on until September, ended with Pryor pleading no contest to a lesser, misdemeanor charge of malicious mischief. Superior Court Commissioner Sherman Juster, who said he had never seen Pryor perform and was paying "no regard to who he is," pronounced a sentence that was not unfamiliar to Pryor. He was fined five hundred dollars and placed on three years probation, during which he was not to possess guns or other deadly weapons. He was ordered to pay restitution to the two women involved in the incident and directed to seek psychiatric care. He was also given a choice of three additional punishments: four hundred and eighty hours of community service; or ten benefit shows, the first five to take place within the next six months; or four months in jail. He chose to give the benefit performances.

Pryor was not happy with any part of this multi-part sentence, but he chose not to share his feelings with reporters. In statements to the press he was positively beatific: "Do I think that's justice? Well, I feel I'm a servant of God and to be placed in a position to serve God's work is fine with me. Its almost like being in His arms. I've always enjoyed helping people in my life and to be made to do something I like is all right with me." But the more hip reporters remembered how he had recalled his sentence on income tax charges in his Just Us routine: "And the judge said, 'What are you doing the next couple of months, Mr. Pryor?'

" 'Well, I'll be helping crippled children ... anything I can do for humanity, sir. . . .'

"I had my pants all down by my ankles when he was finished."

During all the hearings and arraignments back in January, February, and March, Pryor's work schedule had been disrupted hardly at all. He'd completed filming of the title role in The Wiz—his first singing part, for which, he says, composer and producer Quincy Jones coached him endlessly and patiently. Neither the movie, nor Pryor as The Wiz, was a success. The hugely expensive production will in fact go down in film history as a colossal flop and is thought by some to have set back black film-industry participation by making other producers and studios wary of spending big money on black films. Pryor was accorded the back-handed compliment of doing the best he could with a weak role. Pauline Kael thought he should have been cast as the Cowardly Lion instead.

California Suite was next on Pryor's film agenda. Filming began in February for Neil Simon's latest movie, which consisted of four comedy vignettes about separate groups of people who all happened to be staying at the Beverly Hills Hotel. Three of the skits starred whites—Jane Fonda and Alan Alda; Maggie Smith and Michael Caine; and Walter Matthau and Elaine May. The fourth skit, which featured two couples not one, starred Pryor, Bill Cosby, Sheila Frazier, and Gloria Gifford.

Pryor and Cosby play doctors vacationing with their wives. The foursome have been traveling around the country, and they have just about had it with communal living. The comedy is slapstick—almost literally so at times—and many critics were turned off. Pauline Kael charged racism in the fumbling bumblings of the two supposedly sophisticated doctors, and this reaction angered Pryor and Cosby. Cosby took out a full-page ad in Variety to give his point of view: "Are we (comedians/actors) to be denied a right to romp through hotels, bite noses, and, in general, beat up one another in the way Abbott and Costello, Laurel and Hardy, Martin and Lewis, Buster Keaton and Charlie Chaplin did—and more recently as those actors in the movie, Animal House?

"I heard no cries of racism in those reviews. If my work is not funny—it's not funny. But this industry does not need projected racism from critics."

Pryor chose the Tonight show as the forum in which to air his views. "It's white people who have found this offensive," he pointed out. "They got their consciousness all of a sudden. We in no way meant to be anything but funny."

It seemed that there was no way blacks in the film industry could win. They were not supposed to play exploitive Super Fly–type characters, but they weren't supposed to be Abbot and Costello types either. Kael and other white critics who had objected to the Pryor-Cosby segment of California Suite notwithstanding, the movie was a box-office success, and Pryor never regretted doing it. "You have to make changes, transitions," he explained. "You can't just stay in a mold. If you don't keep moving and stretching, you never find out what you can do." Besides, in the course of filming California Suite he and Sheila Frazier got together.

Although Pryor was feeling very anti-marriage, he was not anti-women. He still needed women as much as ever, but he had decided to try to form friendships with women and thereby to gain a better understanding of them. Sheila Frazier, an actress who'd had the misfortune—or fortune, depending on one's perspective—to arrive on the Hollywood scene as the era of blaxploitation movies was waning, was a real friend to Richard Pryor. He could have a good time with her and not feel pressured to make an emotional commitment. From that time in early 1978 until the fire, Pryor and Frazier were close but not an "item."

"I remember one Father's Day, he called my house," says D'Urville Martin. "He was having a big party for all of his kids and the mothers, and he wanted my wife and kids to be there. Sheila Frazier and her kid were going to be there. Each kid had his or her own limousine."

A woman whose position increased in importance in Pryor's life again was Jennifer Lee, who had decorated his house and who he had dated before marrying Deboragh. Bob Lucas remembers that she was at Pryor's house when he and photographer Candi Ward had breakfast with Pryor. She also began acting as hostess at some of his parties.

Pryor had time to plan big parties in the spring and early summer of 1978. Whether he'd planned his schedule that way or whether it was just a matter of the vagaries of film scheduling, he did not have the crush of movie work that he had both enjoyed and suffered through during the same time a year earlier. It is unlikely that studios or directors or casting agents had backed off from Richard Pryor just because he'd murdered a car. By this time Pryor's craziness had become an integral part of his legend—and not an entirely negative part. In some ways it bolstered his reputation. Pryor aficionados did not desert him. In fact Richard Pryor himself probably took the New Year's Day events more seriously than anyone else—except, of course, for the women who were directly involved. He did not let himself off the hook by pleading the eccentricity of genius.

Remembering his uncle's advice, he laid out for a while, taking time to look at himself and his actions and to accept responsibility for them. As he thought about the recent events of his life, his ever agile mind started making connections, and before long he was putting his most devastating experiences into a comic framework.

He had neglected the comedian aspect of his persona in favor of films and television. His most recent albums had comprised primarily old material because he'd been too busy to create new material, and in the back of his mind he'd harbored some guilt over this neglect. Toward the end of January 1978 he learned that his comedy album *Are You Serious???* released by Laff the previous year, was up for a Grammy, and amid the legal hassles over the car murder and the end of his marriage to Deboragh he had found the time to lobby against his receiving the award. On January 26 he ran full-page ads in the entertainment periodicals asking members of the National Academy of Record Arts and Sciences (NARAS) *not* to vote for his album:

AN OPEN LETTER TO MEMBERS OF NARAS

When I recently received notification that I had been voted a Grammy nomination by the members of NARAS I was, and continue to be, appreciative of the recognition given to me. I would like to publicly thank NARAS for this nomination.

My appreciation of the honor of this nomination is, however, tainted by my knowledge that the material under consideration was recorded 10 years ago and recently repackaged and released.

My appreciation of the honor you have given me with your nomination is real. My unwillingness to have 10 year old material up for consideration is just as real. Therefore, I intend to cast my vote for one of the other nominees, and I urge you to do the same.

Sincerely,
Richard Pryor

Whether it was successful lobbying on his part, or whether the members of NARAS simply did not think the album was the best comedy record that had been released the previous year, Pryor did not win a Grammy in 1978.

By the summer of 1978 Richard Pryor had quite a bit of new comedy material in his head. He insists he did not deliberately set out to make a comeback on the concert stage at this time; rather, that one night he simply felt a powerful urge to make an impromptu visit to the Comedy Store, where he took the stage and new material just started spewing forth. Some Pryor watchers have only half-facetiously suggested that his New Year's Day craziness was his way of developing new material. The truth is probably somewhere in the middle.

In the mid-summer of 1978 Pryor arranged to do a seven-week stint at the Comedy Store. He forbade any publicity about his gig and said no to all free passes, but the local grapevine was as efficient as ever and he sold out every night he appeared. The limousines would pull up, and the celebrities emerge—Redd Foxx, Sammy Davis, Don Rickles, David Brenner, among them. His closing shows were packed with stars, including one night Stevie Wonder, whom Pryor pitied from the stage for never having seen a porno movie.

Absent on any night was Freddie Prinz. The previous January he'd been found in his apartment gravely wounded from a self-inflicted gunshot. He'd died a few hours later. A couple of weeks before that he'd been arrested for driving under the influence of methaqualone. He'd been under medical treatment for depression. Knowing that her son had worshipped Richard Pryor, Prinz's mother blamed Pryor for influencing her son to take drugs. Pryor refused to accept that blame.

Controversy continued to dog Pryor that summer, however. In August local police raided the headquarters of a radical Philadelphia-based black group called MOVE and in the ensuing shootout one officer died and eighteen people were injured. Before demolishing the group's headquarters, the police searched it and reportedly found a diary listing contributors to the cause, a list that included the names of Richard Pryor and singer Gil Scott-Heron. Investigators were trying to find out if they could link the donations to the purchase of weapons used by MOVE in the shootout. The diary notations listed the receipt of a five hundred dollar check from Pryor on August 14, 1974, and a one hundred dollar cash contribution from Scott-Heron on May 20, 1978. Representatives of both celebrities denied that such contributions had been made. Murray Swartz, president of Great Eastern Management, which coordinated Pryor's personal appearances, said, "MOVE came to see him in about May 1974, while he was at the Latin Casino. They asked him to do a benefit. He was not impressed with what they were telling him that night. He said No." On August 14, 1974, Pryor had been at the Bijou in Philadelphia, Swartz allowed, but he had not made a donation to MOVE. A spokesman for Arista Records stated that Scott-Heron had done a benefit for the group but had never given them any money. Philadelphia investigators were unable to document the diary entries or tie in the alleged donations with monies used by the group to purchase the guns used in the shootout.

Then in September the car-murder case was decided, and Pryor's name was once again linked with scandal. But none of this adverse publicity seemed to affect attendance at the concerts he began to give in a number of cities starting in the late summer of 1978. If anything, his reception during this first comedy tour in more than three and a half years, proved that he was bigger on the concert stage than ever before.

The concerts Pryor began to give in the late summer of 1978 were different from the ones he had given before. There were no characters, like Mudbone and Black Bertha and the wino and the junkie. Now, the character Richard Pryor played was himself, talking truth and making it funny. Much of his act was embroidered and fictionalized autobiography, inspired not by the pain he saw around him but by the pain he had experienced himself.

"I really mean I'm happy to see people come out, especially all the shit I been in," he would begin. "I mean it from my heart. It makes me feel good, as a person. . . . It makes me say, The shit wasn't *that* bad. All I did was kill a car.

"My wife was gonna leave me. . . . But not in *this* motherfucker you ain't. . . . I'm killing this here. . . . I had a magnum, too, man. . . . I shot one of them tires—*booooom*. . . . It got good to me so I shot another one—*booooom*.

"That vodka I was drinking told me, Go on, shoot something else. . . . I shot the motor—the motor fell out of the motherfucker! Motor say, Fuck it!"

Thus comically rendered, the whole incident seemed not so grievous after all. In fact, killing a car seemed a perfectly natural thing to do, under the circumstances.

Pryor even made a heart attack seem funny. Although he continues to insist he did not have a heart attack in Peoria in the fall of 1977, and the Methodist Medical Center spokesmen back him up, he embroidered on his attack of chest pains and made it all seem hilarious.

"Them motherfuckers *hurt!* I was walkin' in the yard and somethin' say, 'Don't breathe no more!'

"I say, 'huh?'

" 'Don't breathe no motherfuckin' more—you heard me.'

" 'Okay, okay. I won't breathe. I won't breathe.'

" 'Shut the fuck up! You thinkin' 'bout dyin', aincha nigger?'

" 'Yeah, yeah, yeah!'

" 'Why didn't you think about it when you was eatin' that pork, nigger, drinkin' that whiskey and snortin' that cocaine, nigger?'

" 'I'm thinkin' 'bout it; I'm thinkin' 'bout it.'

" 'You put in an emergency call to God.' "

The audiences that laughed uproariously at these routines were sometimes up to seventy-five percent white. Onstage, he would crack, "My God, white people? You motherfuckers came anyway." But offstage he also expressed surprise and some discomfort. "It makes me feel odd, a little odd." Of course, offstage he always felt nervous about performing, but his nervousness left him as soon as he got before an audience. He didn't feel strange at all about playing to a sea of white faces and went right for the jugular of racism: "The fun part for me is when white people come back after intermission and find out niggers stole their seats." And, "You ever notice how white folks always buy their tickets in advance? Black dude gets dressed just before the show. Walks up to the box office, says, 'Hey. Gimme a ticket. What you mean you ain't got no tickets? I got dressed, didn't I?' "

During the course of his peformance he attacked a plethora of racial, cultural, and sexual fears. Among the most noteworthy were his bits about male-female sexual relations. They seemed to reveal a certain amount of growth on Pryor's part, a greater understanding of women. Introducing a new character of sorts, Macho Man, who one suspects is based on Pryor's former self, he would say, "You gotta be cool when you're Macho Man, right? 'Cause you can't be sensitive and care if somebody have a good time in bed—shit. That's too scary. Right? 'Cause men be scared in bed. I don't give a fuck what they tell you women. When the sex is over, men be talkin' shit like, 'Did she come? I wonder if she came. I think she came. I wonder if I was good to her. I hope it was good for her. I'm not gonna ask her, though. I don't give a shit, 'cause if she didn't like it, that's all right. I don't care, 'cause I did the best I could, now fuck her! That's it, she's not gettin' anymore, now that's it!' "

Some of his material was neither sexual nor racial, although even the least objectionable material delivered by Pryor was peppered with profanity. Moving easily from one subject to another, he analyzed Muhammad Ali and Leon Spinks as fighters—"the kind of hand you can strike a match on"—talked about his dogs that were so intelligent that they could read the labels on Alpo cans—"Alpo, all beef . . . very good . . . could you fix this up for us please, Richard . . . and, uh, perhaps a little wine"—and gave advice on what to do when you see a man coming at you with a knife—"Don't try to be macho. You run. And you teach your old lady how to run too, so you don't have to go back for her." He also made fun of squirrel monkeys, horses, and deer, and these bits were as funny as his more scatalogical routines.

Everywhere he went, he played to sold-out audiences. In early September he was at the Kennedy Center in Washington, D.C. Later in the month he was in Chicago; in mid-October he was in Houston; in late October, Detroit. In each city audiences believed they were being treated to the real Richard Pryor. Reviewers referred to his "strangely naked persona." Even in an era of tell all, it was an experience to see a man talk about—and to laugh with him about—the most intimate details of life not to mention his anxieties and fears.

His album *Wanted: Live in Concert* was taped live at one such performance. Released in December, its sales took off immediately, and by April it had gone gold. It was soon followed by *Richard Pryor——Live in Concert*, an audio and visual recording of his concerts at the Terrace Theater in Long Beach, California. Although Pryor had participated in an earlier concert documentary, *Wattstax*, this eighty-minute film was all Richard Pryor.

He had been approached with the idea by Bill Sargent, a peripatetic wheeler-dealer who had promoted concerts, made films, and dabbled in a variety of other forms of mass entertainment. Sargent wanted to use a system of film cameras and TV monitors to record Pryor's performance and release it as a feature-length film. Pryor claims to have said yes out of "pure greed," for the terms Sargent was offering included twelve-and-a-half percent of the profits, and since it was going to be an extremely low-budget film, it was almost guaranteed to start showing a profit very quickly. But Pryor is also very devoted to his art, and Sargent was offering him a unique way to display it. As Sargent explained when the movie was released, "We feel that the film will enable a wider audience to experience the raw power and brilliance of Pryor on stage. TV has always kept a tight lid on Richard's talent. Now, with our film, people can finally see him do what he does best—without a censor looking over his shoulder. There isn't a single word cut out of this film."

Sargent set up his cameras and other recording devices one night in Long Beach, did virtually no editing or rearranging, asked Pryor for some extra footage for his opening credits (Pryor chose to be filmed walking on his property with Jennifer Lee), and in just a couple of months had the film on the market. The film was produced by Hilliard Elkins and Steve Blaunder in association with Compact Video Systems and distributed through Sargent's company SEE (Special Event Entertainment) Theatre Network.

Sargent's was a unique programming technique. Video-taped live entertainment to be shown in movie theaters was so new then that it existed in a gray area between cinema and theater. There was no existing category for it, and thus it sidestepped a number of regulations, among them submitting it for rating by the Motion Picture Association of America. Although Sargent did not submit the film for rating, he did provide a warning to be included in all ads and promotions: "WARNING. This Picture contains Harsh and Very Vulgar Language and May be Considered Shocking and Offensive. No Explicit Sex or Violence is Shown."

Richard Pryor——Live in Concert also fell outside the range of the usual studio-exhibitor agreements. As Sargent explained, "Exhibitors are hurting for quality product. Right now the major studios force the exhibitors to pay outrageous guarantees, in advance, for films which most often lose money—regardless of the cast or story. SEE solves that problem. We capture events which are already big hits in their original form. We know before we start shooting that the event is critically acclaimed and has done big box office business. All we do is film it, curtain to curtain, and give everyone a chance to see it at a fraction of the cost." Ticket price for the film would be $4.50, or one third of the cost of a live concert admission.

Released in early February 1979, *Richard Pryor——Live in Concert* broke box-office records in major cities across the country, taking in $380,996 in its first three days and at one point outgrossing the big-budget, highly hyped *Superman*; eventually, it passed the thirty million dollar mark. Even Bill Sargent had a note of incredulity in his voice when he reflected on the film's success: "One man, on a stage, all alone, with material *he* wrote. He's the scenery; he's the sense; he's the sound effects; he's everything. . . . And why not? Talent and genuis is talent and genius."

What made the film so popular was that it did display both Pryor's talent and his genius at comedy. His comedy, although very successful on records, has always been best when delivered in person, for Pryor is an artist with his body, and he has about a thousand faces. He can act the part of a car, or a deer, or a Doberman as cleverly as he can portray a white man or a black woman. But you have to see him as well as hear him to get a complete idea of his acting virtuosity. *Richard Pryor——Live In Concert* gave the mass audience this chance.

Pryor's concert tour in late 1978 was his most successful ever, but even though he was doing what he loved best—working—he was not happy. He had yet to come to terms with what he had done on New Year's Day, or with his own fame, or with his bad luck with women. His daughter, Elizabeth, aged eleven, wrote a poem about him that fall which read in part;

> *He never seems happy though always so sad*
> *Now they remember him that he's cool and he's bad*
> *He's got the money to do what he wants*
> *Some people want that money to do what they want*
> *They hurt him, they slap him, inside out*
> *But that doesn't matter cause he's Richard Pryor no doubt*
> *It doesn't matter it's the money that counts*
> *This is a story so sad and so true*
> *He has trouble picking his friends*
> *And that makes him blue*
> *My daddy.*

Pryor was finding that money is a cruel mistress. The more he made the more he seemed to need. Although the redecorating of his home in Northridge was not yet complete, he was thinking of getting rid of it. As he told Henry Allen of *The Washington Post*, "It's ridiculous ... when somebody tells you you have to make one million dollars next year just to break even. Well, you gotta maintain, not go for the okeydoke...." In spite of himself he'd hopped right back onto the treadmill, and he was starting to look back; and in the late fall he was forced to look back even further.

On November 1 Pryor canceled a sold-out show at the Fisher Theatre in Detroit to fly back to Los Angeles. He had received word that on her seventy-ninth birthday Marie Bryant had suffered a stroke. Optimistically, Pryor assured Murray Swartz, who was in charge of his tour bookings in the East, that he would be able to go on with the tour, but he made this assurance on the assumption that his grandmother would get better. She did not. For three weeks he commuted between eastern engagements and his home, but finally he could not keep up the pace. Giving exhaustion as his reason, he canceled out the last five days of a week-long engagement at the Shubert Theatre. He realized it was time to take his grandmother back to Peoria.

In Peoria Mrs. Bryant was admitted to Methodist Medical Center, where she died in mid-December. Pryor was with her at the end. "He just stood there shaking like a rag doll," his Aunt Maxine told a reporter for *Jet*. "He had a grip on her hand and they couldn't pry him loose without a struggle. They couldn't get him out of that hospital room and when they did, he broke [away] and come right back in there. . . . And when the wagon table come to take mamma to the morgue, they had to pull Richard out of there. When they pulled him out of there and took him down to the lounge, that's when he really broke down. I tried to console him and he cried, 'Everything I've had and everything I've got is gone. My mamma's gone.' "

It took Pryor nearly two years to get over his grandmother's death and the torrent of emotions it released in him. She had been his rock, his anchor, and the one thing in his life, besides his work, that he could always count on. No matter what trouble he'd gotten into, no matter if he was flying high or in the depths of depression, Marie Bryant had always been there and always the same. She'd died worrying about him and how he was going to survive in such a cruel world. Her death left a void in his life that he knew he could never fill.

And yet he also felt a sense of relief, although he could not admit it at first even to himself. Not until the fall of 1980 was he able to come to terms with his guilt about feeling this way. In the course of an interview with Charles L. Sanders of *Ebony* Pryor tearfully admitted, "I hope people don't misunderstand this, but there's a moment when you're . . . well . . . when you're glad she's dead. You feel that some kind of pressure has been lifted off you, then you feel guilty for feeling that way, then you feel sadness that such a great woman is gone. Does saying that make me an ugly person? I hope not. Do you think people will understand what I'm trying to say about my grandmother?... I'd been afraid to say those things about her death. But that's the way I felt ... that I could finally take care of my own life now."

CHAPTER XII

Pryor on the Edge

AMONG THE PARTS OF the sentence in the car-murder case with which Pryor had no choice but to comply was that he seek psychiatric help. He'd never had much use for shrinks, but he started making regular visits to Dr. Alfred Cannon at Drew Medical Center in Los Angeles. He was relieved to find that therapy was not such a bad experience. He and Cannon became friends.

Cannon had decorated his office with African art, and one day when Pryor admired it, Cannon suggested that Pryor take a trip to Africa. Both therapist and patient were aware that some of Pryor's problems stemmed from unresolved conflicts about being black in a largely white society. Perhaps he would benefit from a personal journey back to his roots.

Filming of Pryor's next movie, titled Family Dreams with Cicely Tyson, had been scheduled to begin in March, but work was delayed until May. Instead for four weeks in March and April Pryor, accompanied by Jennifer Lee, traveled in Africa.

He went without fanfare. No PR campaign preceded his trip, and his whereabouts were not shared with the press. Officials in the countries he visited didn't learn that he had been there until he was gone. He was able to be a regular tourist, and he enjoyed the experience of behaving like a normal person who wasn't recognized by every passerby. Free from autograph hounds and glad-handers, he was able to experience Africa without feeling self-conscious or pressured to be Richard Pryor.

The first thing he noticed was that the black people in Africa behaved much like black people everywhere. The difference was that in Africa they had an automatic dignity because they were in their own liberated lands. In Kenya he visited the museum founded by Dr.

L.S.B. Leakey and looked at the skull of one of the earliest humans. He said later, "It was something to know that it was a black man who probably had the first thought."

As he traveled about, Pryor began to feel the connection between himself and this land, a sense of oneness that transcended the generations and the thousands of geographical miles that separated him from his roots. The climax of this "spiritual awakening" for him came one day when he and Jennifer were driving through a game preserve in Kenya. A pride of lions was resting by the road, and Pryor suddenly stopped the car and got out. Ignoring Jennifer's frightened objections, he walked to within three feet of the lions and stood there staring at them. They stared back.

"They looked at me real curious," he told Lerone Bennett, Jr., of *Ebony* three years later, "and I felt all the Pryors get off—you understand?—and it was, like, they said, 'We can walk home from here. Thank you.' I just felt like I had taken everybody home, *all the spirits home*, you know, and they could rest forever now. All the bloodline from way back when got off at that moment of concentration."

That acute concentration lasted little more than a moment. When one of the lions started stretching, Pryor decided he'd better get himself back to the car, where Jennifer socked him for having worried her with his craziness. But the sense of oneness with his roots stayed with him. He felt as if he had made the journey back to the homeland for all the Pryors, all the ancestors who had been forced to live in an alien land and who had been denied the dignity that is somehow automatic when one lives in a land where he is at home and everyone else is the outsider.

Pryor had another critical experience just as he and Jennifer were about to leave Africa. As he told it later, he was sitting in the lobby of the Nairobi Hilton when a voice seemed to come to him out of nowhere, a voice that asked him if, as he looked around him, he saw any niggers. Pryor answered, no. The voice said that was because there weren't any. In that single breakthrough instant, Pryor says, he stopped using the word nigger. He even stopped *thinking* it.

Later, he thought about the ramifications of this change: he didn't know what his comedy act would be like from then on; he realized that some of his acquaintances would try to bait him by using it. But the problems he expected to encounter seemed small compared to the great sense of relief he felt in unburdening himself of all the guilt and lack of self-esteem that he now realized had caused him to say nigger for so many years. Black folks using the word nigger were, he decided, just trying to take the sting out of an epithet that caused unfathomable pain when used by whites. It was an understandable defense but not a very positive one. He was going to be more positive.

When he first returned from Africa, Pryor shared the feelings and spiritual experiences that it had evoked in him with his analyst and others close to him. As time went on, if the subject came up in interviews, and if he felt comfortable with the interviewer, he would mention that he was not using nigger anymore. But he had no plans to stump for eradication of the word—not from black people's speech, and certainly not from that of white people. He knew that people would come to their own realizations in their own time, and there was no sense trying to preach. Besides, he would feel like a hypocrite, just as he did when he was off drugs and thought about warning young people of their dangers. He returned from Africa with no missionary ideas of changing the world. In fact he returned to the United States, stopping off in Maui, Hawaii, to go fishing before going on to the mainland, as quietly as he had left. For an all too brief time he felt a sense of inner peace that he had not enjoyed in months.

Once he returned to the mainland, that unobstructed sense of peace lasted about two weeks. In retrospect it is even possible to date the start of a new round of Richard Pryor craziness to the completion of that trip to Africa. Although Pryor has chosen to speak only of the positive feelings he garnered from that trip, the way his mind works he generally manages to find the cloud around the silver lining of most positive experiences. He does not trust happiness and feels so much guilt when his life is free of trouble that he is programmed to look for negatives. Not that he had to search very hard for negatives to be gleaned from the experience of going back to his roots. Seeing Kenyans in all their dignity derived from centuries of being in one place and from being rooted in one ongoing culture no matter what historically ephemeral white intruders had tried and failed to do to them, he could not help being struck by the sad state of those Africans who continued to be treated as virtual slaves in lands that were traditionally theirs, as in South Africa. He also found 'it difficult to return to a society where the descendants of Africans, even after so-called emancipation, remained, to quote Jim Brown, "in fourth place from the WASP." It did not take long for the burdens of being black in America to return to rest on Richard Pryor's shoulders as weightily as before. If anything, his anti-white feelings grew stronger.

On May 11 during an appearance on the *Tonight* show, he dropped a potential bombshell. He was speaking about his trip to Africa when he turned directly to the camera and said, "If you want to do anything, if you're black and still here in America, get a gun and go to South Africa and kill some white people, and then you'll probably go to jail again but you'll be doing something besides robbing old ladies."

Across America a few drowsers came suddenly alert, but remarkably, a statement that a few years earlier would probably have made headlines and caused all sorts of flack was given little notice. The Reverend Donald E. Wildmon, head of the National Federation for Decency, based in Tupelo, Mississippi, called for NBC to ban Pryor from the network for one year because of the remark, saying, "Such a statement could come only from a sick mind full of racial hatred. What is more abhorrent is the fact that the program was taped and NBC could have edited the statement out but did not."

Actually, NBC censors had bleeped an expletive Pryor had used earlier in the program. They hadn't done anything about the "get a gun" statement, because they had decided Pryor was just expressing a personal opinion not issuing a call to arms. NBC spokesmen were casual about the whole matter and with good reason, apparently, since there had not been a single telephone call to any NBC affiliate complaining about the statement. The National Federation for Decency wasn't exactly a powerful organization, and the network felt no need to respond to its call. Whether, as *Chicago Tribune* columnist Bob Greene put it, Americans were so numbed by 1979 to be beyond outrage, or whether, as William Brashler suggested, people thought Pryor was joking—"That's the problem with Pryor: We never know when the laughter will stop and he will turn and hiss, 'What you laughin' at, fool?' "—or whether people were no longer inclined to be shocked by anything from Richard Pryor is a moot question.

Pryor was on national television twice that month. On May 29 he was the subject of an interview on one of Barbara Walters's highly rated specials. As the segment in which he was featured opened, he appeared with Jennifer Lee. During the interview with Walters he was at his politest and most ingratiating. His recollections of growing up in whorehouses and his admission of having done crazy things after over-indulging in drink and dope—"Every time I get in trouble, it's because I end up drinking too much, or I end up snorting too much or smoking too much"—drew sympathy from some viewers and apparently from Walters herself. Sympathy from Barbara Walters was highly bankable PR material. But there were not a few observers, both natural cynics and people who knew Pryor quite well, who suspected that he was doing one of his clever put-ons, or that he was trying to cover up his real feelings, attempting to put a cap on the volcanic rage that was welling up inside him.

Pryor tried to keep that cap on during the remainder of the spring and in the summer. He concentrated on his work. He did a guest shot as Pharoah in the Dudley Moore film *Wholly Moses* for Columbia. The picture, released in May 1980, was a dud, and Pryor was lucky to have been only briefly involved. He recorded a couple more albums of material too blue for the airwaves for Laff: *Outrageous* (released in July 1979) and *Insane* (released in February 1980). Somewhat grudgingly, he began giving the benefit concerts that were part of his sentence in the car-murder case and was relieved when, in late 1979, having completed five of them Court Commissioner Sherman Juster who had issued the sentence decided that he had "suffered enough" and dropped the remaining five concerts. He also took steps to make clear that his sense of charity did not extend to motion-picture companies.

There is a tradition in Hollywood that if a performer signs a contract to do a picture for a specified sum of money and for some reason the picture is not produced, the performer still ought to be paid the agreed-upon sum. Such an implicit agreement is called "pay or play." That year Pryor, through his attorneys, took steps to establish that tradition in the courts. A long-running dispute between Pryor and Brut Productions over this issue came to a head in 1979. Back in 1975 Pryor had signed a contract with Brut to play the lead in a remake of

Cyrano de Bergerac for $250,000 plus ten percent of the profits. When Pryor had learned that George Barrie, head of Brut, wanted to direct the film, however, he had balked. In June 1976 a minor factotum at Brut had informed Pryor and his attorney, David Franklin, that the deal had been canceled.

Although Franklin felt that Pryor had grounds for litigation based on the "pay or play" tradition in Hollywood, Pryor didn't really want to get involved in a court suit over the matter. But he did want George Barrie to call personally and say that he had decided not to go forward with the production. When Barrie refused, Pryor got angry. "We're going to be treated like men, right?" he demanded of Franklin. Pryor sued. So did George Peppard, basing his suit on the "pay or play" tradition too.

The case dragged on through 1979, and the experience caused both Franklin and Pryor to decide that the best way to avoid a similar problem in the future was to make sure the tacit understanding of pay or play was written into contracts. Thus, for an as yet untitled film he was to do for producer Frank Yablans at Paramount, Pryor's deal was for $1,350,000 plus points (percentage of box office); but if for some reason the start deadline of April 1980 passed and the picture did not go on as scheduled, he would collect the $1,350,000 as an automatic penalty.

He had a similar deal with Ray Stark at Columbia for a new Neil Simon picture, *Macho Man*, that Simon was writing especially for Pryor. Having seen *Richard Pryor——Live in Concert*, Simon and Stark realized that Pryor was capable of much more than he had been asked to do in *California Suite*, which Simon wrote and Stark produced. They were more than willing to guarantee him a million dollars plus points in the contract.

All this is not to suggest that Pryor was interested in pay to the exclusion of play. He just didn't want to be used, and in the event that he felt he was being used, he wanted monetary satisfaction. By the late summer of 1979 he had already agreed to an extension of the start of principal photography on *Macho Man* because Simon had asked for more time to work on the script. And although Pryor would receive just under one million dollars for his picture for Universal—Family Dreams which was just about to get underway—whether it was made or not, he was prepared to exercise flexibility to the limit in order to ensure that it was made.

By this time Universal might have been just as happy to pay him the one million and not have to go through with the picture, for the studio had serious reservations about its box-office potential. It had a very un-Pryor-like script with a formula plot and a corny ending. According to D'Urville Martin, who was later hired by Universal as a consultant on the picture, "They did it because Richard wanted to do the project, and they didn't want to upset Richard."

Martin continues, "One of the amazing things about Richard that makes me very proud is that the heads of the major studios are frightened of him. Meanwhile, it doesn't seem to me that Richard is all that concerned. Richard will go into a meeting two weeks before the production starts and say, 'I want some black people on this production.' Of course it's too late to hire anyone who will have major responsibility, but they'll rush around and get somebody in as an assistant to the producer or some more extras. But they are frightened to upset him. . . . I remember Jim Brown telling me how this guy had gotten a position as one of the heads of new ventures at Universal because Richard Pryor had told the head of Universal to hire him. There's power in that kind of position and control over a lot of money."

Thus, if Richard Pryor wanted to make a picture, Universal was not about to say no.

Family Dreams, AKA A Family Dream at that time, and ultimately to be called Bustin' Loose, was the first movie for which Pryor originated the idea, collaborated on the script, was involved in the production end, and also starred. He influenced the casting as well, insisting that Paul Mooney have a small part. He wanted Cicely Tyson to be his co-star and in fact he told his collaborators on the script, screenwriter William Simon and playwright Lonnie Elder III, to write the script with her in mind. David Franklin, who with William Greaves was co-producer of the film and who also happened to be Tyson's attorney and manager, was enlisted to help interest Tyson in the role. Franklin had Tyson flown to Atlanta for a special screening of Richard Pryor——Live in Concert, for she was known to disapprove of Pryor's constant use of nigger and motherfucker. Franklin hoped that seeing the film would cause her to understand that, coming from Pryor and in the context of his comedy routines, these words were not as objectionable as she might think.

Tyson had the hoped for reaction to the film. "I was amazed at my reaction to it. I mean, he is, needless to say, a person who uses four-letter words. But somehow when he uses them it takes it out of that realm. I realized that part of his charm, part of his ability to win audiences, was this kind of material. It's like he's a little boy who has heard all the swear words and has seen all the obscene gestures and has no idea of what they mean, but uses them just to be bad!"

Once Tyson had been signed to do the picture, the major casting was complete, for it was the story of an ex-con con man and a prim school marm and how they fall in love in the course of transporting a group of Philadelphia ghetto kids to a farm outside Seattle, Washington. Next in casting importance were the kids, and Pryor had the major influence in this area as well. He wanted the kids to be non-professionals, and he wanted some of them to be from Peoria.

The precasting director in Peoria was none other than Miss Juliette Whittaker, director of the Community Action Agency Day Care Center. When in late October, Maynard Wade, ten, Joab Ortiz, ten, and Eric Alai, twelve, flew out to Seattle for on-location filming, Miss Whittaker was with them.

Pryor had taken pains to make their arrival, and their experience on the set, special. Although he did not personally meet them at the Seattle airport, he had alerted the red-caps and hired a man to walk up and down the airport lobby wearing a sign that said *Family Dreams*. Their rooms at the motel in nearby Bellevue were filled with flowers, and the youngsters were assigned their own special trailer, the sign on which proclaimed, *Dressing rooms for the stars*. He also provided them with spending money; all three bought ten-gallon Stetsons.

While sharing chaperoning duties with Maynard Wade's mother, Whittaker was also involved with the film itself. In the evenings she would go to Seattle to view the day's footage: "I'd look at the film and give them my opinion on what they could do differently. One scene features Cicely Tyson near a closet. Since everything in the closet is brown and she is brown, she fades from view. I pointed out that a key light would make her face more visible. You know, after working for years with stage lighting, you develop an eye for some of these details." Apparently Miss Whittaker took more interest in this part of the filmmaking process than Pryor did. He had said more than once that he didn't care to spend hours on end in an editing room, and he devoted less time and concern than perhaps he should have to this part of his film. He did, however, believe that he had competent people attending to that responsibility.

Meanwhile, it had been decided that Miss Whittaker was a perfect model for a photograph of Cicely Tyson's dead mother. According to Whittaker, "In the beginning of the film Cicely's parents are dead and she shows pictures of them to Richard. They decided they needed pictures of these dead parents for a photo album and for some reason, I was suddenly cast as the mother. I told them I would need a wig since the film is set in the 1960s, and the short hair I wear wasn't in style then." She received a check from Universal Studios for one hour's work, a symbol of how history had come full circle with her appearance in a movie conceived, written, and produced by a man who a quarter century before had appeared in plays conceived, written, and produced by her. In December the Peorians returned home having enjoyed an experience they would never forget, and Juliette Whittaker also had Pryor's promise of support for her new school.

The Learning Tree Day School was a logical outgrowth of the work Whittaker had been doing ever since she'd graduated from college and gone to Peoria to stage plays for kids at the Carver Community Center. A private primary school, it would enroll gifted children, and Whittaker's philosophy was that a gifted child should not suffer because his or her parents happened to be unable to afford private school tuition. Pryor agreed and offered support to the school, in the form of some seventy Richard Pryor scholarships. Since seventy was the approximate number of pupils Whittaker anticipated enrolling when the school opened in the fall of 1980, Pryor's grant to the school would be by far the most extensive of the monetary gifts Whittaker had been able to attract. Per pupil subsidies would range from a minimum of one thousand to the full cost of about two thousand dollars. "It's his commitment to the children of Peoria," Whittaker told a reporter for the *Journal-Star*. "Richard Pryor was a gifted child. He had all the problems a gifted child has."

As 1979 ended, Richard Pryor was having plenty of problems as a gifted grown-up. He still hadn't gotten over his grandmother's death, couldn't synthesize the good and bad feelings that had resulted from his trip to Africa, was having problems with Jennifer, and was agonizing over the first picture over which he had direct responsibility. By the time principal photography on Family Dreams began in September, he was consuming a fifth of liquor a day and combining it with cocaine in unspecified amounts. He had also developed a chronic bronchial condition. But he kept his problems to himself. He had done enough of the naked persona bit. When asked by interviewers, he insisted that everything was fine, and most media mentions of Pryor that fall echoed his public pronouncements. An article in the December issue of *Playboy*, however, did not. Although its author, William Brashler, reported Pryor's statements, he added his own devastating commentary, being a bit peeved when he wrote the article.

Brashler, on whose novel *The Bingo Long Traveling All-Stars and Motor Kings* was based, had originally contracted with *Playboy* to do an interview with Pryor and had been consistently frustrated in his attempts to secure a face-to-face exchange. Having been assured that such a meeting could be arranged, Brashler had gone to Los Angeles, only to be told once he'd got there that the meeting would be impossible at that time. Then Pryor had flown off to Maui. A month later Pryor had called Brashler and talked for almost an hour, never mentioning the fact that he had stood him up. During that conversation Pryor had said he was a very happy man. He was just happy to be alive, and he was with a lady who he cared about and with whom he had an honest relationship. Brashler, remembering that Pryor had expressed similar sentiments to an *Ebony* interviewer about Deboragh in the fall of 1977, remarked that it all sounded vaguely familiar. "Well," said Pryor, "let's just say that I'm happy when I'm happy."

Instead of an interview with Pryor for *Playboy*, Brashler wound up doing a profile for the magazine, including his own problems in trying to get an interview and how he got much of his material from friends and acquaintances, some of whom he did not name. The profile that emerged from Brashler's article was of a man of chronic changeability, who for a time would be open to other people, generous with his time, polite, gracious, and dependable, and then, suddenly and for no apparent reason, cancel appointments, renege on personal commitments, be incommunicado for days. With friends, he could be solicitous and lovable at times but cruel and unreasonable at others. Unidentified friends told Brashler that there was no telling when the violent times would come; but they did tell him what to do when they did come. Wrote Brashler, "I was warned more than once not to stay at Pryor's place if such a situation arose. 'Don't think that who you are or whom you represent means a damn thing. Don't think you can control the situation. Just get out.' "

It was Pryor's changeability that made him so psychologically dominating. Being around him was like being in the same roller-coaster car with him, except that you had to wear a blindfold. People didn't know how he would be from one day to the next, and so the people who lived life with Richard Pryor took it one day at a time and tried to balance the menacing Richard Pryor with the vulnerable one. But, reported Brashler, "Some close to him fear that one day he will push things too far—that probably in the wee hours of the morning in the smog of the drugs and the booze, a scene will go out of control and he will push someone to go after him."

By early 1980 Richard Pryor was again close to the edge. He was embroiled in yet another legal suit, this time about the 35-mm films from which *Richard Pryor——Live in Concert* had been made. In January Compact Video Systems, Inc., which had distributed the film, announced its intention to auction off these and four other films. Pryor, said Compact, had signed a contract surrendering his rights to the film and prints. Pryor disputed the claim and wanted the auction halted until the question of ownership was settled. After a judge delayed the sale of rights to the six films, Compact sued Pryor for one million dollars in punitive and exemplary damages.

He and Jennifer had a falling out and Pryor was back to searching for the unconditional love that his friend Jim Brown says is something that is sought by children of broken homes and broken childhoods. Sheila Frazier become more important to him at this time. He also started seeing Ahneva Ahneva, who had arrived from Chicago as an aspiring actress but eventually turned to catering. She works out of her home and insists she has never advertised—indeed, she is not listed in the L.A. telephone book—but has somehow become known as Caterer to the Stars. With the help of her "spiritual family," by which she means assistants and/or friends with names like Bilalian Rose and Sultan Shah, she prepares vegetarian, chicken, and seafood dishes and specializes in original table arrangements and distinctive brass serving vessels.

"I knew her before anybody," says D'Urville Martin, who met her when she first arrived from Chicago. "She was going to star in my first picture. She catered some of Richard's parties. He has given an awful lot of money to her. He gave her a check for ten thousand dollars one time for catering a party. She went out and rented a yellow Rolls Royce to drive around in, with no place to go. She started being at his house even when there weren't any parties. And in public—one time Richard and I were at the Candy Store, just talking. She walked in, came and sat on his lap, and just took over. We never finished our conversation. She was hoping to marry him. At least she wanted to marry him. It didn't work out."

Jennifer came back, then left again, then came back again. Pryor was still very much in love with her, and she with him, but they were having a hard time working out their differences.

Meanwhile, similar to Pryor's personal relationships, Family Dreams was in a shambles. According to Michael Schultz, who was eventually called in to do repair work, "It was very, very badly produced and directed. They had shot only half scenes—like, they would take a shot on you, but the shot on the other person didn't exist because they hadn't had time, so they'd shoot one person and say, on to the next."

There were problems with the dialogue, too, and Pryor himself had been responsible for some of them. Cicely Tyson would remember the shooting of that movie as quite an experience. She told writers Fred Robbins and David Ragan that the first couple of days of shooting in September 1979 were unsettling for an actress accustomed to working from a prepared script. There was a prepared script for the movie, but Pryor, who had written much of it, seemed not to pay much attention to it. "I would say a line, and he would come up with something new, something not in the script. Then he would come to me and say, 'Listen, I'm awfully sorry, but tomorrow I'm gonna learn my lines and

I'm gonna do it right.' Well, after the third day I said, 'Richard, just do whatever it is you feel you have to do. And I will just roll with the punches.' "

Pryor was not very interested in the first movie over which he had major control. According to D'Urville Martin, "It was supposedly Richard's company that was producing it, but Richard never really paid any attention to actually producing it. He had a title, and he got paid an awful lot of money." By the winter of late 1979 and early 1980 Pryor was not in any emotional state to deal with nitty-gritty problems like half-shot scenes and botched dialogue. Besides, he was worried about his health. His bronchial condition was serious enough for the insurers of his next picture, *Stir Crazy*, to refuse to cover him for the ailment.

Stir Crazy went into principal photography in late February 1980, with cell scenes shot on a Burbank sound stage. Produced by Hannah Weinstein, who had produced the trouble-filled *Greased Lightning* several years before, and directed by Sidney Poitier, who had last directed Pryor in *Uptown Saturday Night* in 1974, the picture again paired Pryor with Gene Wilder. It was a comedy about two New Yorkers who aspire to show business careers and who decide to drive cross-country to California to seek their fortunes. On the way they run short of cash and take jobs as singing, dancing woodpeckers to pro-mote the opening of a new bank. But two hoods steal their costumes and wear them to rob the bank, and Pryor and Wilder are arrested for bank robbery and sentenced to one hundred twenty-five years in prison. As frightened to enter the state penitentiary as they would have been to be thrown into a lion cage, the two try to act like hardened criminals so they can survive long enough in prison to escape.

Much of the filming was done on location at Arizona State Prison in Florence, near Tuscon, where the company moved bag and baggage in mid-March despite recent prison riots in nearby New Mexico. Poitier, Pryor, Wilder, other cast members, and crew all had to sign forms provided by the prison which stated, "I understand that in the event I should be taken hostage or involved in a disturbance, institu-tion authorities will not be expected to make extraordinary or unusual effort to effect my release." The day before filming began there were two stabbings in the prison, and many among the cast and crew were edgy. It was Pryor who loosened up the mood by offering the prisoners soft drinks.

In return the cons started giving Pryor and Wilder some tips. One was, never run in prison unless you want to be shot. Another: new prisoners, especially those who have never been in prison before, tend to stay within view of the guards from fear of their fellow inmates. Pryor and Wilder welcomed these bits of advice, for they were expected to improvise much of the movie. According to Wilder, Sidney Poitier had said to them, "I know what kind of actors you both are, and I want you to follow your instinct for the next three months. Don't stifle one impulse. You're two racehorses. I want to steer you, not tell you how to run."

Although Bruce Jay Friedman wrote the script for *Stir Crazy*, the most famous line in the film was a Pryor improvisation, and Friedman is the first to admit it. It occurs in the scene when Pryor and Wilder first enter the prison. Pryor already knows that if he and his friend are going to survive there, they are going to have to act like they feel at home. He tells the petrified Wilder that they must walk, talk, and look *baaaad*. Summoning their *baaaadest* visages, they jive-walk into the holding cell as Pryor announces, "Thass right, thass right, we bad."

After the movie was released later in 1980, the line was especially popular among young people. Any time they had the opportunity to make an extrance, whether into a classroom, a museum, or even a kitchen, a lot of kids did the jive-walk and repeated the line from the movie. Back in the early spring of 1980, after Pryor delivered that improvised line, members of the cast and crew, not to mention assorted prisoners and guards, immediately took it up.

Unfortunately, that was one of the few bright spots for Pryor in his whole involvement with *Stir Crazy*. While he enjoyed working with Wilder and Poitier, he began, again, to experience the creeping feeling that he was being used, that he was somehow a clown, and began to feel the insidious guilt that he was not supposed to be where he was. No doubt being in the prison environment intensified the latter feeling. He saw the large percentage of black regular inmates, not to mention the death-row inhabitants. He remembered his own prison experience, his own feelings about white prison guards. He hadn't been in the most positive state of mind when he'd started the picture, and at Arizona State Prison his mood grew worse. There the threshold of his racial sensitivity dropped to zero.

At first Pryor's problems seemed to be more physical than mental. He had a flare-up of his bronchial condition and started reporting late—sometimes half a day late—to work. On the set he doubled up coughing at times. Crop dusting of the fields surrounding the prison didn't help his condition. But as time went on, it became clear that bronchitis was not Pryor's only problem. He had altercations with a cameraman that continued after the company returned to Burbank for final cell scenes on the sound stage and that culminated in late April when the cameraman dropped a watermelon at Pryor's feet and Pryor walked off the set. Director Sidney Poitier, meanwhile, was at the end of his patience or at least determined to show Pryor his displeasure. He didn't like the insulting symbolism of the watermelon either, but he was aware that Pryor had done his part in bringing the confrontation to that point. He was talking about replacing Pryor and reshooting earlier scenes in which Pryor had appeared. Given the cost of movies, no one was taking his threat seriously, but he did show the extent of his displeasure by meeting at least once with Columbia brass on the matter. Pryor returned to the set about a week after his walkout, and the picture was completed.

Released later in the year, *Stir Crazy* was a blockbuster, the big, big movie that represented the zenith of Pryor's work in the past decade. It broke box-office records, and critics were nearly unanimous in saying that the film succeeded because of Richard Pryor. Whether the ticket buying public would have attended the picture in such droves if Pryor had not barely escaped death by the time it was released will never be known. It is one of the sad ironies of Richard Pryor's life that even his greatest triumphs are somehow marred by unexpected events.

CHAPTER XIII

The Fire

ON SUNDAY NIGHT, JUNE 8, 1980, Maeotha Rivers, nursemaid to the children of attorney David Franklin, had a bad dream. In it Franklin suffered burns over fifty percent of his body. The next day, Monday, she went out and bought several smoke detectors. Franklin, inquiring about the smoke detectors, learned about the dream and shrugged it off. But when he was awakened at 2 A.M. Tuesday morning with the news that Richard Pryor had been burned in an accident at his Northridge home, he felt a dry ice chill shudder through his body. Maeotha Rivers's dream had been a bona fide premonition. She'd just got the characters mixed up.

On Monday night, June 9, at around 8 P.M. Richard Pryor was entertaining at home in the master bedroom. His Aunt Dee was also in the house. Exactly who else was there remains the subject of controversy and rumor, as does exactly what Pryor and company were doing when the world exploded in front of Richard Pryor and his body was engulfed in flames. The explosion ripped through the master bedroom, and Aunt Dee, who was in another part of the house, came running. She grabbed a blanket and smothered the flames. But she was too late to catch her nephew. He, too, was running, down the palm-lined driveway and into the street. Aunt Dee didn't try to stop him. She ran to a telephone and called an ambulance. Then, she took off down the driveway after Richard.

By the time Pryor reached the street, his clothing was no longer on fire. The tattered remnants of his polyester shirt stuck to his body like napalm, replacing the skin that was no longer there. There was nothing to replace the charred skin on his badly burned hands, the raw pink blotch on his left cheek, the gaping wounds on his jaw and neck, his burned nose, his lacerated lip. The distinct smell of burning flesh pervaded the air around him.

Once out on the street and heading along Parthenia toward Hayvenhurst, Pryor was recognized by the drivers of passing cars. Some slowed and tried to talk to him as he walked quickly along, shoulders hunched forward, head down. L.A. police officers Richard Zielinski and Carl Helm were on routine traffic detail in their patrol car when they noticed the group of cars that had slowed or stopped on Parthenia Street. As they approached to investigate, they, too, recognized Richard Pryor. They pulled over and stopped, and Zielinski, now close enough to see Pryor's tattered shirt and charred skin and to smell the stench, realized that he was hurt.

Aunt Dee had reached them by now. "Auntie, help me!" Pryor cried. "I'm trying!" she cried back, telling the officers that she had called an ambulance. While Helm headed for Pryor's house to direct the ambulance, Zielinski, afraid to touch Pryor for fear of hurting him, tried to talk him into stopping. But Pryor said he couldn't stop. "I gotta keep walking," he mumbled through his lacerated lip. "If I stop, I'll die."

Not knowing what else to do, Zielinski walked along beside him and witnessed what Pryor had once jokingly described as "an emergency call to God." "Lord, give me another chance. There's a lot of good left in me," he pleaded. "Haven't I brought any happiness to anyone in this world?"

Zielinski was still trying to talk him into stopping, but Pryor seemed oblivious to the officer and to the cars and people around him. As the sound of the ambulance siren came closer, Pryor reached the corner of Hayvenhurst and turned south, now breaking into a trot. Zielinski began to trot, too, looking back over his shoulder to see if he could catch sight of the ambulance. Pryor was still mumbling, sometimes unintelligibly, but as the strange pair ran in tandem the officer heard, "They told me yesterday not to smoke that shit, and this is what I get. . . . This is the Lord paying me back. . . . Lord, give me another chance."

Two blocks down Hayvenhurst, the ambulance finally pulled up, and Zielinski made a grab for his charred jogging partner. But Pryor deftly eluded his grasp. Officer Helm and the two ambulance attendants came running with a fluid-treated sheet. Zielinski helped them to throw it over Pryor, like a net over a wild animal. Then they wrestled his hands into leather and cloth restraints. Only after he had been forcibly restrained did Pryor calm down. Saying, "Oh, Lord, I guess you got me now," he gave up, his body relaxed, and he began to whimper from the excruciating pain that he was beginning consciously to feel only now that he had stopped moving.

Aunt Dee and Officer Helm boarded the ambulance bound for Sherman Oaks Community Hospital Burn Center. Officer Zielinski, white member of a predominantly white force that is reputed to regard as anathema black stars like Richard Pryor, was left behind to ponder the most moving experience he'd ever had in his life.

By 10 P.M. that night the news had hit the wire services. But even before the wire services got the story, it had spread like wildfire along the Hollywood grapevine. D'Urville Martin heard about it from Sheila Frazier. "She called me from the hospital to get Jim Brown's number. I knew she was at the hospital, but she wouldn't give me any information. Sheila has never explained to me how, before it was even on the news, she was at the hospital calling me. Minutes after she hung up, it came on TV."

Frazier, Martin says, had been spending some time with Pryor, but it had not been publicly known. Pryor has subsequently made references to "my partner" being with him, but he has never identified that partner.

The early news reports pronounced the accident drug related, using phrases like "drug burns" and "cocaine explosion." The source of this information apparently was a police officer, but accounts differ as to how he came by it. One account holds that he overheard the initial exchange between Dr. Jack Grossman of the Sherman Oaks Burn Center and Pryor as he was wheeled in on the ambulance stretcher. In order to know how to treat Pryor, Grossman asked him what had happened, and according to the officer, Pryor replied that his cigarette lighter had come too close to "freebase," a smokeable combination of cocaine and ether that was enjoying wide use as a new and fashionable high in Hollywood at that time. Ether, a highly volatile chemical, is used to remove the salt from ordinary street cocaine and renders it smokeable. Smoking cocaine gives a quicker and greater rush than inhaling powdered cocaine through the nose.

D'Urville Martin suspects that Jennifer Lee may have confirmed what the officer thought he overheard by informing the police that Pryor was freebasing. "He was trying to put her out around the time of the fire," says Martin. "She refused to leave. Even though she wasn't in the house at the time, she just assumed that the explosion came from freebasing. She's the one who told the police at the hospital that he was freebasing, because he wouldn't see her. . . . She told them all the bad things that he did to her.

"I think that the police department and the fire department went heavy on Richard solely because of Jennifer. Out here, the police are like the gestapo. They don't like homosexuals. They don't like minorities. They don't like integrated groups. They can shoot you in broad daylight in front of witnesses and nothing happens to them. So they went heavy on him, even though he was probably going to die, as far as they knew."

Armed with a shotgun and a "verbal warrant," a team of L.A. police, firemen, and narcotics investigators broke into Pryor's home the next morning. They found no "drug factory" there or any evidence of drug use. They did, however, find a bottle of rum and a broken glass, and when David Franklin arrived that morning on the first L.A. bound plane out of Atlanta, he set about organizing a press conference the following day to try to dispel the freebasing reports.

Pryor, Franklin told reporters, had a glass of rum in one hand and a cigarette lighter in the other. He put a cigarette to his lips, leaned over to light it, and something exploded. Although there was no precedent in history for rum fumes to explode when in contact with an open flame, the reporters, who are paid to be curious, seemed to accept the explanation and never brought up the subject again at later press conferences. Perhaps the reporters disapproved of the L.A. police and firemen and narc squad action. Or perhaps they chose to focus on Pryor's condition rather than on what led to it.

Pryor, meanwhile, was fighting for his life, aided by a team of skilled specialists. The first reports from the hospital had been guarded. Pryor had suffered third-degree burns over fifty percent of his body, and although he was in stable condition Dr. Grossman cautioned that men in Pryor's age group stood only a one in three chance of surviving such massive burns. Going for that thirty percent chance, Grossman and his associates began to treat Pryor early the next morning. He was given hyperbaric treatment, placed in a sealed tube where atmospheric pressure is intensified so as to force oxygen into the blood. He was given whirlpool baths to wash away the charred tissue and polyester fragments from a dermal surface so sensitive that the baths caused Pryor excruciating pain. Afterward he was swathed in antibiotic dressings to reduce the chances of infection, the greatest danger in burn cases. The body burns were the worst—the polyester material of Pryor's shirt had literally melted into his skin—and these were dealt with first. The burns on Pryor's face, being farther away from vital organs like the heart and lungs, would have to wait. Doctors counted on the naturally rich flow of blood to the face to keep the circulation going and natural healing to begin.

Aside from hospital personnel, only Jim Brown was witness to Pryor's pain and to the ravishments of his body. Pryor would not allow anyone else to see him. While former wives Maxine and Deboragh sat together in the waiting room and Jennifer Lee paced the floor in frustration, while Stan Shaw stood vigil and people like Elliott Gould and Cicely Tyson stopped in, while telephone calls by the hundreds, telegrams, cards, and flowers poured into the previously calm 156-bed facility, Pryor would see and hear only Jim Brown. "For three hard weeks he was there," Pryor later told Charles Sanders of *Ebony*. "When I went to sleep, he was there. When I woke up, he was there. And I kept saying to myself, 'I can't give in to the pain . . . not in front of Jim Brown.'" It was almost as if Brown represented for Pryor the only man he knew who could function as a stand-in for God, and Brown accepted that weighty responsibility.

Brown and Pryor had been friends for some fifteen years, but they were not public friends. Some of Pryor's and Brown's long-time acquaintances were surprised to learn that Brown was the only person Pryor wanted with him in the hospital. They hadn't realized the two were so close. Still, it did not seem odd to them that Richard would want Jim with him. Brown is highly respected in Hollywood among both blacks and whites.

"Jim's a very human guy who tries to help black people," says D'Urville Martin. "An often forgotten fact is that he tried to form different organizations to help black people around the world. He tried to form a company where blacks would control the sports in which they are popular: basketball, baseball, boxing, football. He tried to form a kind of loan company to help blacks raise money to make movies. He tries to help individuals, like people who are on drugs. Among people out here in Hollywood, Jim's known as an honest guy—an honest guy who will tell you like it is. He has been around the biggest, wealthiest, most famous people in the world, and so he isn't impressed with a Richard Pryor. Jim Brown just talks to him as people. Jim Brown tells him the truth and tells it straight."

Jim Brown describes his relationship with Richard Pryor as one of "unconditional love," and he demonstrated it unequivocally during Pryor's first few days in the hospital. He stood guard at Pryor's bed night and day, seeing that his friend had peace and quiet, keeping his spirit up, consulting with the doctors about Pryor's condition, fielding questions from the press, and running interference with Pryor's family and friends, not to mention the scores of fans and well-wishers who besieged the hospital with visits, telephone calls, telegrams, and get-well cards. It wasn't easy being the "chosen one." Lack of sleep and the drain on his energy aside, he realized that some among Pryor's friends and family deeply resented him and blamed him for keeping them from seeing Richard.

Among them was Jennifer Lee, who went to the hospital every day but was continually frustrated in her attempts to see Pryor. At last she did secure permission to send him notes, and almost immediately she began to grant exclusive interviews to various members of the press, saying that hospital aides had told her that the notes were helping to bolster Pryor's spirits. Perhaps she hoped that Pryor would read these interviews and that they would underscore her concern for him. If he read the *New York Post* of June 14, he could not have ignored her "spiritual presence." The headline, typically large, read, " 'I Love Him,' Pryor's Gal Tells The Post."

David Franklin, Pryor's attorney, was not allowed to see him either. Interviewed by David Felton for *Rolling Stone*, Franklin had not been in the habit of analyzing Pryor's character and personality. Formerly his statements to the press had been almost exclusively about Pryor's business and career. No doubt, he, too, was miffed about being excluded from Pryor's hospital room, for although he spoke guardedly, he did suggest that there was a pattern of self-destructiveness in his

client's behavior, saying, "The Karma culminated on that night."
Asked if he thought the accident would break the pattern, he was
unable to answer with certainty. "If this doesn't do it, if this doesn't do
it . . . will anything do it?"

Meanwhile, there was still no assurance that Pryor would live to
have the chance to change his pattern of behavior. Over the weekend
of June 14 and 15 he contracted pneumonia. There had been some
injury to his lungs. He was still in critical condition, and his doctors
felt constrained to caution against recent media reports that Pryor's
chances for survival had markedly improved. "He's about as sick as
you can get and be alive for the burns that he has. He's in very critical
condition," said Dr. Jack Grossman.

Still, plans for surgery on Tuesday morning, June 17, went ahead.
Skin grafting had to commence soon, and before any grafting could be
done Pryor had to undergo a surgical procedure called debridement
in which the burnt tissue not sloughed off in the constant whirlpool-
bath treatments had to be removed. They also would use a second
surgical procedure to remove the fluid that had accumulated in his
lungs. Skin grafting operations would begin in three to five days, if
his condition would allow it.

The whirlpool-bath and hyperbaric treatments continued as Pryor
remained in a kind of vacuum-sealed atmosphere, seeing only Jim
Brown, hearing reports from the outside world filtered through
Brown and his doctors. In the outside world some newspaper articles
about him read like premature obituaries. A press release from Twen-
tieth Century-Fox Pictures announced that Gregory Hines, a "bright
new Broadway talent," had been signed to replace Pryor in the role of
Josephus in Mel Brooks's comedy *History of the World-Part I*. Some of
his relatives were helping themselves to mementoes from his house.

Soon he couldn't stand the isolation anymore. He wanted visitors.
One at a time, and briefly, friends and relatives were admitted to see
him. He also began accepting telephone calls. Besides former wives,
girl friends, and relatives, a group as diverse as Sammy Davis, Jr.,
Johnny Carson, Cicely Tyson, Elliot Gould, Bill Cosby, Redd Foxx,
and presidential candidates Senator Edward Kennedy and John Anderson either called or dropped by. Marlon Brando visited several
times, and so did Dan Haggerty. Haggerty, then the star of the televi-

sion show *Grizzly Adams*, was not a friend of Pryor's but the two shared a unique bond. Several years earlier a flaming drink at a birthday party had ignited Haggerty's beard and he had suffered third-degree burns to his face.

On June 19, ten days after Pryor was admitted to the hospital, David Felton was told by a source that he considered "informed and highly reliable" that earlier that day Dr. Richard Grossman, brother of Dr. Jack Grossman and co-owner and operator of the Plastic Surgi-center, had advised members of the hospital staff that Pryor was no longer expected to live, that he could not last more than a week at most. His kidneys had been found to be irreparably damaged by alcohol and drugs. On June 20 Dr. Jack Grossman said that the report that Pryor was near dead was absolutely not true. A kidney-function abnormality that predated the fire *had* been discovered, requiring the services of a kidney specialist, but that there was no basis for the story that drugs and alcohol had anything to do with it. Because of the kidney problems skin-graft operations had been postponed until at least Monday.

Friday evening Pryor watched the first Sugar Ray Leonard–Roberto Duran boxing match from his hospital bed, the special closed-circuit hookup having been arranged by Marlon Brando, who watched the fight with him.

The first skin grafts were made on Monday, June 23. Using skin from Pryor's calves and thighs, doctors began to replace the burnt skin on the upper half of his body and behind his ears. Then they waited to see if the grafts would take. Pryor was still on the critical list, although there was now some talk of moving him off the list and upgrading his condition to serious. Hospital staff also took steps to improve their own procedures for handling the massive outpouring of public sympathy for Pryor, which had increased as the days went by.

Overall, public reaction to Pryor's accident had followed an odd pattern. Initially, the general reaction had been muted, perhaps overshadowed by the reports that Pryor had been freebasing. Whether people believed that he'd gotten what he'd deserved or not, the feeling was that he could not possibly survive. But as the days passed and he clung to life, what had happened or how it had happened became less important than the fact that he was alive and fighting to stay that way. The telephone calls, intermittent in the first few days, were now backing up the hospital switchboard for close to two hours. The mail, managed by one sorter at first, now numbered close to one thousand pieces a day, and two people were required to sort out the letters addressed to Richard Pryor from the other hospital mail. Everything from stuffed animals to three-foot-high post cards to hand-delivered, home-baked cookies arrived at the hospital door at all hours. Richard Pryor, having voluntarily broken the seals of his enforced psychological isolation, said to Jim Brown in some amazement, "People really care."

Although he was not yet out of danger himself, Pryor could not simply accept this outpouring of concern without giving something of himself. Encouraged to walk in order to stimulate his circulation, he visited other patients in the burn ward, and when some of his acquaintances heard about these visits, someone had the idea of staging a telethon to benefit the Sherman Oaks Burn Center. When Pryor heard about the idea, he eagerly endorsed it, agreeing to let the organizers use his name.

Meanwhile, he continued to suffer excruciating pain as the whirlpool-bath and hyperbaric treatments were resumed two days after his first skin-graft operations, and he had been assured that there was much pain ahead for him. His body rejected approximately thirty-five percent of the first skin grafts, and he underwent a second skin-graft operation ten days later. There would be many more before all the skin he had lost on his torso and behind his ears could be fully replaced. His doctors were hoping the skin on his face would heal unaided. If it didn't, still more skin grafts would be necessary—grafts that would have to wait, for there was only so much skin on his thin legs for the taking, and it took a week to regenerate. The problem of cosmetics had not even been addressed as yet. Richard Pryor, human being, was being mended now. Richard Pryor, movie star, face known to millions, had to wait. It might take months of plastic surgery before he would look as he had before the fire, and plastic surgery could not commence until three months after completion of skin grafting. Pryor tried not to think about it. He would not even look in the mirror for six weeks, afraid of what he would see.

Pryor was taken off the critical list and his condition was described as serious, although hospital spokesmen admitted that such changes in condition were more for the benefit of the press than to accurately measure medical progress. Richard Pryor was still very sick. His kidneys were now functioning at the pre-fire level, but that was only about one third of normal functioning. His bout with pneumonia was ending, and his lungs did not require further removal of fluid build-up. But the pressure on his chest from the burned tissue was described by one of his doctors as "like wearing a leather girdle." His legs, though not burned, were sore in the places where skin had been removed for grafts. He could move about only with the aid of a walker, and his walking was a painful shuffle. His entire body was like a huge raw nerve, and he spent his days exchanging one kind of pain for another: the pain of walking for the pain of the twice daily two-hour whirlpool baths, the pain of having antibiotic dressings applied for the pain of just lying helplessly waiting for the next stir of air or movement of a gauze wrapping to cause intense discomfort.

But his spirits were excellent. Jim Brown and other friends and relatives were partly responsible. Although after the first three weeks Brown was not with Pryor round-the-clock, he still visited frequently, as did Richard, Jr., Richard's cousin Denise, and Deboragh. Jennifer Lee was no longer in evidence, and D'Urville Martin believes that it was because Pryor suspected it had been she who told the police he had been freebasing. The report was still circulating and being mentioned in the press, and in late July David Franklin was still feeling constrained to deny publicly that drugs were in any way connected with the accident. Letters and telephone calls from people he'd never met also helped to keep up Pryor's spirits. He told Charles Sanders, "Black people don't just be sitting down writing letters and spending their fifteen cents to mail 'em if you ain't their mama or son or something. But they wrote me by the thousands. And, of course, I could tell when a letter was from a Brother or Sister, 'cause they write a certain way, and it tears your heart out to know that they took the time to do it."

Pryor was encouraged, too, by the idea of the Richard Pryor telethon that was scheduled for the third week in July. Its organizers assured him that it would show how much people cared about him and give them an opportunity to demonstrate it. Unfortunately, the telethon was so poorly organized and publicized that it did not raise either Pryor's spirits or anywhere near the money the organizers hoped for.

From its inception the enterprise was ill-fated. Although the intent was good, it was never really made clear. It was supposed to raise money for the Sherman Oaks Community Hospital Burn Center so more people, and people less wealthy than Pryor, could receive treatment there. It was not supposed to raise money for Richard Pryor's treatment. But Pryor was a patient at the center, and the telethon was called a Richard Pryor telethon, and many people quite naturally assumed that it was being held to raise money for him. Even people who were sympathetic to his pain and his ordeal were not sympathetic to what they mistakenly perceived as an appeal for money for him. Pryor was rich. He didn't need any help paying hospital bills.

The telethon had been Redd Foxx's idea. "I think Redd was sincere about it," says D'Urville Martin, "but he had people around him who were incompetent and unqualified. Redd Foxx is influenced by young, sexy ladies who may not have any brains. And also yes-men, dumb men."

A woman in Foxx's employ was supposed to organize the telethon. Meanwhile Foxx, who held the title of producer, contacted some of his friends. Sammy Davis, Jr., was supposed to co-host the show with Foxx, and among the other stars slated to appear were Muhammad Ali, Alex Haley, Stevie Wonder, Robert Guillaume, Donny Most, and Johnny Cranford. But most of the arrangements were apparently made informally—no contracts were signed—and this informality extended even to the technical arrangements. The first sign of trouble came when Foxx was presented with bills for technical work being done in connection with the show. He refused to pay them, saying that he'd signed no contract that called for him to put up any money. The technical people threatened to sue him, and according to D'Urville Martin, he said, "You don't have anything with my name on it."

When Pryor, still hospitalized, heard about what was happening, he was furious. D'Urville Martin says he blamed Redd Foxx and felt Foxx had tried to use him. Kathi Fearn-Banks recalls, "Because it was so disorganized, Richard decided he didn't want to be associated with it at all. He wrote letters saying he had nothing to do with it."

Somehow, the show went on the air July 18, but it was a fiasco. First, it was delayed for almost two hours in anticipation of the arrival of co-host Redd Foxx. Foxx never showed, pleading back trouble. Nor did the other co-host, Sammy Davis, Jr., show up, although that came as no surprise to Kathi Fearn-Banks. "I knew a week beforehand that Sammy wasn't going to be there," she says. "He sent a cassette." Davis was appearing in Indianapolis the night of the telethon. His wife, Altovise, appeared in his place. Other no-shows included Muhammad Ali and Alex Haley. Altovise Davis, Stevie Wonder, Robert Guillaume, and a few others tried gamely to carry the show, but it was a dismal failure.

According to Kathi Fearn-Banks, even the woman who had organized the telethon did not show up for it. "She left Redd Foxx's employ, and the envelopes with the checks in them were left somewhere," she says. "To this day I don't know what happened to the money."

Having disassociated himself from the telethon, Pryor tried not to concern himself with its failure. He had other things to think about. Within a week after the telethon he was released from the hospital.

The news came as a surprise to many. His release had not been expected for several more days. But hospital spokesmen explained that "basically it wasn't in Mr. Pryor's best interests, medically or otherwise, to have a thousand people waiting outside" as he left the hospital. Besides, Pryor wanted to go home, and his doctors, realizing that his own good spirits had been responsible for the amazing speed of his recovery thus far, were not about to tamper with that very vital part of his cure. Normally a patient with burns like his would have been hospitalized for two-and-a-half to three months. Pryor's release came just six-and-a-half weeks after he'd been admitted with burns over fifty percent of his body and with three-to-one odds that he would not live. Although he would have a nurse–physical-therapist at his home and have physical therapy three times a day, although he would have to visit the burn center once a week and would probably require a couple of touch-up operations to remove scars, and although he was still in great pain, he was at least home and feeling, as he told Barbara Walters who interviewed him there, as if he'd been given a second chance.

Life looked different to him now. He tried to explain his feelings to Walters: "I don't know, just, a fly flew in my room one day, and I talked to it. You know, you just get. . . . The smog is wonderful! You know what I mean; everything just seems different to me. I just feel like a different person. The part [of me] that wanted to die, did. This," pointing to himself, "is the one that wants to live."

He was very proud of the Richard Pryor who had survived. He knew that he deserved much of the credit for not succumbing to death after being burned so badly and that he had started fighting death the moment he'd started running away from his house, although he hadn't realized what he was doing at the time. "I was running because I didn't want to die sitting down," he told Walters. "And I tried to run so that I could bust my heart out. I just wanted to run out. I didn't want to die laid out in the ambulance." Later, his doctors had told him that the running had saved his life, because it had kept his vital organs exercised: heart pumping, blood circulating, lungs heaving. Otherwise, faced with the incredible onslaught of flames to the tissues that surrounded them, these organs might have stopped functioning.

Once in the hospital Pryor had continued to refuse just to lie still and die. Although every exposed nerve in his body screamed for stillness and quiet, he had refused to urinate in a bedpan, and with Jim Brown's help had painfully shuffled the six interminably long feet to the bathroom, ignoring the hysterical nurse who screamed that he wasn't supposed to get out of bed. He had screamed from the pain himself, but he had never complained about it. And when no one around him could see any humor in his situation, he had started to make jokes. On hearing this Deboragh McGuire, sitting out in the waiting room, had commented, "This is his next album."

Pryor's strength, he believed, was given to him by God. He also believed that God had subjected him to his "trial by fire" in order to make him a new man, to force him to see "the real world" and through the falseness of people around him, to make him understand that he need not feel guilty about his success or the material things that success had brought him. As far as Pryor was concerned, he could face life now with the help of God alone and without drugs or alcohol or dependence on false friends.

His friend, Jim Brown, was not so confident. He hoped that Pryor would be a new man, but he also realized that soon Pryor would be right back in the environment that had led him to near self-destruction. "I don't think it's gonna make one bit of difference unless this whole process is fortified by key people in his life," Brown had told David Felton a few weeks earlier. "And as much attention and interest as they give him while he's on his back, they'll have to make that a continuing thing. Those of us who care about him will really have to take some time out and assert ourselves in dealing with him. But if we drop away and leave him out there alone, I don't think this will make up for all the things that have gone before."

CHAPTER XIV

Modern-Day Lazarus

PRYOR HAD JUST BEEN released from the hospital when he learned that a lot of people who were supposed to have cared about him were far more interested in his money and possessions. He told Charles Sanders of *Ebony*, "My watches are missing. My money is missing. Some of my jewelry is gone. . . . Another thing they stole was something my dear grandmother gave me. She had two old one hundred dollar bills and gave one of them to me, but they even took that. People I trusted to take care of my affairs were making deals with other people about my s--t, thinking I was going to die." Although Pryor did not choose to name names at the time, the reference to "people making deals with other people" was no doubt aimed at David Franklin, who ceased to represent Pryor around that time.

Pryor ordered an audit of the accounts of his that had been kept by Franklin, and he later filed suit against Franklin, charging mismanagement. The suit contended, "Literally hundreds of checks have been drawn . . . to various persons . . . many of which do not state the purpose for which they were drawn or the account on which they are paid or whose funds are being used." In August 1982 the California State Labor Commission awarded Pryor $3.1 million in damages against Franklin, finding that Franklin was "guilty of serious moral turpitude" and that he had "willfully misappropriated" monies that should have been paid to Pryor. He was also ordered to return the seventy-five thousand dollar fee he had received from Universal Pictures for acting as executive producer of *Bustin' Loose* (the final title given A Family Dream) for he had not fulfilled his duties in that job.

Pryor also believed that Franklin was the source of some damaging information—and, he charged, incorrect information—that appeared in the *National Enquirer* on September 9, 1981. In one of its legendary exposés the *Enquirer* claimed that Pryor had been freebasing before the explosion, that he had remained high on cocaine for days after he entered the hospital (the implication was that he was somehow getting the drug while there), and that the reason his doctors banned visitors was to keep him from obtaining more cocaine. Pryor brought suit against the *Enquirer*, the reporter on the story, and the distributor of the paper.

New attorneys handled these legal matters. Pryor himself had to concentrate on getting well, and soon it became clear to him that he would not be able to recuperate in California. There, at his Northridge home, the telephones never stopped ringing, and even the ten-foot-high iron gate and guards were not enough to keep unwanted "friends" away. So early in August Pryor put the Northridge house up for sale for $1.2 million and escaped to Maui, Hawaii, the only place where he had been able to find peace.

"I haven't met anyone there who's strange," he told Lois Armstrong of *People*. "There's no wickedness. I went to a festival once and watched them dance. It was so pure and innocent. And they brought children. I like that. When I first saw this place again, I cried. I thanked God for letting me live to see it. . . . You might mildew to death here, but nothin' else is going to happen to you."

He had discovered Maui in the late 1970s and immediately felt a kinship with the long stretches of deserted beach on the wild side of the island that is one of the seven major islands in the Hawaiian group. He had bought land near Hana, an area of tropical rain forests and sun-baked beaches that because of poor roads was a day's travel from the more built-up side of the island. George Harrison and Kris Kristofferson had also bought land there and so, soon after Pryor, did Burt Reynolds. "There goes the neighborhood," Pryor had quipped. Pryor had started building a one-bedroom house on his property during the winter of 1979 and 1980. Construction had come to a halt after the fire, and Pryor felt an urgent need to see it resumed. Accompanied by his nurse–physical-therapist, Larry Murphy, and all the paraphernalia he was using to minimize scarring (greasy medication that he had to keep smeared over the skin grafts, the special gloves and special suit that fit tight over his hands and body to prevent scar overgrowths called keloids from forming), he left Hollywood behind in mid-September and did not return until December.

He probably would have remained on Maui even longer if his picture *Bustin' Loose* had not needed his attention. Michael Schultz, who had been called in by Universal to salvage the picture, had decided that he could not do the job with the existing footage. There were too many half-shot scenes and poor prints and messed-up dialogue. Nothing would do but to reshoot some of the scenes and re-record some of the dialogue.

"It was an extraordinary experience," says Schultz. "It ought to go down in film history. Here was a picture that was made—supposedly finished—and two years after shooting started, more shooting had to be done. A lot had happened in those two years. The kids in it—some of them had grown several inches taller. They looked like different kids. I had to take the half-shot scenes and try to shoot the other half, try to make the weather look the same and the faces look the same. I had to try and make it look like one movie."

The biggest change, of course, had occurred in Richard Pryor. Schultz flew to Maui to talk to him about his ideas for rescuing the picture. "He was still in pain, recovering from the burns. He couldn't walk up the stairs without really being in agony. I just sat marveling at the fact, number one, that he was alive, and number two, that he was not complaining about the suffering that he was going through to get back to a normal level of functioning. I just sat back and watched him in admiration. He was determined to get those joints moving, to get his body back into control. But I didn't think I could shoot the picture with him. I didn't think he had enough stamina. I was really afraid for him to try getting through a normal eight-hour shooting day. . . . But he did it. He would just fall out after a day of shooting, but he never once complained."

Pryor returned to Hollywood and to Universal Studios to do what additional work was needed on the picture. Schultz had done as much advance work as possible: "We were cutting the picture as best we could before I had to go out and shoot it, so I knew what I really needed to shoot, and what I didn't. In order to make it work I had to have him come in and do some dialogue, because a lot of it was messed up in the originals. I had to have him come into the room where you do voice-overs—the automatic dialogue replacement room, the dubbing room.

"He came into the room his first day of work after the accident impeccably dressed. Had somebody park his Rolls-Royce outside, you know. Came into the room, gave me a big hug, and after we did a little chatting he sat down and said, 'Okay, let's do it.'

"He was still weak, still physically not strong enough to do a whole day's work, but I rolled the film. He watched himself up on the screen, and tears came into his eyes. He just started crying, and he wasn't even thinking about trying to do the dialogue. He was watching himself up on the screen.

He started talking to himself: 'Thank you, God, for savin' my ass. Look at that poor creature. . . . He's gone; he's really gone.' He was talking about himself in the third person, and he was so taken with the image of his deteriorated self. It was amazing.

"Then he collected himself and started working, and while he was doing the picture you could see the whole process of his coming to grips with where he had been and where he is now. It's hard to describe in words. You would have to see it. Here was a picture that he'd made before the fire, and you can see how his face was bloated and he must have been twenty pounds overweight, just totally dissipated. There was no way we could make him look the same way for the new frames. We made him up where we could make him up. We tried filling his ears out, because his ears were burned off at the bottoms. It looked so fake; we said forget it. I just shot him and kept him moving so people wouldn't fix on it. There were a lot of tricks and techniques that I used to minimize the difference. It turned out extremely well. The man at the studio was blown away. The whole thing was an extraordinary experience. Someday I may do a film about it."

After his additional work on the film was completed, Pryor seemed to lose all interest in *Bustin' Loose*. Perhaps it held too many painful associations with his life before the fire. Universal naturally wondered how it was supposed to promote the movie without the assistance of Richard Pryor. In desperation the studio hired the Association of Black Motion Picture and Television Producers, of which D'Urville Martin is a member. Martin, who describes his job on *Bustin' Loose* as "consultant after the fact," spent much of his time just trying to find Pryor, who seemed to be leading quite a peripatetic existence for a man who still wasn't entirely well and who still surrounded himself with people who didn't have his best interests at heart.

"When Universal hired the organization, they told us that the problem was that Richard would not do anything to promote the movie. They couldn't reach him; they couldn't find him. I finally found out where he was shooting *Some Kind of Hero*. Sidney Poitier was the director, and one of our members who had worked as an assistant to Richard approached Richard, and Richard told him no. So I went down there with another member, but we had to wait until Richard's flunky left. Always when people reach a certain level, no matter what color they are, they have these people around them who stop everybody else from talking to them, even the ones they should talk to.

"When I finally got to talk to Richard about *Bustin' Loose* and I told him I thought it was ingenious, he looked at me and said, 'You mean that? You're not just saying it? You mean it, really?' He was serious. So many people say so many things that he doesn't know who to believe."

Bustin' Loose opened in February 1981. It was a battered orphan of a picture. Its creator, coproducer, and star, Richard Pryor, had been fickle in his commitment to it. Its first executive producer, David Franklin, had done little but accept that title. The director who had rescued it was not even listed in the credits. Reviewers were cool in their appraisal of it. Still, it was a Richard Pryor movie, and what's more, it was a family movie—a black family movie with more "below the line" black participation than any earlier black movie had had. It was a picture aimed at a black audience but that white people could also enjoy. David Denby wrote in *New York* magazine, "No one could mistake *Bustin' Loose* for a good movie, but it's friendly and good-hearted in a way that's hard to resist." Its star was also hard to resist. Richard Pryor had captured the "crossover" white audience, and that audience stayed loyal, going to see *Bustin' Loose* and paying out with their black counterparts $13.6 million in the film's first thirteen days at 725 theaters across the country.

Richard Pryor was compared with Alan Alda as surefire box-office.

In fact as a black there was no one with whom to compare him. Wrote Dale Pollack in the *Los Angeles Times*, "What ever happened to the black film? It seems to reside these days in the person of Richard Pryor."

Just about the time *Bustin' Loose* was released, yet another motion picture studio decided to bank on Richard Pryor, although its president already knew him well enough to know he was taking no great risk. Guy McElwaine, who had been Pryor's agent, had left International Creative Management to join Rastar and in early March he announced that Rastar would produce Pryor's next concert film. Universal had expected to make his next concert picture, but he'd gone with Rastar instead, promising Universal the next. In addition to the concert film Pryor's contract with Rastar included two more films— *The Toy*, starring Jackie Gleason and a film biography based on the life of Charlie "Yardbird" Parker.

Pryor was fully back in action now and making a serious effort to repay what he evidently considered to be his debt to the Almighty. Early in July he pledged a donation of two hundred thousand dollars to warring Watts gangs if they would agree to a cease fire. Unfortunately, the gangs in question did not take the offer in the way Pryor had intended it. "Mabel King was in charge of getting them together," says D'Urville Martin. "She was the bad witch in *The Wiz* and the mama in the TV series *That's My Mama*; she does a lot of community work in Watts. Mabel set up a meeting, but Richard had to cancel. He called up about a week later and said he could make it the next day, but there wasn't time to get word to the gang leaders. The next day he was there, but the leaders weren't, so he left.

"So, the leaders got together, came for their money. And Richard had to explain that this was not to be put in their hands to do what they wanted with it; this was for a center. But these guys wanted their money. They were going to turn it into billions—buy three hundred kilos and make a big profit. They did get a definite misconception about that money." While the response of the gang leaders was less than appropriate, officials of the Sheenway School and Culture Center in Watts assured Pryor that the money would be put to good use, and he eventually donated about eighty thousand dollars to the center.

Later in the month, perhaps looking for less larcenous recipients of his largesse, he donated fifty thousand dollars to Peoria organizations and charities, among them Miss Whittaker's Learning Tree Day School and an anti–drug abuse program. In the fall he would appear at Sally Struthers's first Christian Children's Fund Country Fair and agree to sponsor ten children. He also did a Comedy Store appearance to benefit the John Wayne Cancer Clinic at UCLA. Given his awareness of the late actor's racial opinions, this was a sure indication of a new mellowness on Pryor's part.

He also got married to Jennifer Lee, although many people who knew him viewed that act as an indication either that the flames had melted his mind or that he was falling back into the same old self-destructive tendencies.

Their relationship had been stormy at best—on again, off again, and more off than on. Jennifer never quite forgave him for refusing to see her when he had first entered the hospital, and he never lost his suspicion that she might have been somehow responsible for telling the police that he'd been freebasing when the fire started or his suspicion that she had a yen for publicity that he did not need. Then, too, Jennifer was white, and Pryor had spent most of his life suffering from unresolved racial conflicts. But, he married her anyway. In a private ceremony on Maui on August 16, 1981, Jennifer Lee became the fourth Mrs. Richard Pryor "on paper."

"She came to me when I was in need," he told a correspondent for Jet. "She stood by me through a lot of pain as most people walked away from me and thought it was over.... I loved her and she loved me and we got to love each other. For real, not just the word part. We went through that part, too, you know.... We went through the racism together. We went through a lot of stuff together and found out that we really have souls and we are people."

They stayed in the Northridge house, which Pryor had taken off the market, until they could find a home to buy, and while Jennifer went house hunting, Richard set about writing the material for his concert film for Rastar. By late September he knew he had to try the material out on a live audience, but it wasn't easy to get back up on a stage, even at the familiar Comedy Store on Sunset Strip. He'd been away for a long time. He wasn't using the word *nigger* anymore. He was going to be talking about some very personal things. He wasn't sure how people would receive him. He was wondering if he was still funny.

His appearances at the Comedy Stores in West Hollywood and

Westwood were not advertised—at his specific request—but word got around anyway. People came in droves to see him. They saw a nervous Pryor, a man who wasn't sure he wanted to be where he was, a man who floundered around on stage and was, at times, visibly ill at ease. Hollywood being what it is, some in the crowd were looking for him to bomb, but the majority were as nervous as he was—like parents at a school assembly, willing the vulnerable person on stage to do well. In the main they were not disappointed. Pryor was obviously uncomfortable; his timing was off; he didn't make transitions well, but his material showed flashes of the old Pryor brilliance.

Some of the best material was about the fire and his experiences recovering in the hospital. He managed to make his audiences feel his pain—and laugh with him about it. Pryor had to be the first—and last—comedian to transport an audience with him into a state where even a breeze caused debilitating pain and to make them laugh and cry at the same time.

He talked about Jennifer, although he did not mention her by name. He spoke of "his lady" and what they'd been through because of their racial difference: "The first two years we went together, she thought her name was White Honky Bitch."

More vintage Pryor resurfaced in bits about the wild animals he encountered in Africa. He *became* the animals—and not just the cheetahs but the gazelles. His performance over all, though no less funny than his pre-fire onstage persona, was gentler.

Unpolished as his performance was, there was no question in the minds of his audiences: Richard Pryor was back. Most were pulling for him all the way. When he faltered, they shouted encouragement. By the middle of November, he felt ready to take his act to San Francisco, and by early December he was at the Los Angeles Palladium doing the shows that photographer Haskell Wexler would capture for the Rastar production *Richard Pryor: Live on the Sunset Strip*. He donated the proceeds from the two sold-out shows to the Reverend Jesse Jackson's Push for Excellence education program.

Unfortunately, the first night's show was a disaster. In the course of trying out the material in the preceding weeks, Pryor had decided to use his Pryor on Fire routine as the finale, but at the last minute he changed his mind and instead opened with it. It worked all right as an opening bit, but the change in sequence left a hole at the end of the show. He found himself up on stage in front of thousands of people and with no finale. He panicked and walked offstage, telling the crowd, "I don't understand some stuff. I'm trying to find out what I want to be and I don't know. . . . I've reached a point in my life where I want to stop. . . . I should be grateful I have a job." Many in the audience were left wondering if he had indeed lost that stage presence that is essential in live performances.

It was extremely difficult for Pryor to return to the Palladium stage the following night, but he went back to his original sequence of routines and was a smash. So was the film version of his performances —*Richard Pryor: Live on the Sunset Strip*—which was released a few months later.

By the time the film was released, Pryor and his fourth wife had separated. Mutual recognition that they were people and had souls was not sufficient to keep them together. The on again, off again nature of their prenuptial relationship continued after they were married, and five months after they exchanged vows, Jennifer left her husband. Within a week columnist Liz Smith was reporting that Jennifer had retained Marvin Mitchelson to represent her. It seemed that word of Jennifer's action had leaked from the camp of the celebrated palimony lawyer, who had represented Michelle Triola against Lee Marvin and been the darling of live-in lovers ever since. Jennifer claimed that it was all a misunderstanding. As she explained the "mistake" to Liz Smith, she and Richard had been vacationing in the Caribbean and she'd left him to return to Los Angeles to do some decorating on their home. During a stopover at Miami International Airport, she'd spotted Mitchelson and introduced herself, saying, "If I ever need to get in touch with you, where do I find you?" She insisted she was only kidding. She and Richard did have an occasional falling out, she admitted to Smith—"After all he is a genius and we don't exactly have a marriage with white-picket-fence values!"—but she had no intention of leaving him. "I hope I'll stay married to Richard forever," she assured Smith. "He is my knight in shining armor, and I'm going to be with this man as long as I live."

In actuality Jennifer left Pryor in the Caribbean not because of house decorating responsibilities but because they'd had a serious fight. Her petition for "Dissolution of Marriage," filed on March 9, 1982, on her behalf by the L.A. law firm of Jaffe, Clemens and Fridkis, stated that she and Richard had separated on January 20, 1982. She cited "irreconcileable differences" as the reason for her petition.

Subsequently Jennifer and Richard tried for a reconciliation, but their egos were larger than their commitment to one another. By late June Jennifer had retained Marvin Mitchelson as counsel and decided to go the palimony route, claiming that while she and Richard had been married for less than a year they had lived together for two years prior to marrying. Pryor claimed that he had an iron-clad premarital contract that prevented Jennifer from suing him. While the matter remained unresolved, he paid her temporary alimony of ten thousand dollars a month.

The matter was resolved in a surprisingly brief time, and out of court, in late June. Jennifer received, tax free, the sum of $750,000. Shortly afterward she moved back to New York, buying a house in Bridgehampton, Long Island, and hoping to resume her career as an actress and songwriter.

Reflecting on his briefest marriage to date and on marriage in general, Pryor said, "I guess I don't know how to do it. I thought this time I was never going to get divorced. I was in love a bunch. I must have made her real mad."

Pryor has been linked with other women since he and Jennifer parted, but he has not become seriously involved with anyone else. And several of the women whom the press has attempted to portray as his lovers have not, in fact, been more than friends or casual dates. The most eager speculation centered around Margot Kidder, Pryor's co-star in Some Kind of Hero, which was filmed in the spring of 1981 and released in the spring of 1982.

The film is the story of a Vietnam POW named Eddie Keller (Pryor) who returns to the United States to find a less than enthusiastic welcome. The government denies him back pay because while in a North Vietnamese prison he signed a denouncement of U.S. activities in the war in order to secure medical attention for his deathly ill cellmate (Ray Sharkey). Keller, broke, robs a bank and while on the run from the police is befriended by a white prostitute (Margot Kidder) and falls in love with her. In the novel on which the movie is based, the returning POW is white.

The script called for some fairly torrid love scenes between Keller and the hooker, and initially director Michael Pressman followed the script and made no adjustments because his Eddie Keller was black and the prostitute white. The gossip columns picked up on the "steamy interracial lovemaking" angle and speculated about Pryor's and Kidder's off-camera relationship. (No doubt, these items did little to help Pryor's relationship with Jennifer.) By the time the film went into the editing stage, Paramount had gotten cold feet. Over the objections of Pressman, the love scenes were drastically edited. Kidder, too, disagreed with the studio's action. "In the last year the movie industry has panicked," she said, "and they've been making films for the lowest common denominator. That basically meant castrating everything. I think that's what happened to *Some Kind of Hero*. . . . They ended up cutting it so as not to offend anyone. As a result, they were left with this little thing that limped along and said nothing." Pryor made no public statements about the editing of the love scenes; he knew that, though he might be box-office, there was a line beyond which he was not allowed to go.

Some Kind of Hero was released in early April 1982 and Pryor, in his first serious dramatic role since *Greased Lightning*, received excellent reviews. In Michael Schultz's opinion Pryor's work in the film showed his considerable growth as an actor: "I thought he did some absolutely brilliant work in that picture, not consistently, but . . . the scene in the bedroom when his wife tells him that she has another man and he's laughing and crying, that was absolutely brilliant. I haven't seen any white actors who could do that scene any better. It was original, fresh, very moving, and funny at the same time. He has an amazing ability to combine both of those qualities. . . . I think he felt more at ease in that picture than in any earlier one, so I see a definite growth pattern there."

Critic Larry Kart, however, did not feel that the film was worthy of Pryor's talents: "Hollywood still doesn't know what to do with the world's funniest man, aside from letting him perform on a concert stage and filming the results," wrote Kart in his review of *Some Kind of Hero*. "On stage, Pryor is funnier, more dramatic and just plain more interesting than any of the characters Hollywood has asked him to portray. . . . A comedy (or even a straight drama) that would meet his genius on his own terms is conceivable, but only if some effort is made to match the material to the master. Why not begin by figuring out who Pryor really is—which should be possible, given his penchant for onstage self-revelation—and then build a movie around that essence?''

Pryor's next movies seemed to prove Kart's point. First, there was the long-awaited *The Toy*, in which he played an out-of-work writer whom tycoon Jackie Gleason buys as a plaything for his spoiled-rotten son. In May 1982, during the filming of the movie in Baton Rouge, Louisiana, Pryor admitted himself to the hospital complaining of a respiratory ailment and remained there for a week. But his respiratory problems did not appear to affect his performance, which critics agreed was the best thing about the simplistic film with its obvious plot and abundant nods to middle-class verities. Wrote Richard Corliss in *Time*, "Even in his lamest movies . . . . Pryor is splendidly funny: whinnying in anger, tiptoeing down the hall like a naughty child, updating Stepin Fetchit's mumbly drawl, or even dispensing sentimental wisdom. Pryor [is] not nearly discriminating enough in his choice of roles."

Then there was *Superman III*. Most critics felt that some of the magic of the first two installments of the Superman series was missing here. But they found Pryor "appealing" in the role of a down-on-his-luck dishwasher who discovers he has a great talent for computers and who creates some quasi-Kryptonite that causes Superman to undergo an identity crisis. And they predicted that with Pryor in the cast, the film, despite its shortcomings, would turn a healthy profit at the box office. Wrote Marilyn Beck, one of many to express this opinion, "Pryor . . . reigns as the single star that can make a winner out of the most mediocre of movies."

Said Pryor on more than one occasion, "I'm better than my movies." He elaborated on this idea to Stephen Farber of *The New York Times*: "Rarely have I read a good script. Maybe there are some good ones out there, but the scripts that come my way are not very good." While he had made some effort in the past to gain more control over the movies in which he appeared, he decided in late 1982 and early 1983 to be more aggressive about working in films on his own terms. Early in 1983 he put himself on the market, in effect, by expressing interest in a deal under which he would star in a few pictures and produce an unspecified number of films in return for several million dollars. Half the studios in Hollywood immediately contacted his representatives. Columbia Pictures, which won out with a multi-million dollar deal (reportedly forty million dollars) calling for Pryor to star in a minimum of three films in the next four to five years and to produce, under the name The Pryor Company, several other modestly budgeted features, considered itself lucky to get him. For his part Pryor weighed the mega-bucks and the idea of helping more blacks to get work in films against the idea of committing himself to yet another long-term deal, and couldn't resist the money and the chance to make a social contribution.

He did, however, decide that his first film for Columbia would be another live-in-concert type of film. That meant holing up on Maui and writing new material—and taking it to the people. And that meant doing what he does best.

He tried his material out first at the Comedy Store. But this time he ranged further afield, making a rare appearance in August on the stage of Radio City Music Hall in New York. He was far more confident than when he had performed the material that was filmed for *Live on the Sunset Strip*; indeed, he had to be, facing the capacity audience of nearly six thousand. Wrote Mel Gussow in *The New York Times*, "Though this is a cavernous theater instead of a cabaret, he worked the audience beautifully, creating his own intimate ambience." Filming of his performance also took place in comparatively alien territory for Pryor—at the Saenger Theater in New Orleans. Pryor himself directed the filming, and his friend Jim Brown was executive producer.

Titled *Richard Pryor: Here and Now*, the film, which like his live routine continued to defy categorization—Mel Gussow called his routine "autobiographical performance art" and that seems an apt description—opened in theaters across the country in late October to critical raves. The material was not new for Pryor, but he showed once again how brilliantly he could handle it.

During his concert someone in the New Orleans audience presented him with a live crab. He made some obvious jokes about it; but he went beyond the expected. He talked to the crab, imagined how it felt creeping around the seat of his stool, suggested that the crab was discovering that the world was round. Spontaneously, he created a brilliant routine by identifying with a crab! Janet Maslin of The New York Times noted that this was a demonstration of Pryor's "amazing and hilarious empathy, of his ability to ascribe feelings to anyone or anything he sees. Together with his relentlessly bawdy wit and his brilliant physical mimcry, this makes him a concert performer of seemingly endless range. It's possible that a dozen more Pryor performance films will leave the format feeling tired, but that doesn't seem very likely. Mr. Pryor appears able to incorporate any subject into his uniquely animated conversation."

At the rate Pryor was going, it would take him a quarter century or longer to do a dozen more such films. Once again he had more projects in development than he could handle, and already he was getting behind on his commitments. He was supposed to have done a film called Color Man for Universal in 1982, but he didn't get to it. The script for the film biography of Charlie Parker, about which he'd been talking for years, was completed, but Columbia had no idea when production might begin. Warner Brothers put out the news that Pryor had promised to play Malcolm X in the film biography of the slain black leader, to be directed by Sidney Lumet. He was supposed to co-star with country music star Willie Nelson in a movie about Depression-era gamblers titled Slim and None. He was supposed to co-star in another comedy with Gene Wilder. As the only black actor in Hollywood who could boast of consistent commercial success, he was the only black actor in Hollywood getting any work to speak of. And unfortunately, for him and for other black actors, he was getting all the work. It was too much for one man to handle.

He began to realize that he was back on the same old treadmill, and he didn't want to be there. But he did not know how to get off. In June he announced that he was making an "unscheduled stop." He told an interviewer, "Now I'm saying, 'Stop the train.' I'm the engineer, and I'm telling the passengers, 'Sorry, folks, we're going to make an unauthorized stop. We'll get going again, but not right now.'" Yet, within a month, he was on the stage of the Comedy Store, trying out his new routines.

Pryor's moods fluctuate from one day to the next. He is honestly unhappy with the movie business. He is aware that he has difficulty handling the Hollywood hype. He told Stephen Farber of *The New York Times*, "There's something dishonest about the whole business. I had these illusions and fantasies about what it would be like, but then I started working and meeting people, I realized there's no brotherhood out there. There are a lot of piranhas. You can become very insensitive if you stay at it too long."

He has a lot of money, and he dreams about getting out of the business altogether, of living quietly on Maui and taking long walks on the beach. He has learned to fly—after the fire, he realized how silly it was to fear flying and he took pilot lessons and bought a single-engine Grumman, which he piloted from Oahu to Maui—and would like to fly his plane more often. He would like to return to Africa and actually live there for a while, having felt a deep, spiritual kinship with the land and people during his one visit. But something keeps him from carrying out his threat to leave the entertainment business.

Perhaps the reason is that he suspects that walking on the beach and flying his plane and traveling to Africa and writing—alone—will not fill up his life. He needs someone with whom to share it. He is not like Flip Wilson, who had a family to go home to when he left show business for several years. The only love that Richard Pryor can count on is the impersonal, but nevertheless gratifying, love he feels when he is on a stage, or when fans who have seen his movies come up to him or write to him. His talent, he has said, is the one thing that has never failed him, and he is reluctant to tamper with the conditions under which it seems to flourish—even though Richard Pryor, human being, often suffers in the process.

There is a saying in Hollywood that the only ones who succeed are those whose talents are greater than their need to self-destruct. But even the most self-assured tinseltown sage is reluctant to forecast the fate of Richard Pryor. He has reached the pinnacle of success and the nadir of self-destructiveness. And he has survived them both.

Discography

Richard Pryor   (1969, Reprise)

Craps After Hours   (1971, Laff)

Pryor Goes Foxx Hunting   (1973, Laff)

That Nigger's Crazy   (1974, Reprise)

Down-N-Dirty   (1975, Laff)

Is It Something I Said?   (1975, Reprise)

Richard Pryor Meets Richard & Willie & the S.L.A   (1976, Laff)

Bicentennial Nigger   (1976, Reprise)

L.A. Jail   (1976, Tiger Lilly)

Are You Serious???   (1977, Laff)

Richard Pryor's Greatest Hits   (1977, Warner Brothers)

Richard Pryor Live   (1977, World Sound)

Who Me? I'm Not Him   (1977, Laff)

Black Ben the Black Smith   (1978, Laff)

The Wizard of Comedy   (1978, Laff)

Outrageous   (1979, Laff)

Wanted: Live in Concert   (1979, Reprise)

Insane   (1980, Laff)

Holy Smoke   (1980, Laff)

Richard Pryor's Greatest Hits   (1980, Reprise)

Rev. Du-Rite   (1981, Laff)

Filmography

The Busy Body   (1968)

Wild in the Streets   (1969)

The Phynx   (1970)

You've Got to Walk It Like You Talk It Or You Lose That Beat   (1971)

Dynamite Chicken   (1972)

Lady Sings the Blues   (1972)

Wattstax   (1973)

Hit   (1973)

The Mack   (1973)

Some Call It Loving   (1973)

Blazing Saddles   (writer, 1974)

Uptown Saturday Night   (1974)

Adios Amigo   (1976)

The Bingo Long Traveling All-Stars and Motor Kings   (1976)

Car Wash   (1976)

Silver Streak   (1976)

Greased Lightning   (1977)

Which Way is Up?   (1977)

Blue Collar   (1978)

The Wiz   (1978)

California Suite   (1978)

Richard Pryor: Live in Concert   (1979)

The Muppet Movie   (1979)
Bustin' Loose   (1981)
Some Kind of Hero   (1982)
Richard Pryor: Live on the Sunset Strip   (1982)
The Toy   (1982)
Superman III   (1983)
Richard Pryor: Here and Now   (1983)

Index